University of St. Francis

W9-AES-355

3 0301 00067617 7

1992

SOCIAL WORK

— A N D —

S·O·C·I·E·T·Y

AN INTRODUCTION

DEAN PIERCE
Delaware State College

LIBRARY
College of St. Francis
JOLIET, ILLINOIS

Longman
New York & London

Social Work and Society: An Introduction, First Edition

Copyright © 1989 by Longman Inc. All rights reserved.
No part of this publication may be reproduced, stored
in a retrieval system, or transmitted in any form
or by any means, electronic, mechanical, photocopying,
recording, or otherwise, without the prior permission
of the publisher.

Longman Inc., 95 Church Street, White Plains, N. Y. 10601

Associated companies:
Longman Group Ltd., London
Longman Cheshire Pty., Melbourne
Longman Paul Pty., Auckland
Copp Clark Pitman, Toronto
Pitman Publishing Inc., New York

"MAN IN THE MIRROR": page 117.
Words and Music by Glen Ballard and Siedah Garrett
© Copyright 1987 by MCA Music Publishing, A Division
of MCA Inc., Aerostation Corporation and Yellowbrick Road Music.
Rights of Aerostation Corporation administered by MCA Music
Publishing, A Division of MCA Inc., New York, NY 10019.
Used by Permission. All Rights Reserved

© 1987, 1988 Yellowbrick Road Music, MCA Music Publishing,
A Division of MCA Inc. & Aerostation Corporation
All rights on behalf of Yellowbrick Road Music, administered
by WB Music Corp.
Rights of Aerostation Corporation administered by MCA Music
Publishing, A Division of MCA Inc., New York, N.Y.
All Rights Reserved. Used by Permission

Senior editor: David J. Estrin
Production editor: Camilla T. K. Palmer
Text design: Jill Francis Wood
Cover design: Anne M. Pompeo
Production supervisor: Judy Stern

Library of Congress Cataloging-in-Publication Data
Pierce, Dean, 1943–
    Social work and society : an introduction / Dean Pierce.
        p. cm.
    Bibliography: p.
    Includes index.
    ISBN 0–582–28665–4 (pbk.)
        1. Social service. 2. Social service—United States. I. Title.
HV10.5.P54 1989   88–22754
362—dc19   CIP

ISBN 0-582-28665-4

94 93 92 91 90 89 9 8 7 6 5 4 3 2 1

361.3
P615

5-26-72 Published $26.57

TO

RONALD CHARLES FEDERICO

for always providing
direction and support
to me as:
—colleague
—companion
—counsel
in my efforts to study
and write about social
work.

143,393

Contents

v

PART II   Social Work and Society   **113**

PART III   Social Workers in Action   **197**

Preface

This book is for those persons seeking to understand social work and to decide if (or how) they want to be part of the profession. Writing about social work is a satisfying and a trying task. Everyone seems to have an opinion about what social work is, but in my experience few understand and appreciate its full scope and complexity. In this book I hope to increase your awareness and understanding of social work by discussing ways in which the profession achieves its purposes within society and ways in which it contributes to society.

When I reply to someone's question, "What do you do?" with the answer, "I teach social work," many naively continue with, "And tell me all about it," as if in a few moments I could do justice to a description of social work. I care so deeply about social work that I want always to present ideas and opinions about it as fully as possible. I also want those with whom I share information to compare and contrast it with their own ideas and to reach their own conclusions.

This book aims to assist you in that inquiry in two ways. First, it offers a range of ideas and beliefs about social work, and second, it provides the opportunities to test your own ideas and values about the profession.

The conclusions offered in this book are mine and sometimes they will differ from those of others. I hope that you will examine carefully the points of view expressed in the book, and that they will stimulate you to formulate your own thoughts about social work.

Three places and the people who occupy them were especially important to me in the development of this book. The first is the Bronx Campus of Mercy College. During the writing of early drafts of the manuscript, the faculty, librarians, and students of that campus helped to create a wonderful work environment. Their laughter and discussions nurtured this project. Special among them are my colleague Graciela Castex and our "assistants," Gloria Delgado, Pat Lang, and Willie LaSalle.

The second place is the School of Social Work at Grambling State University in Grambling, Louisiana, where much support was given to me while I made final revisions to the manuscript. Research assistance was provided by Eddie Cook, Dana Franklin, Neoritha Humphrey, Laura Jones, and Michael Smith; and typing was done by Yolanda Carr, Shirley Lewis, and Sandra Willis.

The third place is my parents' home in Southwestern Idaho. My parents, Cletus Pierce and Charletta Pierce, let me spend several months writing and working on this book there. Their generosity and commentary are greatly appreciated.

Dean Pierce
Caldwell, Idaho

INTRODUCTION

CHAPTER ONE

Definitions and Directions

"In another moment down went Alice after it, never once considering how in the world she was to get out again."

Lewis Carroll
Alice's Adventures in Wonderland.

CHAPTER OVERVIEW

This book begins with a journey whose goal is to discover social work. In discussing how to select a path to follow, this chapter explores how certain words and ideas serve to guide our inquiries and influence the nature of our journey. Several ways of finding social work are identified. Finally, the direction offered to you by this book and the plan of each chapter, which gives you an opportunity to reflect on your reaction to the discussion, is outlined.

FINDING A PLACE IN SOCIAL WORK

This book is for those persons who are seeking to understand social work and to decide if or how they want to be a part of the profession. It will help you to explore several approaches used to define and evaluate social work and to develop a model for learning about social work that is sensitive to the range of ideas used to define it. The assumptions leading to the need for such a model are as follows:

There is no "one" social work that can be learned by rote.
People argue about what social work is and what it ought to be, and such disagreements are okay and useful in trying to explain social work.
The ideas of those who are studying social work are important parts of learning about it.
All the words used to define, evaluate, or criticize social work are key ingredients to understanding and interpreting it.

Any introduction to social work must define it and the terms and ideas related to it. The terms used to portray social work, however, are neither simple in meaning nor universal in usage. We deal with these factors by developing a framework, or model, to guide you in learning about it. We do not begin immediately with a set definition of social work. Instead, we explore some of the reasons for the complexity of the meaning of social work. Then, we use the insight so gained as a basis for a model that we can use in making sense out of the many definitions of social work.

Let's begin by using descriptions of how several social workers "found" social work and their place in it. We can then examine what they say about the profession to come up with some words and ideas that are frequently used to define social work. Their stories also will help you to appreciate how diverse the profession is. You will read more comments from them and other social workers throughout the book (see interviews on pages 4–7).

GRACIELA CASTEX: I never knew there was such a thing as the discipline of social work. All I knew was that certain needs that existed in society should have someone responsible for them. For me, it started out with my thinking about the family. I always felt that society made the family very responsible for both problems as well as their solutions. I always felt that there was a need for some outside intervention. When I went to college, I described social work, without labeling it as such, and they said, "Oh, that's called social work and that's what you want." So it was a matter, I think, of defining for myself what it was I wanted to do, how I wanted to be involved with people, and then going to an admissions counselor in a college and describing what it was I wanted to do. I went to a junior college first. I took an AA in social work and a BSW at another college.

BERNICE GOODMAN: Social work found me. When I finished college I was interested in adult education and went to a faculty member at the Columbia University School of Social Work. I really didn't know what social work was, but after we finished talking it sounded very interesting particularly in relation to group work. I was very naive at that point. I just applied for school. Only after I was accepted and started did I find out how hard it was to get into that school. As I said, social work sort of found me, and I think that is one of the interesting aspects of the profession. Social work involves those things that are most important to all of us in ourselves and in others, a kind of quality of life.

BETTE HARLAN: I am a people-oriented person. As a child, I already knew that I did not want to fill the stereotypical role expectations for a woman from a small- to medium-sized mining town in Southeast Colorado. I knew that I did not want to marry and hence would have to be self-supporting. After looking around at the world I lived in and the so-called "spinster" role models, I decided on college. I went through several majors searching for one that would fit my capabilities and needs. I tried journalism, education, and psychology. After graduation I worked as a substitute teacher. That lasted for two weeks. I saw an ad for a psych tech in a residential treatment facility on the East Coast and decided that it might be a place where I could use my skills. This facility was for the "rich and famous," and my job amounted to glorified baby sitting. Although I liked the job, I decided to return to Colorado where I eventually took a job in public welfare. There I found my niche. I had a diversified caseload and especially liked working with the rural elderly. My supervisor was a graduate of Smith College for Social Work and urged me to go on for further training. I took her advice and finished my MSW there.

JOE HERNANDEZ: I made a career change about five years ago when I was in my late thirties. At that time I was in the trucking industry, doing repairs. I did a lot of diesel and auto mechanics. Prior to that, I drove for a number of years, but I was beginning to get tired, physically and in the sense that I did not see anything for me in the future. Few drivers went beyond their forty-fifth or fiftieth birthdays. I began to think that I needed a change.

About that time, an opportunity came up to manage a garage, do repairs, handle the payroll, and do dispatching. While I was doing that, I got involved in an informal sort of counseling. Although I was not looking for it, quite frequently the drivers or their wives or relatives called me up to talk about a problematic situation. They would ask for advice, some kind of solution. In most cases, I found that I talked to these people a number of times as I tried to help them.

Again, I reflected on the job I was doing and what it meant to me. I started to think about dropping trucking, forgetting about mechanics, and learning something new. I decided to enroll in college again. It was a difficult decision to make in terms of economics, because of the money I stood to lose and because of no experience with or exposure to social work.

What led them to come to me for advice, I do not know. I didn't really question why they sought me out. I provided what I could. They opened up and shared personal matters as if I were their priest or minister. I discovered that the profession of social work could provide me with more of what I wanted to offer people when they approached me. People saw something in me, and social work could strengthen that part of me.

SUSANNA HUESTON: When I completed my undergraduate degree in North Carolina, I decided to take a masters in social work before working. I had a bachelor degree in sociology and had not taken the couple of social welfare courses the department offered as electives. The chair of the sociology undergraduate department was very helpful in getting graduate scholarships for departmental students. I wanted to go as far away from home as possible, if I could get money. I decided on the University of Illinois, which to me represented a different orientation—white, middle America. Actually when I started graduate school, I was still trying to discover what social work was and what field of service I wanted to enter.

Illinois' Jane Addams graduate school had a 16-month program. I received tuition and board free and worked as a resident assistant. From September to May, I took only classes; from June to January there was a full time, four-day-a-week placement, with a seminar day on Friday. My placement was in a social agency run by the school under the auspices of a family services agency funded by the United Way. A university instructor supervised all the students who were placed there.

At first I was nervous. Many of the other students were older and brought social work experience with them. I was one of a few who came directly from undergraduate school. I found the field placement to be extremely useful to me in learning more about myself and about social work. I had a chance to work with lawyers and find out about state law. I had a secondary placement in the schools. I ended up working in the field of school social work.

TRACEY JOHNSON: I became interested in social work because my father and mother had social work jobs. I wanted to be a social worker like them. In high school I volunteered at a community center where I did tutoring. This was a place like the one where my father worked. My mother was a youth leader. I figured it was a chance for me to see for myself what they were doing, what kind of work they did. I found that I enjoyed it. After high school, I went to the University of Cincinnati where I completed an associate degree in social work technology and then a BSW. I started with social work as a major and never changed. From my volunteer experience, I knew it was what I wanted.

IRMA SERRANO: When I came to live in New York City after being a teacher in Puerto Rico, I was looking for a job before I went to graduate school to become a school counselor. I wanted to go back to work in a school but not in the classroom. I was referred by the professional placement program of the state employment service to a hospital to interview for a social work assistant job. When I got there, that job had been taken, so I went to another hospital and got the same type of job. I began working in the department of social services without the least notion of what social work was all about. I had heard about social work, but I really had no idea what it was. They wanted someone who could speak Spanish. That is how I got started. I enjoyed helping people. After four years, I was offered an opportunity to do my graduate degree at Columbia, and I now wanted to be a school social worker. I took an MSW and a job in the mental health field.

ADELE WEINER: My choice of social work as a career was quite accidental. Social work as an undergraduate degree was not an option I had explored. BSW programs were just being accredited as I was preparing to graduate from college. As an undergraduate, I had studied experimental psychology and had enjoyed research. As I was exploring my options for graduate school, I discovered MSW programs. Since I had grown up in a family that had a commitment to social causes, this option seemed particularly suited to me. I applied and was accepted to the program of my choice. I had fully intended to return to psychology for a PhD at a later date. But when I began to explore my options for doctoral study, I discovered that psychology programs would not grant me any credits for my MSW degree work. Essentially they wanted me to begin as if I were a bachelor degree holder going straight to doctoral studies. Since by this time I was a social work educator, I decided to continue my studies in social work and located a PhD program with an emphasis on teaching and research.

These are all social workers. In talking about their profession they use a variety of terms, such as:

social work
profession
needs
problems
intervention
BSW (Bachelor, Social Work)
MSW (Master, Social Work)
advice
counseling
social welfare
graduate study
group work
public welfare
field of service
social agency
field placement
volunteer
community center
social services
mental health
social work assistant
helping

We must not only define these words but develop a framework, or model, that reflects how their differences and variations in meaning can enrich your understanding of social work.

CHOOSING A DIRECTION: THE ROLE OF ASSUMPTIONS, EXPERIENCES, AND VALUES

Because this book introduces you to a new topic of potential interest to you, you should prepare for it in somewhat the same way you would for a journey to an unknown but sought-out new place to avoid an Alice-in-Wonderland style trip and to reach your goal of understanding social work. Such preparation involves determining which path to follow, which guides to depend on, and what precautions to take on the chosen route.

In our search to learn the meaning of social work, certain ideas and the terms used to present them are the guides that provide direction. Words, however, contain at least two hazards, or potential roadblocks, to reaching our intended destination.

First, words reflect the assumptions, experiences, and values of those who use them. You may not share these values with the users, or you may not grasp their significance. Second, if the words are associated with other ideas, either yours or the user's, they can lead both astray. Third, words are limited in the communication of complex, multidimensional phenomena because of the nature of language itself. For social work this is especially true because the words used to define it are often associated with strong positive and negative values and experiences. Moreover, they may be words with which you may associate other meanings that may lead you astray.

Social work is conceived of in different ways by different people. These various conceptions may be accounted for in part by the assumptions, or expectations, people hold about social work and what it should do. Their expectations are influenced by their social class, culture, political viewpoint, sex, race, and age. In these expectations are basic values about which people in our society should get help and how they should be helped. Some people see social work as a necessary evil to control disliked people; others expect it to create better conditions for those in need. Moreover, further differences arise in defining need.

Other differences in definition derive from the various kinds of contact or experiences people may have had with social workers or social work agencies. How practitioners define social work, what consumers of services think it is, or what lay people believe about it can be at odds. Each group has followed a different path in identifying social work. These practitioners, consumers, or taxpayers are looking at social work from the perspective of different experiences.

The story is told of three sightless persons who encountered an elephant, touched different parts of it, and likened the elephant to three different objects. Similarly, those who discuss social work may have come in contact with or encountered different aspects of it, thereby having quite different images of it. The social worker, depending on where he or she practices; the client, depending on his or her needs and service availability; and the layperson, depending on his or her contacts with client, worker, and agency—each can report differing impressions.

Such persons, along with many others, may also hold different opinions about the importance of the activities of social work. They place varying emphases on it and its work. When faced with the recent federal budget cuts that threatened to cut social work services, politicians were divided in their response. Some believed that these services were not essential and could be reduced without any real damage. Many other elected officials vigorously supported social work services as vital to the national well-being. Clearly, the latter placed greater value on social work than did those who went along with the budget cuts.

Even scholars are not unified in their approach to defining social work. What they expect of and the value they place on social work also differ. Some, for example, emphasize social work as part of efforts at social control. Others view it as a vehicle of social change or would like to see a greater emphasis on social action, community involvement, or social reform.

Consider the following typical statements:

> Social work should not continue to foster dependency among poor people. Social workers should deal with those who will help themselves.

This is a common expectation of lay people. It is an unwritten but powerful demand they make of social work. It reflects the values they hold about social work and a large group of people with whom social workers deal.

> In my experience, social work, in collusion with other groups in power, supports a racist society.

Although this statement may be new to you, you will discover that on the basis of their personal interactions some clients (and workers) hold this perspective of social work. The extent to which social work organizations have dealt with racism is not reflected in this statement. By reading policy statements from social work organizations, others might assess social work as being actively opposed to racism.

> Social work can be done by almost anyone, and untrained or part-time workers could do whatever is necessary, because most people don't need social work and/or just need some common-sense advice.

This last statement contains the belief that social work does not contribute a great deal to many people, that social work is not basic to or important in society. The words could be altered to reflect the belief that social work makes a significant impact on a few people, who in turn have a positive impact on society.

Although these examples may appear to represent extreme positions, they contain a variety of expectations, perceptions, and values about social work. They reinforce the conclusion drawn from the earlier statements about a variety of definitions, and they also reflect some of the basic issues for those seeking to find social work:

How is it defined?
Who does social work?
Who else is involved?
What activities are involved in doing social work?
How important is it?

They also raise some basic questions for the reader who is looking for social work, as follows:

What do you expect of social work?
What part(s), if any, of social work have you experienced?
How valuable a contribution to others do you see social work making?

Moreover, when you search for social work, whose expectations should you explore, which perspectives should you pursue, what assumptions about its worth should serve you as guides, whose values should you adopt? Readers of any introductory text are expected to rely on the perspectives and assumptions supplied by the author of the book. Perspectives and assumptions are revealed in the words selected to describe social work. In turn, the words provide the basic direction the readers of the books will follow in discovering social work. Let's examine this issue further.

SCHOLARLY WORDS

Peggy Rosenthal (1983) suggests an important way to consider how words communicate ideas. She points out how dominant words and jargon rob us of our originality as we express our thoughts with them. Because of their availability, such words in part take over our ideas, guide us along their well-used explanatory routes, and add to or subtract from what we intended to say.

An example is the popular, widely used word *feeling*. Although most people feel strongly when facing an emotional situation, the word has come to be applied to many situations and to signify more than emotions. We are asked our feelings about someone close to us, the latest musical fad, or about a current political issue. Wanting to gauge our feeling response has replaced the desire to know our thoughts or opinions about people and issues. Being able to feel or not feel has become one measure of one's personal growth and liberation. Such a word, then, may have meanings for a reader that differ from those intended by an author.

Readers of introductory social work texts seek the meaning of the profession. The words used by authors of textbooks are the readers' guides. But, as Rosenthal points out, words both lead and mislead their users because words are imprecise, bring up other associations, and are value-laden. The ideas imparted by words frequently narrow, expand, or distort our own vision.

In searching for social work, how can we overcome this tendency to look for what we want to find? How can we avoid words that lead us to partial truths or to the limited vision of someone else? A successful search for social work will permit those who seek it to find it in all its dynamic complexity and to explain its totality and differences to others. Readers of a book that proposes to introduce ideas and knowledge about social work must recognize that the words authors use might lead them astray. This is an important insight. Keeping this insight in mind permits the reader to be alert to meanings that lie outside and within the words chosen by the author, to the way the words reflect the author's assumptions and perceptions, and to be aware of how some powerful words add a direction of their own. You should keep all these ideas in mind as you study about social work.

Several ideas are used by scholars in their efforts to help their readers discover social work. Let's consider three used in our introductory statements. Authors look for social work:

Among the so-called professions.
Within the fields of social work practice.
In the institution of social welfare.

The dominant words *profession, fields,* and *social welfare* not only reflect an author's view, but also lend their own direction to a scholar's search. Also, as stated earlier, authors have strong assumptions about what to look for, about what is important or valued. The words they select and use reflect their assumptions.

Think about the words *profession* and *professional,* which are favorites of those who write or talk about social work. To some, a profession is one's life work, the career to which one is devoted. To others, a profession means money, position, social power. The term brings up images of a job well done. Its application lends prestige to a given area of work.

The words *profession* and *professional* can lead to considerations of career, images of high status and educational achievements, or thoughts of doing a job quite well. They focus authors into dealing with how much status social work has vis-à-vis other professions. They lead writers to consider whether or not social work is a profession, how to enhance its position, and how one prepares to become a professional. The focus is on the organization of the profession itself. Excluded from discussion are those persons not within the profession as defined by the so-called true professionals. The words pose the danger of focusing on how social work is a profession and excluding other aspects of its reality. They can make us overemphasize how social work professionals alone view and value social work, and they can lead to a one-sided perspective.

Another frequently used term is that of *fields of practice.* Authors who use this term discuss where social workers practice and what issues and problems they handle for their clients. Fields such as mental health, child welfare, medical, school, and legal rights, and family, industrial, and international services are covered by the term. The focus is on problems or needs areas and the people who face them. It discusses in detail what social workers do in such an area of concern. It has a dangerous way of making us too present-minded, too bound by contemporary practices and issues. It also presents categories of social work that are somewhat rigid in their focus.

Social welfare also has various meanings and values that direct our understanding of social work. For example, the term brings up images of poverty and public assistance, and it may imply the existence of an underclass that is responsible for its misery and that is served by social work. Furthermore, those who work with this underclass are viewed as favorably or unfavorably as are members of the group they serve. Although efforts are made to go beyond the bounds of social welfare in seeking social work, the term itself is limiting and carries the assumption of little worth. (See Document 1.1).

DOCUMENT 1.1

Quotations from Introductory Texts Indicating Their Basic Directions

1. Roy Lubove
The Professional Altruist,
1973, pp. 20–21.

More than any other category of social workers, caseworkers believed that they had at least the beginnings of a scientific knowledge base as well as a specialized skill, technique, and function which differentiated them from the layman or volunteer. Casework formed the basis of a professional identity and forced upon social agencies a consideration of the roles of professional and volunteer.

There was a wide disparity between the professed standards and goals of social work theorists and the day-to-day work in agencies. By the criterion of objective achievement, "scientific" social work remained an elusive ideal rather remote from reality. It did not follow that the efforts of caseworkers and others to establish social work on a scientific professional basis were meaningless gestures. The fact that they had become dissatisfied with their status and equated progress with professionalization and science merits attention. Even if professionalization was not associated necessarily with substantial scientific achievement and control, it was unquestionably associated with changes in the definition of social work functions, the organization of social work services, and the values and institutions of American society. The professionalization of social work is perhaps better understood in relation to these changes, especially the development of a professional subculture, bureaucratization, and specialization than to any unique social work knowledge base rooted in science.

2. Willard C. Richan and Allan R. Mendelsohn
Social Work: The Unloved Profession, 1973, pp. 15–16.

This is a book about social work, a profession that nursed heroic aspirations and wanted to make a real difference in the human condition. Somewhere along the way it ran off course. It became unsure of its direction and ensnared in bureaucratic red tape, the captive of welfare institutions that cared more about their own survival than the people they were intended to serve.

Or had social work always been the flunky of the social welfare industry and a victim of its own obsession with professional prestige? Had the heroic aims been only an illusion—a way for social workers to persuade themselves and others that they were capable of something better?

This is a profession that, as it seeks to free itself from bureaucratic bondage and realize some part of its high purpose, is now being forced to come to terms with its own limitations.

Social work has become the unloved profession—unloved by its clients whom it has ceased to serve, unloved by the system that it has failed to reinforce, unloved by its peers whose respect it has lost, and, most poignantly, since it has not remained true to its own commitments, unloved even by itself.

3. Arthur E. Fink, Jane H. Pfouts, and Andrew W. Dobelstein
The Field of Social Work, 8th edition, 1985, pp. 9–11.

Many students will begin to read this book with some confusion about social work, some uncertainty about whether social work is a possible career for them, and a lot of anxiety about meeting a client face to face, in a social work situation. All of the contributors to this book have faced similar concerns throughout their social work careers. They join to welcome you to explore a career that has great potential for serving others and for bringing personal satisfaction. Through this book we hope to share with you some of the things we learned about social work, but not all of the things you will need to know in order to be a social worker.

It has been said that the more things change, the more they stay the same. This astute observation concerning progress in human affairs (first made in 1849 by Alphonse Karr) seems particularly apt to me as I look back over the forty-year history of the field of social work. The United States has changed enormously over that span of time, and so have social work and the size of its professional membership, its organizational structure, and the sophistication of its practice methods. And yet, because human nature contin-ues to be much as it always was, the same kinds of personal and social problems remain, always recognizable, although sometimes appearing under new labels or in new guises.

These all-too-familiar problems should challenge the present generation of social work students reading the eighth edition of this text, just as they challenged students reading the first edition in the early 1940s. The present edition, like the seven before it, aims to confront students with two basic themes central to the profession: How do we help people deal with personal misfortune? What can we do to help achieve a just society?

4. Jeffry Galper
Social Work Practice: A Radical Perspective,
1980, pp. 3–4, 7, 10–11.

Social work practitioners, students, and teachers share a growing interest in the relationship of radical ideas to social work theory and practice. This interest is a result of the increasingly difficult circumstances arising within Western capitalist countries and their effect on the people working within social service sectors of capitalist economies. It is becoming less and less possible to believe that the conventional processes of reform can create conditions in which the majority of people can have adequate access to the material necessities of life and can have reasonable opportunities for achievement, satisfaction, and personal growth. For social service workers particularly, a manifestation of the broader discon-tent is the growing recognition that the social services offer very limited and imperfect opportunities for service to others, and that they do not support a personally fulfilling and materially rewarding career.

This book is an effort to formulate an approach to social work practice and more generally, to work in the social service sector, by speaking to the underlying discontent. It does so by elaborating the theoretical underpin-nings of what can be called radical social work and by suggesting the kind of practice that flows from such theoretical underpinnings. Specifically the analysis of the dilemmas facing social services and social service workers rests on a socialist perspective, both in the critique of the present system which it develops and in the alternative strategies and outcomes which it proposes.

Most of the people who are likely to read this material do not consider themselves socialists and in fact, may be largely unfamiliar with a socialist model of analysis. I know too that some readers will have more or less hostile, as well as an unformed, reaction to a socialist outlook. I am intentionally directing my writing to these people as well as to those who have thought through the issues and have concluded that a socialist perspective best expresses their desires, concerns, and analysis.

There is by no means complete agreement among leftist social workers about the definition and nature of radical social work practice. To some extent this is desirable, since there is no single, clearly optimal direction for radical change efforts to take at present in the United States. On the other hand, there is need for more clarity, for greater codification of schools of thought, and for more open debate about the alternatives.

My own understanding of the most useful way to define radical social work in the context of present day Western monopoly capitalist societies is to suggest that *radical social work is social work that contributes to building a movement for the transformation to socialism by its efforts in and through the social services. Radical social work, in this understanding, is socialist social work. Those who practice radical social work are those who struggle for socialism from their position within the social services.*

The definition of radical social work offered here also takes into account the fact that radical social workers are both radicals and social workers. Their political commitments are socialist and their specific occupational category is social worker.

5. Beulah R. Compton
Introduction to Social Welfare and Social Work: Structure, Function, and Process,
1980, pp. 3, 5.

This book is about social welfare, social services, and social work as they have developed in the United States over the past centuries. It is written for the person who has not been introduced to the institution of social welfare, to social services as a system found within that institution, and to social work as the dominant profession involved in delivering those social services to consumers. This book is intended to provide a base upon which further understanding of social welfare can be developed, and it has been written to provide breadth rather than depth of comprehension. It is recognized that social welfare problems and programs are worldwide. However, the difficulty of forming an initial comprehension of our social welfare system and of social work as a profession necessitates limiting this book to a consideration of social welfare and social work systems in the United States of America to the exclusion of other systems.

The development of the profession of social work and the growth of the institution of social welfare can hardly be discussed separately. Actually the profession can be seen as growing out of the institution, and they can both be viewed as organized efforts to cope with the problems of life in an industrial society. The profession developed from the institution's need for agents to carry out the welfare programs that were developing. However, today the profession is much more than the agent of the welfare system. It is charged both with the delivery of services to individuals, families, and groups and with attending to the institutional structure within which such services are offered.

6. Armando Morales and Bradford W. Sheafor
Social Work: A Profession of Many Faces,
Third Edition, 1983, p. 5.

The profession of social work is the study of people who are dedicated to helping others change some aspect of their social functioning. In simplest terms, social workers help people improve their interaction with various aspects of their world—their children, parents, spouse, family, friends, coworkers, or even organizations and whole communities. Social work is a profession committed to change.

To deal effectively with such a wide range of individual and institutional changes, social work has necessarily become a profession also characterized by its diversity—diversity of clientele, diversity of knowledge and skills, and diversity of services provided. In addition, the social workers themselves represent a broad sample of the population. They come in all sizes, shapes, colors, ages, and descriptions. What's more, social workers view diversity as a strength. They consider human difference desirable and their own diversity an enrichment to social work, a quality that has created a dynamic profession that strives to respond to human needs in an ever-changing world. Social work is a profession of many faces.

Moreover, it is a profession of doers. Social workers are not hand wringers who contemplate the issues in hopes that they will disappear. Rather, they take action to prevent problems from developing and to help people deal effectively with situations that cannot be changed and with those that can be changed.

Profession, fields of practice, and social welfare are only three terms that are used to define social work. Others were identified in introducing the statements from social workers. Additional terms are used later in this text.

Examine the value and the meaning associations you have with a given word used to present social work so that you can understand fully how these words are used and can assess your own level of comfort with them. It is essential to form your own interpretations of the words and ideas used to present social work to you. You must examine how comfortable you are with an author's conclusions and why you may not be comfortable. This text can facilitate your discovery of social work only if you question and/or expand on the language it uses. The task includes defining social work in such a way that allows us to find as much of its territory as possible, to learn how to define it in the context of the expectations different people have for it, and to appreciate its achievements in light of the significance placed on its contributions to society by taxpayers and consumers.

This text uses popular approaches to find social work, and it presents ideas that can provide you with as complete a picture of social work as possible. Some of these ideas have been touched on briefly in the preceding discussion. These ideas and others will be incorporated into a model to identify and define social work.

THE DIRECTION OF THIS TEXT: A MODEL TO CONNECT SOCIAL WORK AND SOCIETY

Because this book takes you on a journey of discovery about social work and your place in it, you are asked throughout to consider what you and others think about social work. This includes considering what the words and ideas that are selected to lead you to social work may already mean to you and what differences these words may hold for others.

Differences you may have with scholarly or official social work definitions are encouraged. You are also expected to examine how your own preconceptions about social work differ from those presented in this book.

A single sense of social work is difficult to find because to people of different backgrounds it means different things. Therefore, it is difficult and not necessarily desirable to mold all ideas about social work into a single one. Rather than attempt to do that, this book presents ideas about social work and their relationship to one another in a framework that explores social work's connection to society. The framework will emphasize understanding the following:

Social purpose of the social work profession.
Social and human needs it meets.
Societal contexts in which it takes place.

To locate social work in relation to its societal significance involves identifying what purpose it plays in society. Some people may dislike the fact that society and its members must deal with the human needs met by social work. Nonetheless, the activities used to carry out a social purpose make it significant to all members of society.

Moreover, the ways that varying expectations modify social work can be assessed in relation to this social purpose. Tracing the historical development of the profession and its fields of practice in relation to social purpose will fashion for you a way of looking for and looking at what is constant about social work as well as appreciating how it grows and changes. Using purpose as a guide will permit you to trace differing approaches to social work and to understand why social workers are preoccupied with developing public recognition of their work as a profession. This approach avoids developing a static idea of what social work is and helps us to appreciate how it deals with newly emerging needs and social welfare programs.

One way to teach about a subject area is to begin with the concrete and move to the theoretical. Another is to provide a theoretical framework or some model around which the concrete can be ordered. The question is whether to introduce the theoretical, abstract material first or to give concrete examples first. This text has already introduced some abstract notions about directions and words. It has also presented some concrete illustrations as the basis for the more theoretical discussion. Throughout the remainder of the book, the following model is supported by practitioner examples and other illustrative material:

Professional purposes of social work, which indicate its value in society and the basic direction its practice follows and which can be understood by learning about its historical development and contemporary definitions of the profession.

The human and social needs area social work addresses, which stems from people's social functioning or interactions with self, others, and the structures that comprise their social environments and which can be learned by studying conceptions of need and human behavior.

The societal contexts of social services and "societies," within which social work practice takes place and which attempt to shape the profession and which can be understood by learning about social welfare as a social institution, fields of practice, the different expectations people have for social work, and human diversity.

From these elements emerges a framework in which can be presented practice values, knowledge, and interventions as they address within societal contexts people's needs that arise from social interactions. Refer to the preceding three part model as necessary; it is the model for presenting the material in this book.

PLAN OF THE WORK

This chapter has provided you with an overview of some of the difficulties encountered in introducing people to social work. The discussion includes several precautionary notes to be critical and open-minded in your approach to studying social work. The remainder of the book is divided into four parts, each of which further elaborates on the text's approach to social work and how to become involved in it.

Part I, "Finding Social Work," consists of three chapters. The first of these examines several scholarly quests in some detail. The idea of a profession and thoughts about social work as a profession are presented. The concept of fields of practice, the areas where professionals practice, is also examined. Social work is further analyzed in relation to other social welfare or human service professions. The chapter concludes with an assessment of what these ideas can contribute to locating social work in its societal context.

The second chapter in this part explores differing assumptions and ideas that workers, consumers, and the public have about social work.

The last chapter in this part covers the ideas of professional purpose and its utility in connecting social work and society. A brief presentation of the historical development of social work and an overview of how social work meets human need precedes a discussion of social work in society.

Part II, "Social Work and Society," contains three chapters. The first defines individual and societal change and explores how social work meets these needs through its professional purposes. The second chapter presents a model of social work practice based on these purposes. The values, intervention methods, and knowledge required by this model are also covered. The next chapter in this part discusses contexts for practice. Two major ones are covered: a variety of groups that modify purpose, and a number of resources and services used to carry out professional purpose.

Part III, "Social Workers in Action," discusses the ways social workers carry out their purpose in society. The first of three chapters focuses on how contemporary practice confronts significant changes in people's lives. Discussions of how social workers prepare people to meet individual changes in their lives, use resources systems, and help society change service systems complete the chapter. The second and third chapters present examples of workers who have helped people deal with personal change and who also have changed systems.

The last section, "Conclusion," concentrates on helping you to determine your possible role in social work by discussing a number of commitments you may make to it. These commitments range from being a supportive layperson, volunteer, decision maker regarding social work resources, or a social worker who puts all these roles together. The options within each and their rewards and demands are presented for your consideration.

The information presented in these chapters is augmented by several features. Each chapter is preceded by a brief overview of its contents, major objectives, and key points. Immediately following the title of each chapter is a quotation illustrating the basic direction of that chapter. Re-read the quotation after completing the chapter. It will serve as a summary and reflection of the chapter's content. Most chapters also contain a section asking you to explore your own responses, needs, feelings, and attitudes about what you have read.

You have already been introduced to one feature of this book. Illustrations of various aspects of social work are derived from interviews with a number of social work practitioners. The social workers whose interviews appear in this book have a range of degrees in social work: associates, baccalaureates, masters, and doctorates. They are line workers, administrators, educators, and private practitioners. Many are active in professional associations. One is president of a chapter of the National Association of Social Workers. Each has different views about social work and each came to it by a different route. They are diverse in backgrounds and in careers. They represent a range of groups served by social workers, and they themselves serve a range of populations.

They talk about what attracted them to a social work career, what being a professional means to them, how they work on a team, what opinions they think others have about social work, what "change" means to their practice, how they work with special people and shape social responsibility, and what recommendations they have for persons considering a career in social work.

The social workers are:

Graciela Castex
    social work educator
Bernice Goodman
    private practitioner and activist
Bette Harlan
    unit director in a state hospital
Joe Hernandez
    hospital social worker
Susanna Hueston
    school social worker
Tracey Johnson
    child welfare worker
Irma Serrano
    administrator and professional leader
Adele Weiner
    social work educator, researcher, and practitioner

Their stories, it is hoped, will be provocative and stimulating. Their words also provide other viewpoints and ways of addressing social work. Their interviews are used in several ways in the book by providing introductory material and illustrations in several chapters. In Part III, two chapters are based entirely upon them. Their careers are explored in Chapters 9 and 10, in which their interventions, clients, and policy involvement are explored. Actual case illustrations from their practice are used to highlight the ideas developed in the text.

For Further Study

1. What terms, in addition to those used in this chapter, have you heard used to define social work? With which words used in this chapter are you most

(and least) familiar? What meanings do you associate with any of these words?

2. Interview two or more social work practitioners. Ask them how they became interested in social work and how they developed themselves into a social worker. Have them identify words and terms that they think best define social work. How do their concepts compare to the list you developed in answering the first question?

3. Write an essay stating what value you think social work has in society.

4. The social workers' statements presented in this chapter contain several ways in which they "found" social work. In which of the ways that they became social workers can you identify the elements of your own efforts to become one?

5. Compare and contrast the directions for discovering social work offered by the authors' statements in Document 1.1.

Glossary

DOMINANT WORDS. Certain words with the power to shape and direct our ideas because of the frequency with which they are used, the assumptions they convey, and the manner in which they are commonly used.

PROFESSION. A socially recognized, formally and relatively well-organized group of people who use specialized skills and knowledge to meet a need of members of society.

FIELDS OF SOCIAL WORK PRACTICE. Broad classes of social work practice grouped according to where practitioners work, the type of services they offer, or the clients they serve.

INSTITUTION OF SOCIAL WELFARE. The social institution (a patterned structured response to a need of society's population) composed of health, welfare, and social services designed to help people meet those needs not taken care of in other institutions.

Bibliography

Carroll, Lewis (pseudonym of Charles Dodgson). *Alice's Adventures in Wonderland*. New York: H. M. Caldwell, 1922.

Compton, Beulah. *Introduction to Social Welfare and Social Work: Structure, Function, and Process*. Homewood, IL: Dorsey Press, 1980.

Fink, Arthur E., Jane H. Pfouts, and Andrew W. Dobelstein. *The Field of Social Work*. 8th ed. Beverly Hills: Sage, 1985.

Galper, Jeffry. *Social Work Practice: A Radical Perspective*. Englewood Cliffs: NJ: Prentice-Hall, 1980.

Lubove, Roy. *The Professional Altruist.* New York: Atheneum, 1973.

Morales, Armando, and Bradford W. Sheafor. *Social Work: A Profession of Many Faces.* 3rd ed. Boston: Allyn & Bacon, 1983.

Richan, Willard C., and Allan R. Mendelsohn. *Social Work: The Unloved Profession.* New York: New Viewpoints, 1973.

Rosenthal, Peggy. *Words and Values: Some Leading Words and Where They Lead Us.* New York: Oxford University Press, 1983.

=PART I=

FINDING SOCIAL WORK

PART OVERVIEW

What words and ideas are associated with social work? What images and values does the term bring to mind? What meanings are used to describe it? This section explores several sets of values and meanings that are associated with social work.

The first set of ideas consists of those used by scholars who write about social work and by spokespersons for the profession itself. They use the following concepts to define social work and to determine its contributions to society:

Profession.
Social welfare.
Fields of practice.

As a reader of this book, you are asked to reexamine any value and meaning associations that the terms *profession* and *social welfare* hold for you and to explore any differences from those summarized in this section.

A second set of values and meanings associated with social work is also presented in this section—the expectations of various groups, such as client and taxpayer groups. These groups come in contact with social work in quite different ways. You need to be familiar with how such groups view social work because some of them form one of the "contexts" of social work practice. Those whom social workers help, as well as those who create and/or pay for programs, create one context in which social workers must present and explain their profession.

The part also sensitizes you to the need to identify limitations in defining social work and to incorporate your own outlook into your definition. Because social work is subject to many interpretations and because viewpoints about it come from several segments of society, a framework is needed that identifies it from as broad a perspective as possible. This section concludes by offering such an approach. It incorporates several concepts about social work, including:

The social purposes of social work practice.

Meeting human and societal changes as a needs area covered by social work.

"Societies" and services as contexts for social work practice.

CHAPTER TWO

Scholarly Quests:
Finding the Profession,
Its Place in Social Welfare,
and Its Fields of Practice

The increasing trend toward the privatization of social work redirects the traditional concern of the profession from providing services to those in need to competing for those who can afford to pay. Although there is room for both private and public services, it is the present lack of services to 80 percent or more of those with identified needs, as well as the restricted levels of service . . . that should be our major focus.

***

The profession must push assertively—if not in concert with others, then alone—for the development and acceptance of tools that more accurately reflect its domain. It must also continue to refine its education and practice with the latest research. . . . [T]he profession should not forget, minimize, or risk losing the base of its own strength: its person-in-situation perspective and its historical priorities in behalf of people who have the greatest need.

June Gary Hopps (1987)

CHAPTER OVERVIEW

This chapter explores the following in detail:

Profession.
Social welfare.
Fields of practice.

These three terms, alone or in combination, are used frequently to define social work and to help introduce readers to it. Each is assessed in this chapter for the contribution it makes to our effort to connect social work to society. For example, *profession* contributes the notion of carrying out a social purpose. *Social welfare* and *fields of practice* indicate which area of human need the purpose of social work addresses. Profession and social welfare also help to measure the value people place on social work. Finally, social welfare and

143, 393

LIBRARY
College of St. Francis
JOLIET, ILLINOIS

fields of practice help to identify one of the contexts of social work
practice.

THE IDEA OF A PROFESSION AS A WAY OF FINDING SOCIAL WORK

One of the most popular and useful ideas social scientists employ to present
social work is that of a profession. Authors organize their presentations of social work according to the traits of a profession (Morales and Sheafor, 1986).
Those who use this approach identify several major characteristics that distin-
guish a profession and apply these traits to their discussion of social work. In
this fashion, it is possible both to describe the development of social work as
the discipline became more professionalized and to offer some conclusions
about its place among other professions.

Although key features of social work can be highlighted in such an assessment, keep in mind that focusing on how it meets the criteria of a profession
may also lead to overlooking other important aspects of it. Also, to many who
are unfamiliar with the social scientists' use of the word *profession*, it has other
value and meaning associations, especially those of status and accomplishment.
The discovery that the fit of social work with the characteristics of a profession
is less than perfect leaves those trying to discover social work wondering what
it is if it is not a traditional profession. They also may question what this means
for their participation in it. We will return to this issue after exploring the social
scientists' criteria for a profession and how social work meets these.

Social scientists characterize a profession as exhibiting the following characteristics:

A distinctive set of activities in society with the purpose of meeting the
needs of its members.

The development and use of a body of knowledge about such needs and
how to meet them.

A professional subculture to educate, socialize, and organize those of
its members who serve the public.

A binding set of values to guide the behavior of the professionals.

Recognition by the public as experts in their field who are allowed
a large degree of autonomy and rewards.

These attributes derive from those thought to characterize the traditional professions of medicine and law, and to a lesser extent, the ministry (Federico,
1984).

Although any occupation can be distinguished from others by what it does
and what must be known to perform its activities, professions are thought to
involve more complex skills and abilities and to call on knowledge beyond that
required in learning how to perform its routine activities. The additional knowl-

edge needed by professionals is used by them to make decisions about what to do and how to solve the problems brought to them by those they serve. This specialized knowledge requires a lengthy or complex formal education that separates the professions from other occupations.

Another attribute that distinguishes a profession from other jobs is the importance placed on a set of values or a code of ethics whose purpose is to regulate the behavior of the professionals and to help guarantee that those they serve will not be abused or underserved. The Hippocratic Oath of medical doctors is one example of such codes. Members of the medical profession and the public hold its practitioners accountable for any breach of its ethical standards. It is believed also that clients need to be protected from the unethical use of the special knowledge and techniques about which they may know very little. The goal of these ethical standards is to protect the public against the misuse of the trust placed in the professionals.

Connected to the development and use of ethical standards by the professions to protect users of its services is the creation of mechanisms by the public to regulate the entrance into professions and the subsequent behavior of those who enter. Although medical doctors through their professional subculture with its associations and schools select and socialize medical students and practitioners, a state government will require passing scores on medical exams and the completion of licensing procedures before permitting a new medical professional to work. Although members of society are willing to grant a monopoly to a profession, they are also likely to maintain considerable control over it and its members. Each profession tries to define and regulate its own practice in order to control access to it.

Developing a body of knowledge and specialized techniques, being recognized by the public as able to perform a needed function, creating a professional subculture, and emphasizing a regulatory code of ethics are all done in order to meet a specific need of members of society (Popple, 1985). Delineating this needs area and gaining control over helping people meet their needs in it marks the emergence and maturation of a profession. Professions play a key role in defining which needs will be met and how they will be addressed.

Critical to defining a profession is determining its area of expertise within a needs area and the special skills needed to practice that profession. The needs met by the traditional professions of medicine and law are exclusive to each. Medicine handles health and illness and treats those who are sick, and lawyers handle disputes at law and protect the legal rights and interests of their clients. These areas of human and social need are fairly clear-cut and easily distinguishable, although to a greater or lesser extent people can meet some of their own needs in this area.

Overall, each profession deals with a particular (set of) human need(s) that those they serve cannot meet without assistance or inconvenience. Society expects these professionals to be expert and helpful in dealing with concerns in a particular area. In some ways, the profession is granted a near monopoly to gain and use the expertise required to meet the need. According to Maslow (1968), human beings have needs in the following areas:

Physical
Mental
Emotional
Economic
Self-fulfillment
Place in community
Intimacy and love

Within each area of need, or in a combination of them, the professions develop ways to help people meet their needs.

Professionals continue to expand their theoretical and practical knowledge base, becoming ever more sophisticated in their ability to define and meet the needs of those they serve. The development of this expanded knowledge distances the professionals from those they serve and lessens the possibility that clients will be able to use the knowledge and techniques of the professionals to help themselves. The recent advances in medicine are a case in point. The people who develop the knowledge and those who use it are becoming more and more separated. Based in new technologies, the medical profession becomes more specialized within itself and further removed from its clients. Law has also become more specialized with developments of complexity in laws and the legal system paralleling those of medicine. Laws relating to corporations, criminal activities, real estate, mineral and water rights, and consumer interests are examples of only a few of the many areas of specialized legal knowledge. Knowing complex details of the law and using specialized skills in legal research, case preparation, and courtroom presentation are what set lawyers apart from their clients. Access to agency resources and information along with knowledge of special programs for children and the elderly, for example, separate social workers and clients.

In this century, in addition to the traditional professions, a range of other professions has emerged. Librarians, nurses, recreational therapists, psychologists, family therapists, and social workers are a few examples. Each of these has more or less patterned itself after the traditional professions, although the newer ones lack the status of the legal and medical professions. The status of the traditional professions is derived from their strong societal recognition, organizational subculture, and the significant needs they address for members of society. In addition, the knowledge base and specialized skills of the newer professions are not as well developed or as exclusive to them as are those of the traditional professions. Without as exclusive a function in an established and universally recognized needs area, these newer professions are eager for

status and other social rewards and have developed strong organizational subcultures and codes of ethics as a basis for societal recognition. Among the
newer helping or human service professions, social work is conspicuous for its
self-conscious drive to be recognized as a profession.

Remember our caution that dominant words, such as *profession*, have the
power to give direction to our inquiries because other meanings or values are
associated with them. Although social scientists attribute special knowledge
and skills, societal recognition, professional subculture, and values to a profession, members of the newer professions may be motivated by their association
of professions with status and autonomy. Social scientists assess how well a
particular profession fits the categories that characterize any profession. What
emerges from their assessment is the conclusion that there are only a few professions and many other semi- or subprofessions. The semiprofessions are said
to lack one or more attribute of a profession, or they are judged as weak on
some of them.

Hence, members of a discipline that to the scientists does not measure up
as a profession may believe that this rejection means they lack status or competence. They fail to recognize that the conclusion of the social scientists that
their discipline is not among the professions is based on value and meaning
associations different from their own (see interviews on pages 29–31).

I AM A SOCIAL WORKER
"What Being a Professional Means to Me"

GRACIELA CASTEX: Being a professional somehow for me is linked with my
own purpose in life. Being a professional is not so separate from what makes
up my own personhood, what makes my own overall purpose in life. There are
things like being ethical, being truthful, being a good citizen, dealing with social
issues, being timely, and being sensitive to others' needs that are part of me.
Also the educational, scholarly component, including keeping up with the
changes in the profession, with changes in policy and laws that have changed,
and learning about new issues complements for me what is being a professional.

BERNICE GOODMAN: Being a professional means several things to me. First
of all, it means an institutional sanction to put into practice ways of relating to
people and to offer my healing potential to people. It also means that I am given
the sanction to develop myself and my abilities to help heal people. It gives me

the opportunity to link my positive energy to that of others. My being a professional means that I can directly and indirectly address forces to help people and this society address issues of living together, the environment, and justice.

JOE HERNANDEZ: To be a professional, a social worker needs to understand any population he or she is going to work with. Workers need to understand their clients' needs and be empathetic with them. Social workers need to be willing to do as much as they can for their client population, regardless of who their clients are. Sometimes, for example, hospital workers are afraid of various illnesses. Because of this fear, they cannot approach certain patients. They will not work with and they avoid such populations. A professional understands both personal fears and client needs. Professionals try to overcome their fears in order to help others.

SUSANNA HUESTON: I think that the best professional who works with clients is one who serves as a role model for them, displaying ethical, responsible behavior. Such a professional is one who also displays emotions and acts like a human being with feelings. Crying, along with empathy, is not unprofessional. I try to model successful, professional behavior and help children assess the consequences when their own behavior is based in unethical, undisciplined actions.

TRACEY JOHNSON: In working in parks and recreation with workers who had training only in physical education, I quickly realized that I had a different orientation. I guess it came from being a professional that I went beyond the job description. It was as if I could not help relating the kids' lives outside the program to what they did in the program. I also tried to get the program to do something about the kids' problems. It seems to me that a professional is one who uses her or his training to go beyond what is merely required. The professional goes a long way to help people, sometimes confronting the agency or program where they work. The client is first to the true professional. A professional also has to have say-so in how an agency operates. Social workers are usually the ones with the clients, and they need input to the setting of goals for clients and have input to policy matters. Without autonomy and input, regardless of the job's description, workers are not professionals.

IRMA SERRANO: The word professional should not be used as a label to block growth. In the very beginning of my career, although I had a good sense of myself and had worked as a teacher, my first job was as a social work assistant. To me, that was a put down, because in that agency a professional was the beginning for opportunity, while the assistant was a dead end. The idea was that you could not move beyond the assistant job, but in reality you can prove yourself there, can move toward being more of a professional.

ADELE WEINER: Being a professional social worker means that I have internalized a set of ethical and practice guidelines that I operate within. Rather than simply applying actions in a "cookbook" manner, my professional expertise allows me to make judgments and choose among a myriad of options available to me. As a professional, I have made a personal commitment to fulfilling the mandate of the profession to help individuals who are not always able to act in their own behalf. This responsibility includes not only ensuring that current policy is carried out in a humane fashion but that future policy is framed and practitioners are trained to uphold the highest ideals of the profession. One of the reasons that I went into teaching is that I felt that as a practitioner I could touch the lives of only a limited number of clients in a year. As an educator, if I could help develop two good practitioners a year, then I could affect a much larger number of clients and policies.

SOCIAL WORK AS A PROFESSION

Social work is one of the newer professions that often fails to be accorded full professional recognition on the traits used by social scientists. Using these traits, and keeping in mind other value and meaning associations of the word *profession*, what can we learn about social work?

The key to understanding any profession is recognizing its special function in society, the set of activities it performs to meet a particular aspect of human needs (Popple, 1985). Social work helps people to function within their social environment. Social workers are concerned with promoting the effective functioning of society's members in their socially determined environments and in social institutions. Social workers identify and help people to deal with the problems and concerns they develop in their social functioning. They may strengthen people's abilities to function and to solve their problems; help people to identify, obtain, and use concrete resources they may need to function better in their environment; or work to create new resource structures and opportunities for people to use as they interact with other people and systems in their environment. Social workers help people individually and in small groups with their social functioning. They help people confront their problems directly as well as work with the social structural issues that lead to problems in people's social functioning (Constable, 1984). The last chapter in this part and much of the next part of the book expand on this brief overview of social work's purpose in meeting people's needs.

As one of the newer professions, social work has tried especially hard to create a professional subculture that promotes the usefulness of how it helps people deal with their social functioning in their environment (Lubove, 1965).

The efforts of social work to create a professional subculture have been twofold: focusing on educational programs and promoting professional associations.

During the first thirty years of the twentieth century, pioneering social workers created schools of social work out of their initial agency-based educational efforts. The initial focus was on practical skills, and it emphasized learning in the field or agency setting. The social work schools, in turn, spearheaded efforts to develop a knowledge base that was more theoretical in nature and less focused on practical skills. The early efforts to develop a knowledge base attracted the schools to the recently introduced psychological theories of behavior and turned them away from political, sociological, and economic concepts. Today the knowledge base of social workers is composed of information derived from sociology, psychology, political science, economics, biology, anthropology, and other disciplines.

The knowledge base learned by social workers in their educational programs is divided into six broad curriculum areas, as follows:

Human behavior and the social environment.
Social welfare programs and services.
Policy.
Practice methods.
Social research.
Field education.

Field education is an educationally directed experience in social service agencies. Under the guidance of the program's field curriculum and the supervision of a service provider, social work students apply theoretical and practice knowledge in their direct work with clients and in their interactions with other services and other professionals (Council on Social Work, 1984). Their knowledge of practice methods, skills, and techniques is acquired in classroom courses covering theories of practice as well as more practical knowledge. The student in an undergraduate program learns a generalist method of practice, which in part means that they must develop a broad range of social work interventions from a problem-solving perspective. A master's level student concentrates in a practice area such as direct service to children and families or specializes in a field of practice such as agency administration and supervision (Dinerman, 1982). The doctoral level emphasizes research skills. Some doctoral and master's students combine social work with the study of law or of another discipline.

All social workers learn to be consumers of and practitioners of social research in their professional practice. Skills in social research are critical to the scientific assessment by workers of their own practice and the evaluation by them of the effectiveness of service delivery and the usefulness of social programs. Their knowledge of social services and programs is broad-based, covering knowledge about programs of the institutions that provide resources to their clients. The baccalaureate level worker acquires a broad knowledge of such programs and the skills to develop an in-depth knowledge in a given area of practice. The master's level specialist focuses on a specific area in addition to the broad-based knowledge.

Connected both to practice and program knowledge is the social workers' knowledge about policy in systems and institutions that allocate resources to meet the needs of their clients. The generalists learn how policy is made and the details of specific policies. As part of their professional mandate, they also learn how to change existing policies or how to get new ones adopted. The master's level practitioner sometimes specializes in an area of planning and policy making and works as a policy analyst or program development specialist for communities or social agencies.

Practical and theoretical knowledge is in those parts of the social workers' knowledge base that are made up of how to work with people, what programs and services are available to them and the policies that allocate such resources, and how to pose practice and policy questions in a scientific fashion. The knowledge of human behavior learned by social workers is more theoretical in nature. It builds on a strong liberal arts and science background and supports skills in problem assessment, policy development, and research use. Social workers integrate knowledge from the physical and social sciences about how human beings function holistically within their environments. Knowledge of human biology and the various systems of the body; theories of psychological development; concepts of sociological, economic, and political systems and their impact on people's lives; ideas of human diversity and differences—all are brought together during their education to provide social workers with a broad integrated knowledge of human behavior in its environmental context. In order to help people from different backgrounds with their social functioning, social workers learn how diverse people solve problems within their sociopolitical environments. Social workers also learn how the functioning of these systems either offers opportunities to or oppresses such people.

Although the educational programs largely developed this approach to teaching the knowledge base of social work, they were supported in their assessment of what should be taught by the professional associations, which form the second part of social work's subculture. The development of professional associations followed the rise of the schools and accompanied the creation of a knowledge base. Two major professional associations emerged during the 1950s. The National Association of Social Workers (NASW) became the major membership organization for practitioners, and the Council on Social Work Education (CSWE) was its counterpart for educational programs and social work educators.

Initially, the practitioner-oriented organizations were independent, representing separate groups of social workers who were engaged in serving a particular population or who worked in a specific service setting. Organizations of hospital, school, and psychiatric social workers are examples. In the early 1950s, efforts at creating a single organization for practitioners were successful, and the NASW was established in 1955. About 15 years later, membership was opened to those with a baccalaureate degree in social work from an accredited program. Thus membership included workers at both the master's and the baccalaureate level (Lubove, 1965).

The professional association responsible for accrediting educational programs is the Council on Social Work Education. The CSWE grew out of earlier efforts to establish standards for education. By the mid-1930s these efforts resulted in the recognition of the Masters in Social Work (MSW) as the only professional social work degree. In 1932 the Association of Schools of Social Work guided setting and application of standards. A rival organization, the National Association of Schools of Social Work, favored one-year programs unlike the two-year approach promoted by the Association of Schools of Social Work. In the early 1950s, the CSWE was created from these two associations and adopted the two-year graduate education model. Although the MSW did not represent as high a status as medicine's doctorate, the master degree requirement for entry into practice supposedly had more value than the earlier baccalaureate degrees in social work.

Until the late 1960s, the MSW remained as the recognized professional social work degree. At that time, undergraduate degree programs that granted the baccalaureate in social work (BSW) re-emerged. Also characterized as an entry-level professional degree, the BSW emphasized generalist practice, which created a dual-level entry into professional practice. By 1973 the CSWE was applying accreditation standards to the BSW as well as the MSW programs. Doctoral programs (DSW, or PhD) are not accredited by the CSWE (Leighninger, 1984).

The latest CSWE curriculum policy statement and standards, adopted in 1984 and revised in 1988, define current BSW and MSW practice responsibilities. The accreditation standards, as applied by the accrediting process of the CSWE's Commission on Accreditation, ensure consistency and integrity in both parts of professional education. Accreditation standards cover the nature of program content, administration, and structure. Although each program may create its own approach to teaching the required content in relation to its desired outcomes, the standards assure uniformity of social work education (Aigner, 1984; Hokenstad, 1984). The CSWE serves as a primary guardian and gatekeeper for entry into social work practice. Social work educators and practitioners join the CSWE and benefit from its publications as well as the annual program meeting, which sponsors workshops, presentations, and papers on current social work education and practice issues (see Document 2.1).

The NASW also offers extensive benefits to its members. Today the NASW has about 110,000 members and 55 chapters, one in each state and in Washington, DC, New York City, Puerto Rico, the Virgin Islands, and Europe. Membership services include practice liability insurance; professional development opportunities such as continuing education, national conferences, and symposia; numerous journal, book, and encyclopedia publications; professional standard

DOCUMENT 2.1

Curriculum Policy for the Master's Degree and Baccalaureate Degree Programs in Social Work Education

1.0 SCOPE AND INTENT OF THE POLICY STATEMENT

1.1 This document sets forth the official curriculum policy for the accreditation of programs of social work education by the Council on Social Work Education (CSWE). It succeeds the 1969 statement of curriculum policy for master's (MSW) programs in social work and provides the first statement of curriculum policy for social work baccalaureate (BSW) programs.

1.2 The policy statement specifies certain content areas to be covered and requires that they be logically related to each other, to the purposes and values of social work as set forth in this document, and to the stated purposes, mission, resources, and educational context of each professional program. The statement does not prescribe any particular curriculum design.

1.3 The content areas on which all programs of social work education are required to build their curricula are intended to provide social work students with a professional foundation—the basic values, knowledge, and skills required for entry into the profession . . .

* * *

2.0 RELATIONSHIP TO ACCREDITATION STANDARDS

2.1 The commission on Accreditation of CSWE develops standards by which social work education programs are evaluated for accreditation. These standards establish principles for the organization and administration of programs of social work education and include the educational requirements set forth in this Curriculum Policy Statement . . .

* * *

4.4 Social work as an organized profession is practiced in a wide variety of settings and in the major institutions of society, including the family. It is the primary discipline in social services provision and is one of the essential disciplines in income maintenance, health, education, and justice organizations. It is utilized as well in business, industry and government. Social work is necessary in meeting the social needs of diverse population groups with a wide range of problems and aspirations . . .

* * *

4.5 It is essential, therefore, that all professional social workers have, in common, knowledge, values, and skills that are generally transferable from one setting, population group, geographic area, or problem to another. It is also essential that advanced professional social work practitioners have the special knowledge and skills appropriate to a specific role, field of practice, population group, or problem area . . .

* * *

6.2 Social work education takes place in four-year undergraduate and two-year graduate programs and leads to professional degrees at the baccalaureate and master's levels, respectively. These levels of education differ from each other in the level of knowledge and skill they expect students to synthesize in practice competence. These distinctions and the discretion provided by the tradition of academic freedom contribute to the desired uniqueness of each program . . .

* * *

BSW PROGRAMS

6.8 The baccalaureate is the first level of professional education for entry into the profession. The curriculum shall include the knowledge, values, processes, and skills that have proved to be essential for the practice of social work, which is hereafter referred to as the *professional foundation*. The baccalaureate social worker should attain a beginning professional level of proficiency in the self-critical and

accountable use of this social work knowledge and integrate this knowledge with the liberal arts perspective.

* * *

6.9 Students who receive a baccalaureate degree from an accredited social work program should possess the professional judgment and proficiency to apply differentially, with supervision, the common professional foundation to service systems of various sizes and types. There should be special emphasis on direct services to clients which includes organization and provision of resources on clients' behalf. Each program shall explicate the ways in which students are being prepared for generalist practice.

* * *

6.10 The purpose of undergraduate social work education is to prepare students for a beginning professional level of practice. Although some BSW graduates will subsequently pursue additional social work education at the graduate level, this consideration is independent of the primary objectives of the undergraduate curriculum.

* * *

MSW PROGRAMS

6.1 Social work education at the master's level is built on the liberal arts perspective and must include the professional foundation and one or more concentrations. In the master's program, the content relating to the professional foundation is directed toward preparing the student for concentration. Students who graduate from MSW programs are to have advanced analytic and practice skills sufficient for self-critical, accountable, and ultimately autonomous practice.

* * *

6.12 Concentrations at the master's level may be organized in various ways, such as fields of service, population groups, problem areas, professional roles, interventive modes, and advanced generalist practice. Each graduate program shall clearly identify which framework it is using to organize the advanced concentrations and describe the relationship of this framework to its educational philosophy.

* * *

6.13 All MSW programs must require or provide an educational background with a liberal arts perspective. They also must provide all non-BSW students with the professional foundation content on which every concentration is built.

(SOURCE: This material was first published in the *Handbook of Accreditation Standards and Procedures,* 1988, and it is reprinted here with the permission of The Council of Social Work Education.)

---

setting through licensing and job classification efforts along with the Academy of Certified Social Workers; social policy action achieved by influencing policy legislation; and policy development in other systems by lobbying and political action efforts (Colby, 1983). The chapter and local units follow the priorities of the national organization, which is headquartered near Washington, DC. The national organization is directed by a professional staff that is responsible to a board of directors and is required to carry out the policies set by the nationally elected Delegate Assembly.

In addition to these major professional associations, which reflect the educational and other criteria of social scientists, there are other organizations of social workers serving the interests of practitioners. Chief among these is the Association of Black Social Workers (ABSW). Having a career as a social worker, but not necessarily having education as one, is part of the membership requirements. It especially serves the interests of Black social workers and clients. It has its own special code of ethics and focuses on services to the Black community and its families. The ABSW is organized into local units and sponsors workshops and regional and national conferences (see interviews on pages 38–40).

Social work has integrated a strong value base into its professional organizations and its educational programs. The NASW has adopted a Code of Ethics that represents a continuation and culmination of ethical positions taken by its predecessor associations. The present code is divided into several areas cover-

I AM A SOCIAL WORKER
"Professional Growth and Professional Involvement"

GRACIELA CASTEX: There are several ways that I have continued my professional development. One is the fact that I am working on a doctoral degree, which is giving me the opportunity to hear a larger perspective on issues and to look at issues differently than I have looked at them before. There is a whole range of new growth-producing experiences that go along with the structure of a doctoral program, such as becoming acquainted with the literature or interacting with faculty and students in doing the day-to-day classwork.

A lot of my growth comes from my current teaching. The things I do from day to day in the classroom, such as figuring out what students need, dealing with those needs, looking at the students in terms of changes in student populations, teaching differently today than I did five years ago, and learning how students learn, contribute to my growth. In addition, going to professional meetings, such as those of the Council on Social Work Education, the statewide social work organization, National Association of Social Workers, or lectures that are not necessarily conducted by social workers but that touch on social issues, enhance my own understanding. I can bring that into the classroom and into my own research and work.

BERNICE GOODMAN: It seems to me that every day I work with people is a process of growth and development, for them and for me. The spark is the commitment to change and caring about what happens to other people. As a profession, social work is about growth and change. The process I engage in leads to my development.

BETTE HARLAN: Find an agency or a supervisor who will provide opportunity for continued growth. A social worker can never stop trying to learn and grow. It is an important way to avoid burnout. To continue one's education by seminar, conferences, or workshops is quite essential to becoming a better practitioner. Having started out without a social work degree in public welfare, I know the importance to me of an education in social work both as a worker and as a person. Professional growth and development come not only from formal sources but also from informal sharing with my colleagues.

JOE HERNANDEZ: Because of my inexperience in dealing with persons with AIDS, the lack of knowledge about AIDS at that time, working alone with PWAs (persons with AIDS), and my co-workers' and supervisor's fear of AIDS, I had to teach myself. I picked up material and did a lot of reading. I explored with the patients their feelings and needs. I kept documentation about what I did in order to monitor my own practice and how it changed and when it was effective. Keeping these records was instructive to me about how and what I had missed in some cases. I also reached out to others and learned from them. I conducted research with a colleague about social workers serving persons with AIDS.

SUSANNA HUESTON: We never stop growing and learning. Certainly I have learned a tremendous amount from the cases I have had and from interacting with team members. I am fortunate to work in a community where a lot of professional workshops are offered. I participate in these and keep abreast of issues and developments. I am a member of the Association of Black Social Workers and follow the work of this organization. I am also a member of the board of directors of a community mental health center where I live. Being on this board means that I have to keep up with issues in this field.

TRACEY JOHNSON: On my current job, I have an excellent supervisor from whom I've learned a great deal. My cases are not of one type. In addition, time is granted by the agency for me to attend workshops. I've attended several dealing with child welfare issues and practices. It is important to keep up in the field and to find out about it. Reading the literature from professional associations has been very helpful to me. I'm a member of NASW and ABSW. As a student, I was very active.

IRMA SERRANO: Originally, when I finished school my first involvement in a professional organization was in the Association of Puerto Rican Social Workers. The reason I did this was that at the time I, along with other Hispanics, needed a place to share our feelings and frustrations about problems in agencies and a place to ventilate. I found other people with similar problems and that we could support one another. I also saw it as a chance to recruit people who could also take action on issues. I became president of the organization.

From there I was invited to participate in other associations, including the Conference on Social Welfare and the National Association of Social Workers. I was elected to the board of the New York City chapter of NASW. I worked on committees and in other capacities. I did so because I believed that the Hispanic community had little representation or say. I thought being active professionally was a very good avenue. I'd decided that instead of being outside of the organization and raising issues, the only way that you can do things is to be inside. It was an educational process. There were many people who did not know that much about Hispanics. It is necessary to correct false ideas about Hispanics, such as stereotypes that Hispanics are loud and that we make a lot of noise. These false ideas can be removed by example and contact.

I also started teaching about Hispanics in schools of social work. This became a growth process for me as well. I've taught for the past ten years. First the course was called Puerto Rican Lifestyles, but with the increase of other Hispanic populations in New York City, the course is now called Hispanic Lifestyles. For the past six years I have served on the state's Minority Committee on Mental Health helping to develop better services for Hispanics.

ADELE WEINER: Professional organizations play an important role in the life of the social worker. They provide emotional support for workers who often work under very stressful conditions. Continuing education programs offer the opportunity for professional growth and development. Recognition from one's peers is rewarding. Additionally, the organization of social workers into large national organizations offers a power base for lobbying for policy changes and funding.

---

ing the social worker's behavior in a range of practice situations and relationships. The Code of Ethics emphasizes that the primary concern of social workers is their clients and the interests of their clients. The right of clients to determine their own lives and the guarantee of client involvement in problem assessment and solution are to be protected by social workers. Whether in agency or private practice, worker regard for clients is called for by the Code of Ethics (National Association of Social Workers, 1980).

This primary ethical responsibility of social workers is buttressed by ethical commitments to those who employ them, to their colleagues with whom they practice, and to the profession itself. Social workers also are called on by the Code to promote the profession and its effort to develop better programs and better strategies for the delivery of service. Moreover, social workers are expected to promote the general welfare by advocating social policy and social legislation in line with the best interest of their clients.

The creation of a professional subculture with associations and educational programs to educate and socialize workers and to promote the profession have been successful in bringing the majority of social workers together. Less successful than these efforts, but extremely important to the profession, has been gaining public recognition for expertise in a significant area of needs and for autonomy in practicing to meet these needs. The public has not responded consistently to efforts to license social workers as being especially qualified to help people function in their environment (see Document 2.2).

Although accreditation standards assure the public of uniformity and cohesiveness in education, and although the NASW presses for licensure and the classification of state social work jobs to include a social work degree in their requirements, the majority of the public does not see these two efforts as important or essential to society (Pecora and Austin, 1983). This viewpoint stems in part from misconceptions about the worth of social work for society and differ-

DOCUMENT 2.2

Louisiana Board Certified Social Work Practice Act

2701. LEGISLATURE PURPOSE

The legislature declares that, in order to safeguard the public health, safety and welfare to the people of this state against unauthorized, unqualified, and improper practice of board certified social work, it is necessary that a proper regulatory authority be established and adequately provided for.

2702. SHORT TITLE

This chapter shall be known and may be cited as the Board Certified Social Work Practice Act.

2703. DEFINITIONS

As used in this chapter, unless the context clearly requires otherwise, and except as otherwise expressly provided:

(1) "Board" means the Louisiana State Board of Board Certified Social Work Examiners.

(2) "Board Certified Social Work" means a practice or service which a special knowledge of social resources, social systems, human capabilities, and the part that past experiences play in determining present behavior is directed at helping people to achieve more adequate, satisfying, productive, and self-realizing social adjustments. The application of social work princi-ples and methods includes, but is not restricted to, casework and the use of social work methodology of nonmedical nature with individuals, families, and groups and other measures to help people modify behavior or personal and family adjustment; providing information and referral services; explaining and interpreting the psychosocial aspects in the situation of individuals, families, or groups; helping communities to analyze social problems and human needs and the direct delivery of human services; and education and research related to the practice of board certified social work.

(3) "Social Work Methodology" means the use of psychosocial methods within a professional relationship to assist the person or persons to achieve a better psychosocial adaptation, to acquire greater human realization of psychosocial potential and adaption, to modify internal and external conditions which affect individuals, groups, or communities in respect to behavior, emotions, and thinking, in respect to their intrapersonal and interpersonal processes.

(4) "Board certified social worker" means persons licensed under the provisions of this chapter.

(5) "Graduate school of social work" means any university or other institution of higher learning offering a full-

time graduate course of study in social work, granting the degree Master of Social Work or Social Welfare, and approved by the Council on Social Work Education or its predecessor or successor organization.

2704. BOARD OF SOCIAL WORK EXAMINERS

A. There is hereby created a Louisiana state board of board certified social work examiners, consisting of five members, who are citizens of the United States and residents of the state of Louisiana. The members shall be appointed by the governor within thirty days from the effective date of this chapter to serve the following terms; one member for a term of one year; two members for a term of two years; and two members for a term of three years. All appointees shall be selected from one list compiled by the Louisiana Society for Clinical Social Work and the state council of the National Association of Social Workers.

B. Each board member shall be certified under this chapter, except that members comprising the board as first appointed shall be persons who have rendered service, education, training or research in social work for at least five years and who hold a master's degree from an approved graduate school of social work. At all times the board shall have at least three members who are engaged primarily in rendering direct services in board certified social work and/or at least one member who is engaged primarily in education, training, or research in social work.

2706. QUALIFICATIONS; EXAMINATION; LICENSING

A. The board shall license as a board certified social worker and issue an appropriate certificate to any person who files a verified application therefor, accompanied by such fee as is required by Section 2712, and who submits evidence verified by oath and satisfactory to the board that he:

(1) is at least twenty-one years of age;

(2) is of good moral character;

(3) has obtained a master's degree from an accredited graduate school of social work;

(4) is a resident of the state of Louisiana;

(5) demonstrates professional competence by passing a satisfactory examination in social work which shall require demonstration of special knowledge and skill in inventive methods and techniques and the underlying theories including psychopathology, group dynamics, human growth and behavior and health and welfare resource systems and which shall be written and oral as prescribed by the board; and

(6) has at least two accumulated years of postmaster's experience after the effective date of this chapter in a setting practicing social work under the supervision of a board certified social worker or a physician licensed to practice medicine in the state of Louisiana and certified by the American Board of Neurology and Psychiatry who must countersign all work, provided that the board has the right to review supervi-

sion to standardize its quality and quantity.

B. Upon investigation of the application and other evidence submitted, the board shall, not less than thirty days prior to the examination, notify each applicant that the application and evidence submitted for consideration is satisfactory and accepted, or unsatisfactory and rejected. If an application is rejected said notice shall state the reasons for such rejection.

C. The place of examination shall be designated in advance by the board. The examination shall be given annually at such time and place and under such supervision as the board may determine, and specifically at such other times, as in the opinion of the board, the number of applicants warrants.

D. Each applicant shall pass an examination approved by the board. The board shall assign the passing grade point to any examination administered after having promulgated rules and regulations. To insure impartiality, written examinations shall be by numbers, and no paper shall bear the name of the applicant.

E. If an applicant fails the examination, he may retake the examination at the next opportunity given by the board, upon payment of such fee as is required by R.S. 37:2712.

F. The board shall assure that copies of written examination papers and transcripts of the questions and answers, as well as the grade assigned to each answer thereof, shall be maintained for at least two years subsequent to the date of the examination.

G. The board shall reserve the right to administer and grade oral examinations when the applicant is physically impaired, in addition to any written examination administered to the applicant.

2707. LICENSE WITHOUT EXAMINATION

A. Persons practicing board certified social work in Louisiana who wish to continue the practice of board certified social work in Louisiana must apply for a license under the provisions of this chapter within one year subsequent to the effective date of this chapter.

B. At any time within one year from the effective date of this chapter, the board shall waive the examination requirement and shall issue a certificate as a board certified social worker to any person who files a verified application therefor, accompanied by such fee as is required by Section 2712, and who submits evidence verified by oath and satisfactory to the board that he complies with the requirements of R.S.37:2706 A (1) - 37:2706 A (4).

2708. CERTIFICATION BY RECIPROCITY

The board may certify as a board certified social worker without examination any person who submits the appropriate verified application accompanied by such fee as is required by Section 2712 and who possesses a valid, unsuspended and unrevoked license on the basis of any examination by a duly constituted examining board under the laws of any other state or any territory of the United States or of the District of Columbia, which state or territory in the judgment of the board has requirements substantially equivalent to those in this chapter.

* * *

2711. RIGHTS AND PRIVILEGES OF LICENSEE

Any person who possesses a valid, unsuspended, and unrevoked certificate as a board certified social worker shall have the right to practice and use the title, Board Certified Social Worker, and the abbreviation, BCSW. No other person shall assume such title, use such abbreviation, or use any work, letter, signs, figures, or devices to indicate that he or she is a board certified social worker.

* * *

2713. DENIAL; SUSPENSION; REVOCATION; PROBATION

A. The board shall have the power to deny, revoke, or suspend any certificate issued by the board or applied for in accordance with this chapter, or otherwise discipline a board certified social worker for any of the following causes:

(1) a final conviction of any felony upon a plea or verdict of guilty or following a plea of nolo contendere;

(2) use of drugs or intoxicating liquors to an extent which affects his professional competence;

(3) obtaining or attempting to obtain a certificate by fraud or deception;

(4) willfully or repeatedly violating any of the provisions of this chapter;

(5) being adjudged a mental incompetent;

(6) being grossly negligent in practice as a board certified social worker.

B. No certificate shall be suspended or revoked until a hearing is held before the board, after notice of at least thirty days to the board certified social worker.

* * *

2714. PRIVILEGED COMMUNICATIONS

A. A board certified social worker shall not be examined without the consent of his client as to any communication made by the client to him, or his advice given thereon in the course of professional employment, nor shall the secretary, stenographer or clerk of a board certified social worker be examined without the consent of his employer on any fact, the knowledge of which he has acquired in such capacity, nor shall any person who has participated in any social work therapy conducted under the supervision of a person authorized by law to conduct such therapy, including but not limited to group therapy sessions, be examined concerning any knowledge gained during the course of such therapy without the consent of the person or persons to whom the testimony sought relates.

B. No board certified social worker may disclose any information he may have acquired from persons consulting him in his professional capacity that was necessary to enable him to render services to those persons except:

(1) with the written consent of the client, or in the case of death or disability, with the written consent of his personal representative, other person authorized to sue, or the beneficiary of any insurance policy on his life, health or physical condition; or

(2) when the person is a minor under the age of twenty-one and the information acquired by the board certified social worker indicated that the child was the victim or subject of a crime, then the board certified social worker may be required to testify fully in relation thereto upon any examination, trial, or other proceeding in which the commission of such crime is a subject of inquiry; or

(3) when a communication reveals the contemplation of a crime or harmful act; or

(4) when the person waives the privilege of bringing charges against the board certified social worker for breach of the privilege.

C. Nothing in this section shall be construed, however, to prohibit any board certified social worker from testifying in juvenile court hearings concerning matters of adoption, child abuse, child neglect, or other matters pertaining to the welfare of children.

2715. DISCRIMINATION

No certificate shall be denied any applicant based upon the applicant's race, religion, creed, national origin, sex or physical impairment so long as the physical impairment does not interfere with the performance of professional duties.

* * *

(SOURCE: Louisiana Board Certified Social Work Act-Public Domain.)

---

ent understandings about what social workers are attempting to contribute. Social workers have created an association that is quite inclusive of its members, but they have not created a clear or widely accepted image of what they do or how what they do is important to members of society. The importance of social work is taken up in the next chapter.

SOCIAL WORK AND SOCIAL WELFARE

Social work can be further identified by its place in social welfare, the social institution that provides the resources and assistance to help people maintain their interaction with other people and with systems in society. Social institutions such as the family and the economy are described as a set of patterned activities that are a formal and recognized means of meeting needs of people in a given society. Social institutions as such are abstractions, but they are made up of real, tangible agencies and organizations such as hospitals, schools, family units, bureaucracies, and the people who occupy specific positions and perform certain tasks within them (Federico, 1984). One does not see a social institution intrinsically. Instead, one should consider the institution as the compound of social units and people that collectively meets a given set of needs:

Physical needs for food, clothing, and shelter.
Health needs.
Emotional needs.
Communal needs.
Love and Intimacy needs.
Security needs.

A social institution is the pattern of activities developed in a given society to meet some or all of the needs in a given area.

The family, for example, provides love and emotional support to children who, in turn, are socialized to do the same for their children. By producing and distributing goods and services, the economy meets some of the physical needs of people. One way of defining social welfare views it as helping some people meet needs that have not been met by some other social institution. Social welfare provides mutual support to people to help them meet needs not provided elsewhere, such as in the family or the economy. Social welfare functions to assist people to overcome the problems or concerns they have in functioning within other social institutions.

As a social institution, social welfare offers a range of programs to a variety of people. It assists farm families to deal with economic dislocation. A number of services and programs are offered to children, adolescents, and parents to augment family functioning. These services substitute for or supplement what the family ordinarily provides. Similarly, those whose sustenance needs are not met in the economy or family receive income maintenance support through the institution of social welfare, including money, food, food stamps, public housing, temporary shelter, clothing vouchers, and meals from public and private sources. The social action programs of social welfare challenge the functioning of the economic and political institutions when these institutions ignore the needs of people or when they oppress certain groups of people.

Social welfare, along with the notion of "societies" (defined in Part II as the range of diverse groups and subcultures with whom social work professionals interact), form the context of social work practice. Social welfare offers many of the programs social workers use and contains many of the agencies in which social workers practice.

Many negative values and meanings are also associated with social welfare by many people (Stoesz, 1984). Although historically, social work and other helping professions are associated with the development of social welfare, the strong link between social welfare and social work leads to discomfort on the part of some practitioners. Hence, efforts are made to broaden everyone's outlook on social welfare to include all socioeconomic groups in those it covers in its programs, especially the middle class (Abramovitz, 1983). Efforts to include everyone in the needs area covered by social welfare in order to upgrade its image parallel similar efforts within social work to extend professional services to all members of society.

To be bothered by the question of who receives social welfare is to miss the point of a social institution. The needs a social institution meets and the people who exhibit those needs are neither good nor bad. The needs and the institution that develops to meet those needs are an outcome of the interactions of all parts and people within a given society. To blame those who are in need and to put a stigma on them is to hold them accountable for the outcome of a social process to which they alone did not have input. The part social work plays in meeting the needs of people within the institution of social welfare is a natural and useful one within society. Such meanings and values associated with social welfare should be carefully examined. Social workers must constantly deal with people who are devalued by society and deal with a society which devalues social workers.

FIELDS OF PRACTICE

The human service programs of social welfare are far-reaching in the problems and people they cover. Nearly every age group, socioeconomic class, and culture are covered by such programs and services. Not all these programs involve social workers; those in which social workers practice may also include other helping professionals. Some social workers are based in social agencies or other service delivery organizations such as hospitals, day-care centers, senior service centers, or departments of public welfare. Other social workers maintain a private practice either alone or in association with colleagues from social work or other disciplines.

Social workers' fields of practice are clustered by type of client population, social problem covered, intervention method, kind of service delivery organization, or area of human need. Regardless of the field of practice, the social worker attempts to help people function better and to resolve difficulties within their social environment (Fink, Pfouts, and Dobelstein, 1985).

It is not possible to discuss all the fields of social work practice. You can, however, be introduced to several of the major practice fields and to some emerging ones. The following overview, with a brief description of each field and some of the issues confronting social work practice within it, gives examples of clients of different ages, needs in the areas of physical and mental health, methods of practice, new fields of practice, and social work education.

Child Welfare Services

Social workers serve people of all ages. The fields of child welfare, adolescent services, and work with the elderly are examples of three age groups with which social workers practice. Child welfare includes working in day-care, foster care, adoption, group home, and unwed parent programs. Each of these programs supports or restores the social functioning of children and parents or provides a service that is needed by their families.

Day Care   Day care provides full- or part-time care to a wide range of children whose parents' work or other responsibilities prevent them from giving daytime care to their children. Special educational, supportive, recreational, and social-ization programs are provided in private homes or day-care centers. The social worker helps children; adjusts, orients, and supports parents and children in the program; and deals with program- or home-based problems the children encounter in day care.

Foster Care and Group Homes   Foster care and group homes provide tempo-rary replacement for a child's home or other child-rearing unit when child or parental functioning prevents the home from meeting the needs of the child. Social workers help both parents/caretakers and their children to adjust to the new situation and to resolve the issues that led to the need for foster care place-ment. The worker must be sensitive to the policy issues of parental rights and the tendency of foster placements to become permanent. Permanency planning aimed at determining as soon as possible the best place for the child have at-tempted to balance the issues of parental rights and children's needs (Jenkins and Diamond, 1985).

Adoptive Services   Social workers in adoptive services place children in per-manent adoptive homes when children are without parents or when parents cannot or will not rear their children. Practitioners locate potential parents, manage the adoption and matching processes, and support the new parents. The background and motivation of the applicant and the needs of the child are investigated, and support is given as needed after the child has been placed in the adoptive home. Revealing the identity of their natural parents to adoptees, finding homes for so-called hard-to-place children, placing Native American and Black children outside their culture in adoptive homes, and subsidizing adoptions for poor applicants are a few of the policy issues facing social work-ers in this field of practice (Knight, 1985).

Protective Services   As mandated by law, protective services involve social workers in a different part of child welfare. Practitioners in this area monitor and support families who are or may be suspected of abusing or neglecting their children. Working with foster home services, protective services aim to prevent such abuse. With the emergence of physical, emotional, and sexual abuse of children as a major social problem, work in protective services has emerged as a significant but stressful field of social work practice (Besharov, 1985).

Unwed Parents   Babies of unwed parents who choose to keep their children are also the beneficiaries of social work services that try to improve the parent-child relationship, identifying for the parents and connecting them to needed resources, and counseling and supporting the new parents. Services for unwed parents may also involve counseling to terminate the pregnancy, discussing whether or not to place the child for adoption, or finding needed resources such as shelter and employment.

Other Areas Other areas of child welfare practice also exist, including work in prisons, community outreach, and prevention. Generally speaking, the problems facing social workers in this field emerge when society creates barriers to family functioning or when the family unit cannot continue to function adequately enough to rear its children, consistently fails to protect and/or provide for them, or does not wish to rear children. Similar to child welfare services are those provided by social workers to adolescents.

These services may be delivered through community-based agencies, schools, or the juvenile court system. Workers who provide these services confront specific age-related problems that arise from family life and from the interaction of adolescents with other systems of society. For example, the youth they work with may not attend school or may be involved with crime. Their involvement with drugs may be another avenue leading to contact with a social worker (Fox, 1985).

Services to the Elderly

Senior Centers Services also arise from unmet needs in the family that involve elderly people whose contact with social workers may take place in senior centers where supportive group and individual counseling are offered along with a range of concrete services. The elderly come to the center for the services and programs it offers and to gain companionship or to eat meals. Once at the center, if they have a need for services, the elderly may contact a social worker. Examples of service needs can involve helping to reach a decision on a lawyer to write a will or applying for an insurance policy to supplement Medicare benefits. Needed counseling may involve how to handle the death of a loved one or how to deal with the elderly person's fear of his or her own death. Supportive groups for recreational outings or for dealing with feelings on a common issue can be developed and led by a social worker.

Nursing Homes Social workers also do outreach from agencies that provide services to the homebound frail elderly and work in residential facilities that serve the elderly. The elderly may not be ill but may require the support and care offered by the staff of a residential program. In such facilities, social workers complete intake interviews to collect information about clients' background and needs, assess the needs of the residents, interview and orient the residents and their children to determine needs and interests, arrange admission, and help the new resident become comfortable in the facility. Social workers also help family members maintain contact and assist residents to become involved in appropriate programs at the facility.

Mental Health, Hospitals, and Practice Methods

In addition to being able to work with age-related groups of services, social workers also are experts in such fields of practice as physical and mental health. Mental health wards of hospitals, community mental health centers, family service agencies, and private therapy services are some places where psychiatric or clinical social services are offered to potential clients. Individually or in groups, social workers help such clients to deal with mental health issues that impair their social functioning. Social workers also help clients to locate the concrete resources, such as income or employment, they need to live better, more complete lives. Social workers also offer preventive services to children, the elderly, or the mentally ill to reduce the impact of problems or to stop them from occurring (Bloom, 1983).

Hospital social workers are one example of practitioners who deal with physical illness. They handle the adjustment needs of those who are in hospitals, help family members and/or other loved ones deal with the person who is ill, and obtain the needed resources such as financial aid or living arrangements for those who leave the hosptial. Moreover, the death of a hospital patient may require the social worker to help the patient's loved ones manage this crisis.

Fields of practice may also be identified according to practice method or technique—for example, casework (work with individual client systems) or group work (provision of support or education or assistance in solving group needs). Community social workers are associated with the planning and organizing method of social work, and they function as outreach workers or planners who identify their client as a neighborhood or a larger community. They identify community-wide needs for basic services such as schools, banks and/ or other businesses, or better treatment by existing agencies and bureaucracies. They create new programs or bring members of a given community together to help them create and support each other in their efforts to obtain needed services. The communities served are usually impoverished.

Social workers are also associated with income maintenance programs such as Aid to Families with Dependent Children (AFDC), Medicaid (health benefits for lower income), or Supplementary Security Income (SSI). The involvement of social workers in income maintenance programs is less in the area of direct client contact, which is handled by eligibility technicians, and more in the administration of such programs. There is a strong social work component in some of the specialized income maintenance support programs. Examples are Meals on Wheels, a program designed to deliver meals to shut-in poor elderly, and WIC, a nutrition program for women and infants. The social work component determines need for the program and other concrete services, and it identifies and offers other supportive or counseling services.

New Fields of Service

In addition to these fields of practice, social workers are becoming involved in re-emerging fields of practice such as industrial social work. In this field, they work with employees to assist them in meeting job-related needs such as care of children, work-related stress, alcoholism, or financial problems (see Document 2.3).

DOCUMENT 2.3

Practice Commissions Draft Action Plans: First Meetings Mark NASW's New Structure

Four of NASW's five new practice commissions hammered out action plans at initial meetings in late 1985. In separate sessions, the commissions on family and primary associations, education, and health/mental health met, organized, sifted through suggested plans, and settled on goals for their first year. The Commission on Employment and Economic Support was to meet as the *NEWS* went to press.

The fifth commission, which addresses social work practice in the field of criminal justice, is scheduled to become operational sometime later this year.

In preliminary remarks to each, NASW Executive Director Mark G. Battle asked commission members to select social policy boundaries, update annual legislative issues, develop state-of-the-art data bases, review existing practice standards and set new ones if necessary, consider advanced practice certification and credentialing, help the National Center for Social Policy and Practice plan research and set priorities, and represent NASW with other national professional groups.

The Commission on Family and Primary Associations, meeting October 31 and November 1, began by defining families as either "a traditional family wherein two or more individuals are in a relationship which is based on kinship and/or legal sanctions, or two or more individuals who are in a self-defined relationship. Self-defined families may not always be sufficiently recognized by societal institutions and in policy formulation."

The commission decided to explore the status of Social Service Block Grants and to follow social and governmental policy affecting single-parent families as major, long-term legislative priorities.

The group decided to devise a conceptual framework, update current policy statements, and prepare for the 1987 Delegate Assembly. It will develop a resource bank, describe the state-of-the-art in family practice, establish commission files in NASW's new management information system, describe and evaluate elements of the Social Service Block Grant program, and accept a report on single-parent families being prepared for NASW's Women's Issues Conference in Atlanta in May. It will also identify and eventually sanction subfields, collect data, and establish networks of social workers practicing with the aged, children, and families and primary associations, both within and outside NASW.

The commission reaffirmed NASW's commitment to the field, planned to set standards where necessary, and to institutionalize existing standards. Concerning advanced-practice certification, the commission will consider examining standards, setting directions for continuing education, and increasing visibility for the concept.

The commission's members include Chairwoman Lennie-Marie P. Tolliver of Oklahoma, Adrienne A. Haeuser of Wisconsin, David Kennedy of Virginia, Nancy S. Nicol of Indiana, Donald R. Bardill of Florida, and Juanita C. Evans of Maryland. NASW Senior Staff Associate Roberta Green staffs the commission.

The Commission on Education met November 4 and 5 in Chicago before the 1985 NASW Symposium. Members set eight goals for the coming program year. They hope to affect education legislation by strengthening Delegate Assembly support for NASW's legislative activity in general and particularly for education. They will help NASW legislative staff lobby for legislation which backs "total education of children," and includes social workers as pupil personnel workers.

Commission members will actively build networks with school social workers nationally and with outside organizations such as the National Education Association, Parent-Teachers Association, American Association for Counseling and Development, Council for Exceptional Children, National Association of School Psychologists, and National Association of State Directors of Special Education. The group encouraged national staff and commis-

sion members in the Washington, D.C. area to continue active participation in coalitions such as the National Alliance for Pupil Service Organizations.

The commissioners divided the states among themselves so that individual commission members would be responsible for contacting school social workers in NASW chapters, state associations, state education departments and schools of social work. The resulting network will serve as a basis for identifying personal and programmatic expertise on special areas of school social work.

The knowledge and skill base for the practice area of school social work will be further developed through improving curriculum in preservice education, providing continuing education opportunities, and suggesting collaborative research projects for academicians and practitioners.

Commission members will begin identifying issues and developing policies with potential for implementation in school social work practice which can be followed up and used as models.

The commission hopes to promote greater public awareness of school social work by identifying the "ingredients for success," developing brochures and posters, and through other means.

They will begin data collection and identify effective school social work practice and will also develop effective interorganizational relationships in the professional community.

The commission also formulated a policy on children with AIDS in schools and reviewed a resource guide on implementing NASW's new policy on combating corporal punishment in schools and residential institutions. NASW staff are currently compiling this guide, which will be available in the spring.

Commission members include Chairwoman Joyce A. Cunningham of Pennsylvania, Anne M. Mitchell of Colorado, Alvin J. Flieder of Iowa, Esther Glasser of Washington, D.C., Frances E. Smalls Caple of California, Emilie Barrilleaux of Louisiana, and Eleida Gomez of Illinois. NASW Senior Staff Associate Isadora Hare staffs the commission.

The Commission on Health/Mental Health met November 14 and 15, setting as an overall goal the building of links and networks in what commission members felt is a very large practice domain. In order to begin, commission members will personally represent NASW on professional technical advisory committees of the Joint Commission on Accreditation of Hospitals as well as other advisory boards or committees of health and mental health organizations which request NASW representation.

The commission will ask chapters to identify key persons to be liaisons with the commission and their states as activities develop. It also approved a subcommittee devoted to home health care. This group will develop a national home health care network and tackle regulatory and reimbursement issues affecting the delivery of home health care social work services.

The commission chose three new program efforts. The first priority is the development of a position paper on the cost benefit of social work services in health and mental health settings, reflecting the commission's view that questions of economics currently are dominating and driving health and mental health delivery systems and require a careful response from the profession.

Commission members selected the psychosocial implications of acquired immune deficiency syndrome (AIDS) as a second priority, since this public health issue affects all segments of the American population. It also endorsed continuing NASW's efforts regarding the Health Care Financing Administration's development of new regulations for hospitals under Medicaid and Medicare.

On the legislative front, the commission set as a priority support for broadening social work reimbursement under the Federal Employees Health Benefits Program (see separate story), Medicare and Medicaid, and in health maintenance organizations (HMOs), as well as protection of the Health/Mental Health Block Grants in the federal budget process.

Commission members include Chairman Carl G. Luekefeld of Maryland, Marcella Baird of Ohio, Janie Salinas Farris of Texas, Leland K. Hall of Washington, D.C., Phyllis Nash of West Virginia, Thomas O. Carlton of Virginia, and Mary J. Demory of Maryland. NASW Senior Staff Associate Betsy Vourlekis staffs the commission.

(SOURCE: Copyright 1986, National Association of Social Workers, Inc. Reprinted with permission from "Practice Commissions Draft Action Plans," Vol. 31, No. 1.)

New social problems that become a new field of practice or a highly specialized aspect of an existing field are also occupying the attention of social
workers. New services in the areas of spouse abuse, chemical addictions, issues
of immigration, and the AIDS crisis have emerged (Anderson, 1984; Furstenberg and Olson, 1984; Salcido, 1984). The development of rural social work has
taken on a new meaning with the economic dislocation of farmers. Counseling
about stress and feelings related to the loss of their land and about problems
connected to new jobs and relocation are handled by some social workers.

A specialized field of practice is social work education. Social workers with
practice experience and advanced training direct graduate, undergraduate, and
continuing education programs, teach field and classroom courses, coordinate
field education programs, and conduct research. Social work educators may
also be actively involved in the curriculum and program development activities
of the Council on Social Work Education.

This brief description of selected fields of practice also offers guides for
those seeking to understand social work in its various practice areas. As discussed, a setting, social problem, needs area, method, or client population is
common to a field. Each field may involve different programs or services, but
the goal of each field is to improve, restore, or create opportunities for the
social/environmental functioning of their clients.

CONNECTING SOCIAL WORK AND SOCIETY

The concepts of profession, social welfare, and fields of practice are useful in
understanding social work. If each were considered independently, several
questions about social work might be left unanswered. Summarizing and connecting ideas from each of the three helps to direct us to the connections between social work and society.

A profession defines a group of educated, skilled people who are guided by
a code of ethics and whose service is carried out with a degree of societal sanction and support to meet a significant social need. The overall function or purpose of the profession of social work is to help people to meet their needs in
the area of social functioning.

The institution of social welfare has developed regular, ongoing programs and services to meet the mutual support and social functioning needs
of a variety of people who are unable to use other institutions to meet these
needs. Social welfare provides one of the social contexts for understanding
social work.

Fields of practice cluster the practice of social work according to service
delivery, social problem, special needs area, or client population. The fields
further highlight one of the social contexts for practice: the locations where
practice takes place within the institution of social welfare. The three ideas
together point to the need to explore further the links of social work to society.

The next chapter in Part II discusses the second part of the societal context of practice—the expectations of those served by social work and the expectations of those to whom practitioners must constantly interpret their profession.

For Further Study

1. List those occupations and/or career fields you have always considered as being professional. Use the attributes discussed in this chapter to analyze the occupations on your list. How well do they fit these attributes?

2. What does "being professional" mean to you? How do you think your ideas of being professional would apply to the profession of social work?

3. Obtain a copy of the *Handbook of Accreditation Standards and Procedures of the Commission on Accreditation of the Council on Social Work Education* from a member of your school's social work faculty. Review it to familiarize yourself with its policies, procedures, and practices.

4. Attend a meeting of a professional association. Outline what benefit such meetings have to members of the association.

5. Think about the field of social work practice of greatest interest to you. Identify a person who works in this field. Interview that person regarding his or her preparation for and work within this field of service.

6. Each of the social workers quoted in this chapter presents one or more ideas about the meaning of being a professional. Summarize their comments.

7. Bernice Goodman offers a slightly different idea about professional growth and development as coming from client and colleague interactions. Susanna Hueston offers the same idea along with another. Compare this idea of professional growth with those presented by the other workers.

8. Compare and contrast MSW and BSW workers as described in the material presented in Document 2.1.

9. Discuss the fields of service as identified in Document 2.3, and compare them to those discussed in the text.

Glossary

PROFESSIONAL ATTRIBUTES. Distinctive set of activities; body of scientific knowledge; subculture to educate and socialize; value or ethical base; public recognition.

NEED CATEGORIES. Physical and mental health; emotional gratification; economic security; self-fulfillment; a sense of community; intimacy and love. (See also Human Needs.)

SEMIPROFESSION OR SUBPROFESSION. A particular profession, usually one that has developed more recently, that does not meet all the attributes of a profession as defined by social scientists.

PROFESSIONAL FUNCTION OR PURPOSE. The set of activities a profession performs in meeting a particular aspect of human needs.

FIELD EDUCATION. An educationally directed learning experience carried out in a social service agency or setting as part of the training of a professional social worker.

GENERALIST METHOD OF PRACTICE. A method used by practitioners who use a broad range of skills and interventions within a problem-solving method to help individuals, groups, families, and communities meet their needs.

SOCIAL WORK KNOWLEDGE BASE. The knowledge of human behavior and the social environment that is composed of knowledge from sociology, psychology, political science, economics, biology, anthropology, and other disciplines and that is used by social workers in their practice.

NATIONAL ASSOCIATION OF SOCIAL WORKERS (NASW). With more than 110,000 members, the major association of social work practitioners was founded in 1955.

COUNCIL ON SOCIAL WORK EDUCATION (CSWE). The professional association responsible for accrediting educational programs in social work and providing educational leadership to the profession.

ASSOCIATION OF BLACK SOCIAL WORKERS (ABSW). A national social work association focusing on black workers, clients, issues, communities, and families.

CODE OF ETHICS. A compilation of the ethical and value positions of social work that stresses commitment to clients and professional responsibility to agency, society, and the creation of a just and humane system of social welfare.

SOCIAL INSTITUTION. A set of patterned activities and structures in society that are a formal and recognized means of meeting the basic human needs.

HUMAN NEEDS. Basic human needs according to accepted standards in the areas of health, emotions, community interaction, and security.

CONTEXTS OF SOCIAL WORK. Contexts such as social welfare services and "societies," which are major forces attempting to shape the profession and practice of social work.

FIELDS OF PRACTICE. Where social workers practice, as determined by client population, social problem, method of practice used, type of social agency, or area of human need.

CASEWORK. A traditional field of practice that uses a method of working with individuals to meet their needs.

GROUP WORK. Social work that provides support or education or assistance in solving group issues or needs by using a group method of practice.

COMMUNITY ORGANIZATION OR COMMUNITY WORK. A traditional method of social work practice that involves planning and organizing with neighborhoods and other communities to create new services or to bring about improved living conditions for members of a particular community.

Bibliography

Abramovitz, M. "Everyone Is on Welfare: 'The Role of Redistribution in Social Policy' Revisited." *Social Work* 28(6): 440–445, 1983.

Aigner, S.M. "The Curriculum Policy: Implications of an Emergent Consensus." *Journal of Education for Social Work* 20(1): 5–14, 1984.

Anderson, G.R. "Children and AIDS: Implications for Child Welfare." *Child Welfare* 63 (1): 62–73, 1984.

Besharov, D.J. "Right versus Rights: The Dilemma of Child Protection." *Public Welfare* 43(2): 19–24, 1985.

Bloom, M. "Primary Prevention: A Crisis in Policy and Planning." *Human Services in the Rural Environment* 8(4): 17–22, 1983.

Colby, I.C. "A National Survey of the Small Chapters of the National Association of Social Workers." *Human Services in the Rural Environment* 8(4): 4–9, 1983.

Constable, R.T. "Social Work Education: Current Issues and Future Promise." *Social Work* 29(4): 366–371, 1984.

Council on Social Work Education. *Handbook of Accreditation Standards and Procedures.* Washington, D.C.: CSWE, 1984. Revised 1988.

Dinerman, M. "A Study of Baccalaureate and Master's Curricula in Social Work." *Journal of Education for Social Work* 18(2): 84–92, 1982.

Federico, Ronald C. *The Social Welfare Institution: An Introduction.* 4th ed. Lexington, MA: Heath, 1984.

Fink, Arthur E., Jane H. Pfouts, and Andrew W. Dobelstein. *The Field of Social Work.* 8th ed. Beverley Hills: Sage, 1985.

Fox, J.R. "Mission Impossible? Social Work Practice with Black Urban Youth Gangs." *Social Work* 30(1): 25–31, 1985.

Furstenberg, A.L., and M.M. Olson. "Social Work and AIDS." *Social Work in Health Care* 9(4): 45–62, 1984.

Hokenstad, M.C., Jr., "Curriculum Directions for the 1980s: Implications of the New Curriculum Policy Statement." *Journal of Education for Social Work* 20(1): 15–22, 1984.

Hopps, June Gary. "Who's Setting Social Work's Priorities?" *Social Work* 32(2): 99–100, 1987.

Jenkins, S., and B. Diamond. "Ethnicity and Foster Care: Census Data as Predictors of Placement Variables." *American Journal of Orthopsychiatry* 55(2): 267–276, 1985.

Knight, M.R. "Termination Visits in Closed Adoptions." *Child Welfare* 64(1): 37–45, 1985.

Leighninger, L. "Graduate and Undergraduate Social Work Education: Roots of Conflict." *Journal of Education for Social Work* 20(3): 66–77, 1984.

Louisiana Statutes. Title 37, Chapter 35. Baton Rouge, LA.

Lubove, Roy. *The Professional Altruist: The Emergence of Social Work as a Career, 1880–1930.* Cambridge, MA: Harvard University Press, 1965.

Maslow, Abraham. *Toward a Psychology of Being.* 2d ed. Princeton, NJ: Van Nostrand, 1968.

Morales, Armando, and Bradford W. Sheafor. *Social Work: A Profession of Many Faces.* 4th ed. Boston: Allyn & Bacon, 1986.

National Association of Social Workers. *Code of Ethics.* Washington, DC, 1980.

Pecora, P.J., and M.J. Austin. "Declassification of Social Service Jobs: Issues and Strategies," *Social Work* 28(6): 421–426, 1983.

Popple, P.R. "The Social Work Profession: A Reconceptualization." *Social Service Review* 59(4): 560–577, 1985.

Salcido, R.M. "Social Work Practice with Undocumented Mexican Aliens." In *Color in a White Society.* Silver Spring, MD: National Association of Social Workers, 1984, pp. 74–82.

Stoesz, D. "The Rise of Corporate Welfare," *Social Development Issues* 8(3): 15–49, 1984.

CHAPTER THREE

Diverging Paths: Colleague, Client, and Public Perspectives

There is a social message to be noted in the fact that, in this country, work is more highly regarded than is social welfare. The restrictions placed on professional practices in the public sector can be contrasted with the freedoms described in the corporate sector . . .

* * *

Social work always is in an anomalous situation; it is not like medicine and law, for example. Physicians and lawyers can choose their work sites and never fear that their cause will be lost to bureaucrats, and no one would believe that the work they do could be done by less than an expert. Social services are different, as we all know. It is thought that anyone with common sense can "deliver" them and that when professional social workers take charge, they must be held strictly accountable to the community's requirements because the community's requirements are, after all, part of the definition of social work as a social institution.

Carol H. Meyer (1985)

CHAPTER OVERVIEW

To further our search for social work and to explore other values and meanings associated with the term, this chapter examines what different groups of people who interact with social work expect it to do and what importance they place on it. This exploration also enables you to begin to come to grips with part of what you face as a practitioner. The previous chapter covered ideas about what social work is, what its function and activities are, and what constitutes its knowledge and value base.

This chapter focuses more on what the response of another person might be if you said, "I am a social worker." It also extends our notion of examining a range of value and meaning associations of a given word. You have already read about what social work means to the scholar and members of the profession, but you also need to examine the meaning social work holds for other groups to whom you will present yourself as a social worker. Such groups make up one of the critical societal contexts of social work practice. Their perceptions and expectations of social work reveal much about its place in

society and offer several routes to follow in expanding your understanding of social work.

PERCEPTIONS OF SOCIAL WORK

Social workers practice in the institution of social welfare. Social work is a
people-oriented profession, and groups of people with different investments in
social work form another societal context for social work. Social workers represent their profession in interactions with other professionals in the agencies
and programs in which they work. Practitioners also deal with a variety of clients, as indicated in our overview of the fields of social work practice. In addition, in their effort to change systems within society or to seek resources for
their clients, social workers face politicians, policymakers, and other members
of the public. Groups of colleagues, clients, and laypeople cooperate with, benefit from, or resist the efforts of social workers. The differences in these various
relationships that exist between social workers and members of groups in society stem partly from the nature of the relationship itself but also from what
members of other groups think of social work.

   This chapter discusses some of these groups and the ways social workers
relate to them. It also describes what perceptions these groups have of social
work and explores some of their expectations of the profession. Although diverse groups of clients are discussed, along with colleague and public groups,
Part II more fully describes the relationship of social workers and their clients.
Clients maintain a special relationship with social workers and hold expectations for social work that are important to understand. This chapter emphasizes
that aspect of worker-client interactions. In describing expectations of clients,
as well as those of colleagues and the public, any differences in outlook that
help to account for a lack of cooperation with or a resistance to social work are
noted, as well as factors providing support from society. Benefits accruing to
colleagues, clients, and the public from their interaction with social work are
discussed.

WHAT COLLEAGUES SEE

Although some social workers practice alone and have relatively few contacts
with other professionals, many social workers interact with other disciplines
and professions on a daily basis in their agencies. This frequently involves
working as a member of a team. Social workers also interact with nonprofessionals who are important to service delivery in their agencies. Nonprofessionals include receptionists, some program and agency directors, secretaries,
aides, community and outreach workers, and some members of agency boards.
Social workers also maintain contact with professionals in agencies and programs other than their own. They maintain regular contact with workers outside their agency to benefit their clients (Barth, 1985; Mallory, 1979). These con-

tacts take place through activities in professional associations and by means of networks of colleagues.

In the broadest use of the word, all those who interact with social workers are their colleagues. Their colleagues are a significant group for social workers, and the ideas their colleagues have about social work reveal much about its place in society. One way social workers interact with colleagues is through teamwork.

Teamwork is important in the delivery of many human services (Toseland, Palmer-Ganeles, and Chapman, 1986). Depending on the agency or service involved, the team is composed of a variety of disciplines, including social work. Schools, for example, may group guidance counselors, nurses, psychologists, and teachers into a professional team. In a hospital, nurses, psychiatrists, medical doctors from many specialties, physical therapists, and social workers may work together on service delivery. A group of professionals involved in program development may include researchers, economists, specialized planners, and social workers. A team at a mental health facility may involve psychologists, psychiatrists, social workers, nurses, and mental health technicians.

The team acts as a unit in assessing what the client needs, in setting goals to meet those needs, and in developing, implementing, and evaluating their plans to achieve those goals. Each member of the team represents his or her profession or discipline and is responsible for contributing special skills and knowledge to the team effort (Watt, 1985; Abramson, 1984).

For example, a school-age child who is having problems in attendance and difficulty in peer relationships in school may be assessed as needing testing, possible counseling, and the involvement of family members in the treatment plan. Counselors, psychologists, and nurses do the testing and provide some of the support. The social worker is supportive of the child and responsible for involving the family members and working with them to assist the child achieve better attendance and functioning in the school environment.

In a hospital, the diagnostic and health-related care of the doctors and nurses is coordinated with the efforts to promote the patient's physical, emotional, and social recovery that are carried out by therapists, psychiatrists, and social workers. The members of each profession are responsible for their area of specialization and expertise. The social worker may coordinate services, identify needed resources, and work with family members or loved ones on problem resolution.

The degree to which the team's delivery of services is characterized by a cooperative and supportive environment varies in part with the personalities of team members. Some professionals with a hierarchical sense of professional relationships that is based on education and social rewards rank social work with other human service professionals and not as high as medical doctors or psychiatrists. Persons holding such an outlook may expect deference from those with lower rank during the assessing and planning efforts of the team. Social workers, on the other hand, may expect to provide leadership in the area of care coordination and/or involvement of environmental factors in case discussions (Watt, 1985).

Cooperation on the team varies with the importance team members assign to the expertise of the various disciplines and professions involved and the individual status accorded a given member of the team (Dove, Schneider, and Gitelson, 1985). From these inputs emerge the perceptions or expectations other professionals hold about social work. If medical doctors, for example, do not perceive the practice domain of social workers as extending beyond the problems of poor people, they are unlikely to refer their middle-class patients to the hospital's social work staff (see Document 3.1).

DOCUMENT 3.1

Social Work and Medicine: Shared Interests
Robert F. Schilling II and Robert F. Schilling

The relationships between social workers and physicians have always been ambivalent, although social workers have sought to improve their professional status by emulating physicians.[1] They still criticize the medical model and object to the status and authority of physicians, and, according to Kane, use large amounts of energy to assert the legitimacy and importance of their role in health care.[2] Physicians have long espoused the importance of social factors in the prevention and treatment of disease, but for the most part, they have not welcomed social workers as major allies. Changes within social work and medicine, however, may point toward an increasing collaboration between the professions. Citing recent developments in health care, the present authors argue that social workers and physicians have much to gain by emphasizing their mutual concerns and complementary roles.

DISEASE AND DISABILITY

The changing nature of disease in the United States may affect how social workers and physicians value and interact with each other. As the population ages, health care professionals will increasingly treat chronic ailments. For many chronic and degenerative conditions, the principal intervention may be arranging care in the patient's own home, in long-term care facilities, or in hospices. In the future, social workers may have pivotal roles in coordinating health care for older patients.

Disabled adults and handicapped children, also a growing proportion of the population, will require the attention of the health care system, and in many instances, the role of the physicians may be limited to diagnosing the disease and prescribing medication.[3] In contrast, social workers may help physically and mentally handicapped persons close the gap between their daily needs and their environment. For a patient who must depend on assistance from others, it is often the social worker who can best determine the degree to which family members are willing and able to provide the required physical care and emotional support; thus, social workers and physicians must work together if disabled persons and their families are to function optimally.

Social workers may be called on to facilitate treatment of the increasing number of patients who do not hold majority values or follow majority customs.[4] Many medical conditions—for example, heart disease, some forms of cancer, and respiratory ailments—are more prevalent among low-income individuals and some ethnic minority groups.[5] Language, cultural, and educational barriers often interfere with the diagnosis and treatment of special populations.[6] Patient compliance, which often related to social and cultural attitudes, is a relatively new area of social work practice. To increase compliance, social workers work to reduce incongruent patient-provider expectations,[7] to teach self-care,[8] and to ensure that family members support the indicated treatment.[9] As the costs of disease and disability rise, the health care system is likely to make a greater effort to insure that treatments known to be effective are carried out by patients or their families.

CHANGES IN THE DELIVERY OF HEALTH CARE

The major social changes taking place in the system of health care delivery may require a restructuring of hierar-chies, alliances, and collaborative relationships. One possible outcome of such restructuring would be more and better professional links between social workers and physicians. Among the changes in process are constraints on practice, new payment structures, and preventive health care.

Constraints and Practice

New physicians are entering a tight job market, and in many areas of the United States, physicians are in oversupply.[10] They realize that their services are subject to market conditions and other forces beyond their control, and that they must increasingly consider malpractice claims and government regulations and peer review boards and consumer groups. Never as autonomous as physicians, social workers are also subject to regulation, budgetary constraints, public scrutiny, and civil liability.[11] Medicine and social work are becoming more alike in terms of the social complexity of their work environment. The rise of private practice notwithstanding, social work has always been and continues to be an agency-based profession. For physicians, the entrepreneurial model of practice is losing ground to health maintenance organizations, preferred provider organizations, and salaried positions;[12] which affect their control and prestige.[13] One result may be that physicians and social workers will see themselves, more often than in the past, as interdependent professionals cooperating within broadly defined health care organizations.

Financing of Health Care Costs

Traditionally, social workers and physicians have been philosophically distant from each other in terms of financing and distributing health care resources. After decades of resisting any movement toward socialized medicine, physician groups have lately acknowledged the need for distributing health care resources through means other than fee-for-service schemes.[14] As government, industry, and consumer groups press for reform, physicians will have to accept cost containment measures that limit fees and restrict practitioner autonomy.[15]

Social workers may at first welcome such changes in health care financing. Their continued satisfaction will depend, in part, on the extent to which social work services are deemed cost-effective. Paradoxically, cost-based reimbursement—a faulty health care policy from the social work perspective—has increased the demand for social services.[16] As payment structures change, social workers will have to demonstrate that their services improve health care at a reasonable cost.[17] To the extent that social workers believe that illegitimate criteria are used to reduce their services, they may align themselves with practitioners of similar persuasion. For example, if certain preventive or mental health practices are excluded from prepaid health schemes, social workers may join with family practitioners or psychiatrists in an effort to secure coverage for such services.[18]

Prevention

Social workers were among the first to call for prevention of disease through social intervention.[19] Bracht asserted that "the major diseases of affluent America . . . are susceptible to the con-trol of risk factors that are almost entirely behavioral or social."[20] As the social and behavioral prevention of disease gains acceptance, social work stands to become a more influential profession.[21] Although prevention through social intervention has great promise, the long-term efficacy of such strategies has not been demonstrated. Nevertheless, social workers have begun testing innovative approaches to prevent unhealthy behavior in various settings. School-based strategies have delayed the onset of tobacco and alcohol use in children.[22] Skills-building groups have helped parents of handicapped children deal with stress.[23] Social workers have also presented dieting strategies on network television[24] and have developed techniques to increase the use of pediatric dental services.[25]

Physicians and social workers have a common interest in preventing disease and unhealthy behavior. Their roles could be complementary. Physicians are in the position to assess prevention needs, such as observing what types of injuries occur among which populations, and to apply certain preventive measures, such as immunization to prevent contagious diseases. Increasingly, social workers are involved in designing prevention strategies aimed at high-risk and underserved populations.[26] If social workers initiate prevention programs, they increase their opportunities for collaboration with physicians. But if they continue to focus on the psychosocial consequences of physical illness, and not on the prevention of disease, social workers will continue to be involved in supportive tasks.

CHANGES WITHIN
SOCIAL WORK

Social work, no less than medicine, is changing rapidly. Developments within the profession have implications for how social workers interact with physicians, which include the incorporation of scientific methods into practice and the rising stature of social workers.

Scientific Practice

Kane argued that just as physicians could improve patient care by incorporating psychosocial awareness into their practice, so too could social workers profitably emulate the scientific traditions of medicine.[27] The strengths of medicine have been listed by Kane; several bear repeating. Their relationship to social work are noted.

Empiricism. Social work has made considerable progress in data-based practice.[28] Empiricism will likely result in changes in the delivery of social work services within health care settings. Plausibly, social workers who see themselves as scientific practitioners will develop a degree of simpatico with physicians who have an established scientific tradition. Physicians may better understand social work and appreciate the difficulty of measuring complex personal, social, and organizational variables.

Iatrogenesis. Social workers are beginning to recognize that if their interventions can be helped, they can also be harmful. Concern for the client cannot, in itself, justify social intervention: Potential benefits must outweigh likely risks. As social workers are better able to identify such risks, they may have more influence over patient care.

Balancing Utilization and Risk. Resources should be used to help patients who need them most and who stand to gain from intervention. Weighing potential costs and benefits will be particularly challenging for prevention practitioners. Advocates of prevention or treatment programs should be required to evaluate the association between risk markers and subsequent illness or dysfunction, the efficacy of the proposed strategy, and the relative cost of intervention.[29]

Rising Status

Social workers still answer to physicians, at least indirectly, in most medical settings. Increasingly, however, social workers are assuming positions in which they can influence physicians. In nursing homes, mental health centers, and residential care facilities, social workers often have authority over doctors. They head hospital boards, hold seats in state legislatures, and in the U.S. Senate. In some states, social workers, not psychiatrists, determine when emotionally ill persons may be temporarily held against their will. Courts now call on social workers for expert opinions whereas only psychiatrists would have been called to testify in the past.[30] Licensure has allowed social workers to serve private patients who often would otherwise have sought care from physicians. As these examples suggest, social workers are closing the status gap between social work and medicine. With larger numbers of social workers earning doctoral degrees, this trend should accelerate.

Physicians and social workers are collaborating in teaching and research, with social workers teaching in departments of psychiatry, rehabilitative medicine, family practice, and pediatrics.[31] If prevention commands a larger proportion of the medical curriculum, social workers with prevention credentials could become more visible on medical school faculties. Similarly, prevention-oriented physicians have much to offer social work students pursuing careers in health care. Social workers now conduct research with psychiatrists, pediatricians, and family practitioners,[32] and as medical social workers become more involved in research, they will publish more in a wider range of professional journals. Social work scholars, too, may attract a larger audience, as other health care professions become more interested in the social determinants of health and disease.

CHALLENGE AND OPPORTUNITY

It would be naive to suggest that physicians and social workers are inexorably moving toward a happy, productive alliance. Social workers and physicians will perhaps always have different interests, values, and perspectives. Doubtless, social workers will continue to be concerned with who defines social work in medical settings[33] and with how to gain more autonomy in the health care system.[34] If physicians believe that their authority and livelihood are being threatened, they may act to limit social workers' influence over and

share of the health care dollar. Nevertheless, changes within health care pose opportunities for social workers and physicians to establish closer working relationships.

One area open to collaboration between medicine and social work is health care delivery to special populations. As health care moves away from the entrepreneurial model, both physicians and social workers could influence the design of clinics and programs aimed at low-income, immigrant, aged, and handicapped populations. Physicians are knowledgeable about disease, disability, and treatment. Social workers understand social characteristics and other social phenomena and how they affect patient access, communication, compliance, and comfort. Examples of collaboration between medicine and social work need not be hypothetical. Hospices depend upon the physician's knowledge of such physical aspects of incurable disease as the progressive failure of organs and the necessity of large doses of pain killers and upon the social worker's understanding of personal coping, social support, and family dynamics.

Disease prevention affords many opportunities for collaboration between social workers and physicians; for instance, maternal and child health specialists recognize that many pregnant adolescents do not receive adequate prenatal care. Because school- and agency-based social workers often are in regular contact with pregnant young women, they are in a strategic position to collect information that could lead to better prenatal outreach programs. Informed social workers could design strategies for reaching out to pregnant adolescents and for increasing adolescents' compliance with the medical regime. Physicians could suggest ways of incorporating questions on physical health into social histories gathered by social workers, which could point up potential health problems.

Along with physicians and other health care professionals, social workers could run pilot programs designed to prevent disease and disability among high-risk groups. For instance, physicians can determine when average cholesterol levels of various populations are dangerously high. Social workers, in concert with nutritionists, could design culturally sensitive interventions to reduce cholesterol levels among high risk populations.

Physicians and social workers, working together, could obtain impressive results. One potential area of collaborative research is the effect of social support on the prevention and treatment of disease. Social workers could operationalize such concepts as social support and other coping resources. Similarly, physicians could provide information on prognoses and survival rates of certain diseases. Working together, social workers and physicians could launch innovative, descriptive prevention and treatment studies involving many social aspects of health.

The present authors have argued that changes within social work and medicine could enhance cooperation between these sometimes adversarial professions, which would benefit patients, physicians, and social workers. Perhaps social workers, with their un-derstanding of social systems and interpersonal relationships, will take the lead in this new collaboration.

NOTES AND REFERENCES

1. D. M. Austin, "The Flexner Myth and the History of Social Work," *Social Service Review,* 57 (September 1983), pp. 357–377.
2. R. A. Kane, "Lessons for Social Work from the Medical Model: A Viewpoint for Practice," *Social Work,* 27 (July 1982), pp. 315–321.
3. N. F. Bracht, "The Social Nature of Chronic Disease and Disability," *Social Work in Health Care,* 5 (Winter 1979), pp. 129–144; and R. F. Schilling and S. P. Schinke, "Social Support Networks in Developmental Disabilities," in J. K. Whittaker, J. Garbarino, et al. *Social Support Networks: Informal Helping in the Human Services* (New York: Aldine, 1983), pp. 383–404.
4. U. S. Bureau of the Census, *Statistical Abstract of the United States 1984* (Washington, D.C.: U.S. Government Printing Office, 1983); P. A. Wilson, "Expanding the Role of Social Workers in Coordination of Health Services," *Health and Social Work,* 6 (February 1981), pp. 57–64; and P. A. Wilson, "Health Planning Structure Processes, and Social Work Involvement," *Social Work in Health Care,* 7 (Fall 1981), pp. 87–97.
5. L. S. Cunningham and J. L. Kelsey, "Epidemiology of Musculoskeletal Impairments and Associated Disability," *American Journal of Public Health,* 74 (June 1984), pp. 574–579.
6. R. M. Becerra, "Knowledge and Use of Child Health Services by Chinese-Americans," *Health and Social Work,* 6 (August 1981), pp. 29–38; M. Del-

gado and D. Humm-Delgado. "Natural Support Systems: Source of Strength in Hispanic Communities," *Social Work,* 27 (January 1982), pp. 83–89: and K. Goodman and B. Rothman, "Group Work in Infertility Treatment," *Social Work with Groups,* 7 (Spring 1984), pp. 79–97.

7. R. L. Levy, J. McCann, and C. S. Lee, "A Methodology for the Study of Congruence in Parent/Provider Treatment Expectations," *Social Work in Health Care,* 5 (Spring 1980), pp. 279–286.

8. R. L. Levy, D. Lodish, and C. Pawlak-Floyd, "Teaching Children To Take More Responsibility for Their Own Dental Treatment," *Social Work in Health Care,* 7 (Spring 1982), pp. 69–76.

9. D. N. Noble and A. K. Hamilton, "Coping and Complying: A Challenge in Health Care," *Social Work,* 28 (November-December 1982), pp. 462–466; and S. K. Schultz, "Compliance with Therapeutic Regimens in Pediatrics: A Review of Implications for Social Work Practice," *Social Work in Health Care,* 5 (Spring 1980), pp. 267–279.

10. D. O. Nutter, "Medical Education in the United States: A Resource for the Third World?" *Health Affairs,* 3 (Spring 1984), pp. 6–20.

11. D. J. Besharov, "Liability in Child Welfare," *Public Welfare* (Spring 1984), pp. 28–49.

12. S. A. Freedman, "Sounding Board: Megacorporate Health Care," *New England Journal of Medicine,* 312 (February 29, 1985), pp. 579–582; and P. Starr, *The Social Transformation of American Medicine* (New York: Basic Books, 1982).

13. S. L. Fielding, "Organizational Impact on Medicine: The HMO Concept," *Social Science and Medicine,* 18, No. 8 (1984), pp. 615–620; and J. A. Morone

and A. B. Dunham, "The Waning of Professional Dominance: DRGs and the Hospitals," *Health Affairs,* 3 (Spring 1984), pp. 73–87.

14. E. L. Schor, J. M. Neff, and J. L. LaAsmar, "The Chesapeake Health Plan: An HMO Model for Foster Children," *Child Welfare,* 63 (September-October 1984), pp. 431–440; and Starr, *The Social Transformation of American Medicine.*

15. H. Pardes, "Commentary: Prospective Payment and Psychiatry," *Hospital and Community Psychiatry,* 35 (May 1984), p. 419.

16. "Health Experts Take Policy to Task: Ballis Says Practice and Politics Mix," *NASW News,* 29 (July 1984), p. 1.

17. C. J. Coulton and N. Butler, "Measuring Social Work Productivity in Health Care," *Health and Social Work,* 6 (August 1981), pp. 4–12; and P. J. Volland, "Costing for Social Work Services," *Social Work in Health Care,* 6 (Fall 1980), pp. 73–87.

18. D. L. Poole and L. J. Braja, "Does Social Work in HMOs Measure Up to Professional Standards?" *Health and Social Work,* 9 (Fall 1984), pp. 305–313; and F. G. Reamer, "Facing Up to the Challenge of DRGs," *Health and Social Work,* 10 (Spring 1985), pp. 85–94.

19. K. Siefert, "An Exemplar of Primary Prevention in Social Work: The Sheppard Towner Act of 1921," *Social Work in Health Care,* 9 (Fall 1983), pp. 87–103.

20. N. F. Bracht, "Preparing New Generations of Social Workers for Practice in Health Settings," *Social Work in Health Care,* 8 (Spring 1983), pp. 29–44.

21. C. J. Coulton, "Factors Related to Preventive Health Behavior: Implications for Social Work Intervention," *Social Work in Health Care,* 3 (Spring

1978), pp. 297–311; and R. Shanker, "Occupational Disease, Workers' Compensation, and the Social Work Advocate," 28 (January-February 1983), pp. 24–35.

22. S. P. Schinke and L. D. Gilchrist, "Preventing Cigarette Smoking with Youth," *Journal of Primary Prevention,* 5 (Fall 1984), pp. 48–56; and S. P. Schinke, R. F. Schilling, L. D. Gilchrist, R. P. Barth, J. K. Bobo, J. E. Trimble, and G. T. Cvetkovich, "Preventing Substance Abuse with American Indian Youth," *Social Casework,* 66 (April 1985), pp. 213–217.

23. R. F. Schilling, L. D. Gilchrist, and S. P. Schinke, "Coping and Social Support in Families of Developmentally Disabled Children," *Family Relations,* 33 (January 1984), pp. 47–54.

24. A. J. Frankel, J. C. Birkimer, J. H. Brown, and G. K. Cunningham, "A Behavioral Diet on Network Television," *Behavioral Counseling and Community Interventions,* 3 (Spring-Summer 1983), pp. 91–101.

25. D. G. Olson, R. L. Levy, C. A. Evans, Jr., and S. K. Olson, "Enhancement of High Risk Children's Utilization of Dental Services," *American Journal of Public Health,* 71 (June 1981), pp. 631–634.

26. T. D. Royer and R. P. Barth. "Improving the Outcome of Pregnancy," *Social Work,* 29 (September-October 1984), pp. 471–475; and R. Merino, E. Fischer, and S. J. Bosch, "Technical Assistance Offered to Community Health Programs through a Resource Model," *Public Health Reports,* 100 (January-February 1985), pp. 25–30.

27. Kane, "Lessons for Social Work from the Medical Model."

28. D. Christie and G. Weigall, "Social Work Effectiveness in Two-Year Stroke Survivors, A Randomised Controlled Trial," *Community Health Studies,* 8, No. 1 (1984), pp. 26–32, and W. J. Reid and P. Hanrahan, "Recent Evaluations of Social Work: Grounds for Optimism," *Social Work,* 27 (July 1982), pp. 328–340.

29. C. B. Germain, "Social Work Identity, Competence, and Autonomy: The Ecological Perspective," *Social Work in Health Care,* 6 (Fall 1980), pp. 1–10.

30. D. S. Hughes and B. C. O'Neal, "A Survey of Current Forensic Social Work," *Social Work,* 28 (September-October 1983), pp. 393–394.

31. A. S. Bergman and G. K. Fritz, "Psychiatric and Social Work Collaboration in a Pediatric Chronic Illness Hospital," *Social Work in Health Care,* 7 (Fall 1981), pp. 45–55; R. Contreras and L. Scheingold, "Couples Groups in Family Medicine Training," *The Journal of Family Practice,* 18, No. 2 (1984), pp. 293–296; O. A. Cordoba, W. Wilson, and J. D. Orten, "Psychotropic Medications for Children," *Social Work,* 28 (November-December 1983), pp. 448–453: and H. Hess, "Social Work Clinical Practice in Family Medicine Centers: The Need for a Practice Model," *Journal of Social Work Education,* 21 (Winter 1985), pp. 56–65.

32. R. Fischler, G. Comerci, A. Yates, and B. Dover, "Evaluation, Treatment, and Follow-Up of Child Abuse." *The Journal of Family Practice,* 17, No. 3 (1983), pp. 387–403; and M. J. Monfils and F. J. Menolascino, "Mental Illness in the Mentally Retarded: Challenges for Social Work," *Social Work in Health Care,* 9 (Fall 1983), pp. 71–85.

33. Z. H. Carrigan, "Social Workers in Medical Settings: Who Defines Us?" *Social Work in Health Care,* 4 (Winter 1978), pp. 149–163; and A. M. Gross, J. Gross, and A. R. Eisenstein-Naveh, "Defining the Role of the Social

Worker in Primary Health Care,"
Health and Social Work, 8 (Summer
1983), pp. 174–181.
34. A. D. Murdach, "Skills and Tactics
in Hospital Practice," *Social Work*,
28 (July-August 1983), pp. 279–284.

(SOURCE: Copyright 1987, National
Association of Social Workers, Inc.
Reprinted with permission, from
"Social Work and Medicine: Shared
Interests," Vol. 32, No. 2, pp. 231-234.)

Teamwork takes place within an agency or some service unit of it. Teams are characterized by a group of professionals operating as a single entity to deliver coordinated service that is focused on agreed-on goals. Social work practice is also marked by contact with professionals in other agencies. If their contact with other professionals in their field of practice is developed and systematically maintained by social workers, they have created a network (see interviews on pages 70–73).

I AM A SOCIAL WORKER
"My Work with a Team"

GRACIELA CASTEX: I had two quite different experiences with teams. At the psychiatric center, the team had a psychiatrist, MSWs, and people who were hired to transport clients. At that time in Miami the public transportation system was not good, and people without cars could not get to the clinic. The driver was very important. In this model at the clinic we did function well as a team; everyone's input was seen as essential. If one goes to pick up the family and one family member is consistently not ready, that becomes important information for the clinician to have.

In my first post-MSW experience, I worked with a team on a medical unit in a hospital. This team was based in a very medical model. There the team approach was one where we would have team meetings where all the disciplines providing services to patients would come in. Basically the physician, the MD, was the person who directed, or wanted to direct, the outcome of the services being provided to the patient. At that point as a social worker I had to be a lot more assertive. Not only did I have to do my job, but I also had to educate the other team members. On the psychiatric center's team, I had only to do my job because the people on the team understood the role of the social worker. The concept of a social worker on the team did not have to be explained over and over again. At the hospital I had to do so. Moreover, since the hospital was a teaching hospital, the MDs also rotated constantly while the other team members (nurses, dieticians, social workers, physical and occupational therapists) remained constant. So the education was aimed at the physicians.

BERNICE GOODMAN: In my practice itself, I practice alone with my clients. Team work is not a concern there. However, certainly in my other efforts to establish organizations and create task forces in existing organizations I work on teams. These efforts involve working with people from a variety of disciplines including psychiatry and psychology. In some ways the interdisciplinary setting was easier. Sometimes in a situation where everyone was a social worker it seemed to me as if the social workers were not operating from the same value base. On the other hand, in my interdisciplinary efforts a similarity of outlook and values facilitated our efforts. In working on a team it is much more important that everyone share similar attitudes, values, and commitments about what is important to the quality of life of people. If this is so, then whatever the professional skills, be it social work, medicine, or another discipline, they will be added to the team's effort and make the team more effective.

BETTE HARLAN: In my experience, attitudes to social work have varied from psychiatrists who absolutely value social work to psychiatrists who want to see social work off the team entirely. Nurses have been the main supporter of the social worker role. Like psychiatrists, lawyers seem to be on one side or the other. Some view social workers as capable of a sound assessment; others expect social workers to behave like bureaucrats instead of acting like advocates for clients.

JOE HERNANDEZ: Later in my work at the hospital I worked with a team. The team was composed of psychiatrists, psychologists, a social work supervisor, caseworker, social worker, nurse, and epidemiologist. On this team the only real conflicts were among the social workers. The staff who were not social workers, especially the psychiatrists and psychologists, saw social work as important. I got tremendous support from all team members. I checked all the team's patients on all wards and was more aware than anyone on the team what was going on with the patients, socially and mentally. I identified many of their needs and could provide real input to others. The nurse and I also worked closely together.

They seemed to appreciate what I could do for our patients. Their attitudes about other social workers in the hospital did not seem to be so positive. They knew the other social workers were reluctant to deal with the AIDS population. This reluctance colored the outlook of the team members. The team members assessed the competence and attitudes of individual social workers.

SUSANNA HUESTON: The school district is quite fortunate. We have a full child study team in each of our schools. In my school I work with a school psychologist, school nurse, guidance counselor, and learning specialists. For each grade level and for special education, we have a unit chairperson who coordinates the work of the team. This means that we have four meetings, one for each grade and one for special education.

I feel the attitude of team members is very positive about social work. Initially, I had to help them understand what my role as a social worker was, that I did not have a bag of tricks to make the student's problems go away immediately. I had to work with the teachers and other staff, as well as with the families, in trying to enable a given child to function in a traditional school setting. Initially, the staff referred almost any kind of case to me. Now I find, having been in the school for such a long time, that the referrals are more appropriate in terms of what a social worker can do. Their attitude about and understanding of social work changed as I worked with them.

IRMA SERRANO: In coordinating the various units of the childrens' services, we have social workers, nurses, psychiatrists, psychologists, teachers (in specific programs), assistant teachers, and psychiatric nurses (in the clinic program). Each of these various disciplines makes a contribution. One of the reasons I have remained here as long as I have is that, in my experience, our psychiatric program, of all those within the entire medical complex and its psychiatric departments, is one of the few where social work is seen as contributing professionally. The fact that I am on the faculty of the hospital, without a PhD, says a lot about how the profession is looked on. In the department they see social work as equal. Elsewhere, usually, it is the MD against everyone else, the whole "physician versus the rest of the services" syndrome, but here is one of the few places were social work is looked on equally.

ADELE WEINER: Throughout my professional career I have had the opportunity to work on several interdisciplinary teams. As the director of social services of a nonprofit nursing home, I was the designated discharge coordinator and therefore, ran the interdisciplinary team responsible for reviewing patient care. The team was composed of the patient's doctor, nurses, dietician, physical therapist, recreation therapist, and social worker. The team played an active role in planning, coordinating, and implementing patient care plans. This was extremely important so that the total person was served in a complementary manner by the members of the team.

In my current consultant position, I am coordinating the development of an Elder Abuse Awareness and Training Project in Brooklyn, New York. The funding for this project focuses on identification, education, and the development of an interdisciplinary network. No one particular agency has been designated as serving all the needs of the abused elderly. Rather, certain agencies have been identified as case management agencies, which will coordinate the many services needed by clients. Other agencies will continue to provide the services they already offer such as: reimbursement or compensation for victims, criminal prosecution, medical treatment, new locks and repairs for housing, home health care, respite care, psychological services. The case manager will have to play a very important role in coordinating the team that provides services for each client.

Networks are created to assist workers in meeting the needs of their clients through an alliance of cooperative, helpful professionals. The cooperation of network members may take the form of using member influence within their own agency to assist the worker, providing ideas on how to proceed within their program, sharing approaches or strategies to use in a given situation, exchanging information about newly discovered resources, or providing support to one another during difficult situations. The network develops out of a common geographic area or work with a common client population—not, as in teamwork, out of a shared client system.

For example, a social worker in a shelter for the homeless could create a network composed of those persons and organizations who make referrals to the shelter, among whom are the following:

Public welfare workers.
Police officers.
Staff members of community mental health programs.
Volunteers in a local church's soup kitchen.
The staff of a county hospital.
Providers of needed resources, including members of local churches, owners of businesses who donate food and clothing, and staff of the local department of public welfare.
Volunteers from a college social work program faculty and community programs volunteers.

Specific people would be well known by the worker and active contact would be maintained with them. The network could serve as the nucleus of an action group to lobby and advocate for better services and programs for the homeless.

Social workers develop similar networks that are made up of people who deal with the same client population as do the social workers. Examples of such populations include abused women, the chronically mentally ill, the homebound elderly, and farmers in danger of losing their land and livelihood. Social workers also create networks in new fields of practice for the purpose of developing new practice knowledge and to provide support with difficult cases. Networks of this nature have been developed by hospital social workers faced with problems in dealing with the AIDS crisis. Networks include professionals and nonprofessionals, but regardless of professional standing, their members share common interests and a need for information and support.

In addition to contacts with professionals within and outside their own agency, the practice of social workers involves nonprofessionals. In large agencies, nonprofessionals often hold jobs that are critical to the operation of a given program. Nursing homes, for example, use nurses' aides who have a great deal of contact with patients. Similarly, aides are used in community outreach programs, day-care services, and community mental health programs. They may supplement the work of nursing, teaching, and other helping professionals.

In smaller agencies or rural areas, well-trained aides are essential for effective delivery of service. They may have the associate degrees from two- or four-year colleges in child care, human behavior, or human services. Working closely with aides is advantageous for a social worker. Many nonprofessionals in fields quite similar to social work aspire to become social workers. Their observations of and contributions to the social worker's practice can be quite useful as they develop their own careers.

Nonprofessionals within the agency where the social worker is employed or outside it in another program can express enthusiasm for the professional behavior of individual social workers. Without sharing, as other professionals do, an educational and socialization experience similar to social workers, nonprofessionals may be more impressed by the practice of an especially competent (or incompetent) social worker. Thus, their perception of, and expectations for, social work is derived from their interactions with individual social workers, along with any attitudes they have developed and share with members of the public who are of a similar background. Nonprofessionals who work closely with social workers benefit from learning new approaches to problem solving and new ways of dealing with clients. It is incumbent on the social worker, therefore, not only to practice as professionally as possible but also to interpret social work to the nonprofessionals with whom they practice.

A social worker's practice can be a shared experience if the worker is assigned to an agency or unit's team or if he or she creates and/or participates in a network. Teams and networks are composed of colleagues who may be social workers, other professionals, and nonprofessionals. These groups of people may perceive the social worker as a professional in an important profession who is doing an effective job. However, others may have little respect for social work as a profession. They may see social work as having low status. Their viewpoint may be based on the competence and professional actions of the individual social worker or from their attitude about the profession of social work. Such differences can lead to their treating social workers with deference or with the disdain they hold for someone with lower status than they. Finally, their view might stem from taking a hierarchical approach to working with social workers on a team or in a network. For the social worker, awareness of and action on the potential difference in perceptions and expectations on the part of colleagues can lead to improved collegial relationships and heightened cooperation in helping clients. The benefits are better services for clients and an easier and more effective practice for colleagues. Social workers can offer to their colleagues useful environmental information and the skills to enhance the social functioning of clients. Moreover, social workers can provide strategies to reduce some of the structural inadequacies that contribute to the problems of their shared clients.

WHAT CONSUMERS EXPECT

Social work serves a diversity of client populations and encounters a variety of problems in helping them. Clients differ from one another by age, culture, ethnicity, socioeconomic class, physical ability, emotional state, and sexual orientation. Clients also differ according to the type of problem they have and the nature of the program or service offered to them by the social worker to deal with the problem. In the previous discussion of social welfare programs and fields of practice in social work, some of these various kinds of client populations were discussed.

Clients expect their problem to be solved by the social worker. They may hope for a quick solution or, if the problem is severe and of long standing, a miraculous turnaround. To them the professional social worker is somewhat like a savior who will get them back on their feet, make their concerns go away, or bring about a hoped-for miraculous change in their lives.

The parent grateful for help with a troubled child, the unwed mother relieved over reaching a decision about her pregnancy, the unemployed person happy about a promising job-training program, and the elderly shut-in who feels safer with new door locks provided from a social worker's referral can each come to relate to the social worker as if to a miracle worker.

Other clients, however, are neither very helpful to or even very willing to work with their social worker. These persons are called *involuntary clients*. Legal mandate or program functioning requires their participation, whether or not they wish to do so. Social work is part of an institutional effort to control them. They may be resistant initially. Some of these clients never cease to be so. Their resistance to their social worker might take many forms, ranging from refusal to cooperate to active efforts to "con," or manipulate, their social worker (Cingolani, 1984).

Examples of involuntary clients are abusive parents, some drug addicts, people in prison, many clients who have been institutionalized for their emotional or mental problems, and some of the homeless. They may simply remain passive, expressing no expectations of or interest in the social worker's efforts. Many are hostile, acting as if their social worker shares blame with others for causing their problems (see Document 3.2).

DOCUMENT 3.2

Doonesbury   BY GARRY TRUDEAU

(SOURCE: Doonesbury © G. B.
Trudeau. Reprinted with permission
of Universal Press Syndicate. All
rights reserved.)

Clients are uncooperative for other reasons as well. Some conceive of social workers as agents of control. Although they may be ambivalent in their willingness to work with a social worker, they see little hope for change in their life. To them social workers represent the interests and intentions of other segments of society that the clients believe are seeking to keep them oppressed. Well-intentioned workers who initiate interaction with some economically disadvantaged clients are confronted with the clients' perception that the social workers are involved with them only to control and keep them in their place, not to help them change their environment through more money, better services, or better jobs. In such cases, clients' expectations create relationships with insufficient trust and little outlook for change (Hasenfeld, 1985).

On the other hand, some clients see social workers as agents of change because of their commitment to helping create changes in the environment of clients, not in the clients themselves. These social workers conceive of their clients not simply as individuals or small groups but as members of entire communities.

Community organizers (and program developers who have contact with community members) are expected by their clients to create new organizations and opportunities within a given community. For example, a rural community in need of a health clinic may turn to a social worker to develop proposals to organize and fund a clinic. Lesbian and gay communities have used social work planners, among others, to create community-based programs and service centers.

Outside their roles as clients, people served by social workers also have differing expectations and perceptions of social work that are based on their backgrounds. Older persons may have never encountered social workers before their initial request for service. More affluent groups probably have used professionals other than social workers to help them with their problems. Members of some groups, however, will have had a great deal of contact with so-called social workers, although these workers were not members of the profession by education or membership in professional associations. Many members of Black, urban poor families, for example, recall social workers as the snooping, stingy caseworkers from public welfare departments. Some members of lesbian or gay communities recall social workers as part of mental health efforts to stigmatize and "cure" them.

Rural areas have conflicting ideas about and experiences with social work and social welfare services. On the one hand, residents of small towns and farming areas believe that they have been extremely self-sufficient in meeting their own needs. Social work as a profession developed in early twentieth-century urban areas populated by new immigrants and poor people. Persons who migrated to farming areas engaged in mutual help efforts on an informal family or community basis, which created a different institutional structure and response to problems. Today, their ideas of individualism and of nonpublic, somewhat ad hoc approaches to helping others conflict with their perceptions of social work as an urban, bureaucratic, publicly funded profession. As noted in our discussion about social work fields of practice, rural social work has emerged quite strongly in recent times but still faces these conflicting images of social work.

Overall, clients of social workers are not a homogeneous group and do not have common expectations of social work. Even when they are clients, their perceptions and expectations of their relationship with a social worker vary greatly. Involuntary clients, however, may be hostile. Other clients are ambivalent about working with social workers, because they hold the pessimistic outlook that social workers are primarily agents of control and, hence, incapable of helping them on their own terms. In social work relationships with some communities, the client views social workers as powerful agents of change.

Differing ideas and expectations aside, clients benefit from social workers through the individual help they receive and the social changes social workers help to create. For some clients, the benefits are unexpected and derive from the nature of professional social work practice, which aims to leave clients stronger and more capable of managing their own lives.

For all clients, regardless of background or area of concern, a benefit of social work that lies beyond the resolution of an immediate concern is an increase in confidence and problem-solving ability. Individual clients and sometimes entire communities expect problems to be dealt with in some fashion. Few expect that social work practice also seeks to strengthen the person or the community. Regardless of client expectation of the client-worker relationship, and often in spite of client hostility or hopelessness, the benefit to clients lies in the unexpected and quite useful direction of enhancing problem solving abilities of clients.

WHAT THE PUBLIC WANTS

Clients and, to a lesser extent, colleagues are two groups nearly everyone thinks of in relation to social work. Few, however, realize how significant members of the public and their elected or appointed representatives are for social work practice. Reflection on the relationship between the public and other professions, such as medicine or law, points out that the public has a clearer idea of what those professions are and holds a more universal acceptance of their worth than it does of social work. Although medical doctors may be thought of as charging too much and offering too little in the way of personalized attention and lawyers as too self-aggrandizing in their actions, the public consensus is that the medical and legal professions are essential to society and its members.

What lay people as well as what politicians and other policymakers believe about a profession is essential for its practice. Public ideas form the basis for supporting or opposing allocation of money to pay for the delivery of professional services. As noted, social work and the needs areas it deals with in the institution of social welfare and in its fields of practice are not fully accepted by the public as significant (Abramovitz and Blau, 1984). The profession plays an active role in defining need.

Also covered in those discussions is the public's perception that the institution of social welfare is not universal in its coverage, being limited to programs for the poor only. Although social welfare also covers the middle class, it remains limited to those, regardless of class, who have not met their needs in other social institutions. Hence, social welfare is believed to be less universal than other social institutions regarding those who potentially might benefit from its programs and services.

It is believed that any member of society *potentially* may become sick and require medical services. It is not believed that all people are potential recipients of help with problems in their social functioning.

Compounding this situation is the attribution of what causes problems in areas of need. The public will accept responsibility to meet certain needs but not others (Taylor-Gooby, 1983). Those who become sick can often meet some of their medical needs and are usually not held responsible for making themselves ill. Society assumes the responsibility for protecting its members, fearing that anyone could be faced with the same situation. The potential vulnerability to, and lack of responsibility for, illness is applied universally. Those persons who fail to meet their own needs for shelter or love or sustenance or proper socialization in other areas and who must turn to social welfare or a social worker are held responsible for their problems. The stigma associated with social work's first clients, the impoverished immigrants, has carried over to today. Most members of the public believe they somehow are immune from having similar problems in dealing with their own environments. Hence, the public does not entirely or even uniformly hold itself responsible for meeting needs dealt with by social workers.

Some members of the public, however, have come to believe that the needs met by social work practice within social welfare are similar to the needs met by professionals in other social institutions. Although they may never use what it offers, to these members of the public their potential need for social welfare service is little different from their potential need for legal or medical services. Moreover, others recognize that regardless of personal need, the significance of social work comes from its availability to those in need. Its help does not have to include everyone in order for its services to be critical for society. What has emerged among lay people is an ongoing, unresolved public debate about the importance of the needs, the clients, and the professions in social welfare (Auclaire, 1984). The inconclusiveness of this debate extends to attitudes about the importance of social work (see Document 3.3).

DOCUMENT 3.3

Image of Social Workers in Fiction
Beverly B. Nichols

Oh wad some power the giftie gie us
To see oursel's as other see us!
It was frae monie a blunder free us
And foolish notion.

Robert Burns
"To a Louse"

Physicians, lawyers, nurses, and teachers have long since made their mark in fiction. As individuals, their personality is portrayed, their character developed, and their essence depicted. And even if they seem unreal as people, these professionals still influence others. Fictional social workers have never achieved a similar status. One can search through whole libraries and find no more than a handful of such workers with whom to identify.

A social worker is the main character in Konrád's *The Case Worker,* first published in Hungary in 1969 and then translated into English in 1974.[1] He works in a governmental child-family welfare agency in a large city in Hungary. Nameless, his self-awareness, warmth, frustration, anger, and helplessness become increasingly clear to and painful for the reader. The reader also appreciates his cutting, but insightful, remarks about the social system. Eventually, the caseworker loses his professional direction, abandoning, for a while, not only his work but also his wife and children so that he can care for an unteachable idiot for whom he cannot find foster parents.

Konrád's novel gives shape to an ordinary caseworker's work environment. Knowledge of the reality depicted in this environment would hardly ever swell the ranks of applicants to schools of social work, although few social workers expect to remain long in the bailiwick of the poor and disadvantaged.

At the other end of the spectrum is the humorist Peter DeVries. DeVries *likes* social workers—they lend themselves well to ridicule. In one of his novels, the main character is even married to a caseworker.[2] In another, *The Tunnel of Love,* DeVries deals with the process of adoption, which he finds ludicrous, and has a heyday with the likes of Mrs. Mash, who has "a mouth like a mail slot," and Miss Tercle, both of whom are social workers.[3] DeVries's social workers "snoop," but those on whom they snoop are much more clever and ingenious and, or course, have the last word and laugh.

In general, other fictional social workers are busybodies, self-serving types, or social isolates. Introducing the social worker in *A Forest of Feathers,* Hoffman writes the following:

> I can see the wheels go round in their smug little empty minds. I try to tell them something important and they say to themselves, H'm this girl is a mental patient. Why? Because she's off her rocker, that's why. And are you supposed to listen to the aimless prattle

of someone who is off her rocker? No. How do you know she's off her rocker? She's a mental patient. That's how. Next case.[4]

Gallant begins her story "Orphan's Progress" by writing this:

> When the Collier children were six and ten, a social worker came and shortly after that, they were taken away from their mother, whom they loved without knowing what the word implied. . . . whether it is the right thing or the wrong thing as far as the children were concerned, it is the end of love.[5]

Where Mist Clothes Dream and Song Runs Naked, by Sara, is about a young Jewish immigrant family struggling during the depression.[6] The main character is an 11-year-old girl. The family lives in a slum area, in which life is primitive and rough. The girl believes she has had a sensitive and caring sexual experience, through which she changes from an immature to a self-aware person. When providing "help," the professionals portrayed in the book quickly violate her much more insidiously than her sexual partner had.

Because social workers intimately touch the lives and affairs of many people, their untenable portrayals in fiction are disconcerning and puzzling. Writers depict them as narrow and stereotyped characters, blending person and role. Paradoxically, when social workers describe themselves and their work in the professional literature, they show an obtuse blindness, usually reporting on their successes as though nothing could be learned from examining their failures. However much social workers wish that others would see them as they see themselves, this will not occur without the realistic self-appraisal and insight that they seek to evoke in others.

1. George Konrád, *The Case Worker,* Paul Aston, trans. (New York: Harcourt Brace Jovanovich, 1974).
2. Peter DeVries, *The Glory of the Hummingbird* (Boston: Little, Brown & Co., 1974).
3. Peter DeVries, *The Tunnel of Love* (Boston: Little, Brown & Co., 1949), p. 9.
4. Peggy Hoffman, *A Forest of Feathers* (New York: Harcourt, Brace & World, 1966), p. 17.
5. Mavis Gallant, "Orphan's Progress," *New Yorker Magazine,* April 13, 1965, p. 49.
6. Sara, *"Where Mist Clothes Dream and Song Runs Naked* (New York: McGraw-Hill Book Co., 1965).

(SOURCE: Copyright 1979, National Association of Social Workers, Inc. Reprinted with permission, from "Images of Social Workers in Fiction," Vol. 24, No. 5, pp. 419–420.)

Social Workers in Fiction: A Brighter Image

Irene Glasser

The article "The Image of Social Workers in Fiction," by Beverly B. Nichols (September 1979 issue), both stunned and fascinated me. Yes, as Nichols says, we are portrayed as callous bureaucrats, like the worker in *The Case Worker* (who, by the way, is suffering from a classic, full-blown literary version of the "burnout" syndrome). Or else we are shown to be comical, meddlesome creatures, as in the movie *A Thousand Clowns,* in which Ms. "Do-Good" comes to interfere with the genuine, though somewat offbeat, relationship of father and son.

But are we always portrayed as such grotesque figures of ridicule or disdain? This is of more than academic interest, since we know that many people interested in human emotions and struggles are also avid readers of fiction; thus our image of ourselves is affected. Also, young people often find their professional role models as characters in a story. And finally, the members of society who are empowered to support or not support social work, through funding and legislation, are surely also subject to the emotional impact of fiction. Therefore, I would like to offer a few examples of sensitive insights or effective work by people in social work–type jobs in fiction.

PERCEPTION OF 'CLIENTS'

In the recent book *Final Payments* by Mary Gordon, Isabel Moore is engaged in a follow-up assessment of an adult foster care program for the elderly.[1]

Although she is not educated formally for her work, the reader can appreciate the sensitivity of Ms. Moore's observations in the following description of a home visit to Rose Gerardi, her four children, and her three elderly house guests, for whom she receives stipends. This novice social worker's ability to perceive the emotional life among her "clients" in this brief, informational type of exchange becomes clear in this passage.

Rose Gerardi was wearing white high heels in the middle of November. She teetered into the kitchen in a worrisome way for a woman of her age. The house smelled of polish but was cluttered with racing forms. Everywhere I looked there were pages of newspaper, either spread out or crumpled, with firm, decisive-looking circles around horses' names in different-colored inks. A very elegant-looking old man sat in front of the television in the living room. A large woman with purplish hair sat next to him. She cleared some newspapers off a black leather chair for me.

"Sit down, honey. You must be dead tired."

Four children ran through the living room, scattering papers and furniture. They were all thin and dark and nervous, and they made straight for the kitchen. There was a loud crash. One of the dark children came into the living room.

"Ruth dropped a pitcher," he said.

"So," said their mother, "it's the last pitcher in the world. Clean it up."

I was surprised to hear an old woman's voice say from the kitchen, "The frigging thing slipped right out of my hand."

The old woman with the purplish hair said to me. "Ruth never spoke like that before she moved here."

"But I always wanted to, Alice," said the voice in the kitchen. "That's what you've never known, my dear."

"She picks it up from my kids," said Rose. "They all talk like sailors."

"Yes, but they're wonderful children," said the woman named Alice with some concern, as if she were afraid I might misunderstand. "We never had so much fun in our lives, did we, Richard?" she said, turning to the old man.

. . . . .

"Miss Moore, we hope you don't have to report this particular aspect of our lives [betting on horse races] to the county as we are aware that it is quite illegal. We rely on your discretion. We've found, however, that it is an excellent way of supplementing our pensions as well as keeping our minds alert."

"You must excuse my sister," said the old man. "She was a schoolteacher and she tends to talk to one as if she were teaching the three-times table."

"Nonsense, Richard," said his sister. "The young lady and I were merely having a conversation."

. . . . .

One of the children ran through the living room. Rose caught him by the waist of his pants. "Did you rip your jacket again, you hooligan? Didn't Alice just sew it for you yesterday? Change it so you don't look like you live in a slum, and put it on top of Alice's sewing pile."

"Try to be careful in the future," said Alice.

"Yes, Alice," said the boy, hugging her roughly. "Thank God you're around or we'd all be bare-assed."

No one had addressed any remarks to me in some minutes. They were obviously absorbed in each other, and their absorption shielded them from the consciousness of a stranger. This is love, I thought, this is happiness; going on, ignoring the one who has come to judge you. It struck me that this was the nature of my work; it was this that I was paid for, to judge these people and their happiness (welfare, the county called it, but it was happiness they meant), to make general statements about the nature of happiness.

. . . . .

Mrs. Blake, the medical report said, had cancer of the colon; within a year she would be dead. She had been told. She had a colostomy that required daily changing by Rose; she had refused cobalt treatments. There was a queer time-bomb effect about the old woman, sewing and betting and waiting to die. Coloring her hair in that mistaken way.

When I went into the kitchen, Rose was crying. She rubbed her wet cheeks with the heels of her hands.

"It's Alice," she said. "I can't stand it, you know what I mean, knowing she's not going to be around."

I looked out the door at the three old people, who were arguing about whether to put a comma or a semi-colon somewhere in their report. To care about punctuation with death about to go off like that was a way of saying life is good. Life is valuable.

PRACTICAL HELP

From these very personal observations, let us move to the less sensitive but yet very practical help offered to Deborah

Blau in her recovery and eventual return to the community in *I Never Promised You A Rose Garden*.[2]

"Oh, Miss Blau—" a voice called behind her. It was one of the social workers. (What now? she wondered. I have a room, so I don't need a room-tracker, unless there's one to rescind the other's trackings.) "Doctor Oster was talking to me about you going to the high school." (There it was again, the lock-step-lock of the world; they had reassigned her to her place under the juggernaut.) Redness seethed upward from the tumor until she was hot to the eyes with its pain.

"I should have thought of it right away," the social worker was saying. "There's a place in the city that might be able to prepare you for them."

"For what?" Deborah said.

"For the examinations."

"What examinations?"

"Why, the high-school equivalency. As I was saying, it seems the practical way."

The benefits of the social worker's facilitating Deborah's studies for the high school equivalency examination are seen later on.

Miraculously, her need had been seen by earth ones. Deborah found that her exceptional problem was common enough to be covered by a statute. If she could prove to the Board of Regents her conquest of high-school subjects, she could get a certificate of equivalency without having to undergo three years in the big stone school. If she could ride the two hours to and two hours back between the hospital and the city's Remedial and Tutorial School, there might be a quicker and less perilous bridge between Never and

Maybe. She fell into her work dizzily and full of doubt, found her balance, took the books, and dove into them. Buried in pages, she sounded to the bottom like a whale, rose, took breath, and plunged again. Despite the dangerously hypnotic effect of the double two-hour ride each day, pride in the stubborn battle gave her the strength she needed. She struggled to stay up to the demands of the study and travel. In time the teachers were able to open a tiny crack in the wall of her separation. During the month that she went to school from B Ward the nurse woke her before full light. Each morning before she was ready to leave for school, she was allowed by doctor's order (medicinal) one cup of coffee, and after a week of fidelity to the early hour, the night nurse added toast and a glass of juice on her own responsibility. Deborah was proud of the respect that the little extras showed. Except for the extraordinary ones, the hospital workers tended to give the flat requirements and no more, but lately, at the moment when she stood at the door with her morning schoolbooks—symbols of responsible sanity—and waited for it to be unlocked with the large "madhouse" key, the attendant would say, "Good-by, now," or even, "Have a good day." [Pp. 243–244]

And still later, the full significance for Deborah emerges.

At the end of the month the Regents of the State called her out of the springtime to open their letter. She had passed well—well enough to be certified by the state as having an education equivalent to that of students who had attended high school—and there were enough points over to make her an acceptable applicant to any college. She phoned home especially proud to give

her parents that second bit of news, and glad that their time of pride, while hedged-about and deferred, was still possible.

"Wonderful! It's wonderful! Oh, wait until I call all the family! They are all going to be so proud!" Esther said.

Jacob, by comparison, was almost still. " . . . very proud," he said. "It's fine, just fine." His voice seemed on the verge of breaking. [Pp. 250–251]

"ONLY A CONVERSATION"

Finally, consider the excerpt from an interview in a work of fiction, "Only a Conversation," by Viola I. Paradise.[3] It takes place in the early 1900s; the issue is child labor and working conditions in an oyster farming camp. This excerpt captures the crucial initial movements of the encounter between a working woman and the interviewer.

Mrs. Kazalski struggled hard against despair. If only she had never left Baltimore!

And now the government, the government was sending inspectors, to fine them, to starve them, to take the work away from their children! Twenty-five dollars! Suppose they discovered that her children worked, that she had not the twenty-five dollars? Some of the neighbors might let it out. Well, the government lady would get nothing from her, not a thing. She would be civil, but not a word about the work!

The government lady was in the door. "It's not a man, dressed as a woman," was Mrs. Kazalski's first thought. "Annie Oshinsky is a fool!" She responded, unsmiling, to the "Good afternoon, Mrs. Kazalski. I'm Miss Egmont of the Children's Bureau. May I come in?"

"Sit down," she said in a dull voice. But she thought, as she looked at the short, slight, brown-clad figure, the pointed piquant face under the close-fitting little round hat. "She looks—almost—as if she could be happy!" It came as a revelation to her that any adult could look like this.

Afterward, thinking of her, Mrs. Kazalski wondered why she had seemed so remarkable. She was not pretty, nor yet clever; apparently she had not noticed Mrs. Kazalski's hostility, had acted as if she were welcome. She had said, easily, "May I take off my hat? It fits a little too tight"; and, without waiting for permission had removed it and hung it on the knob of the chair.

Afterward, as during the interview, Mrs. Kazalski felt about in her sparsely furnished mind for a word to explain this visitor, so unlike anyone she had ever met. The Polish word for "separate" kept coming to her mind; but, being unused to abstract thinking, she did not recognize it as exactly the word to express Miss Egmont's detachment—detachment for herself, apparent freedom from problems of her own—which was a quality that puzzled and attracted Mrs. Kazalski.

A little later, we glimpse the effect of asking a person to reflect on her situation.

"I'd like to know," Miss Egmont went on, in her soft, even voice, "about the work you and the children do in the cannery—just what you do, and how much you earn, and what time you go to work, and some other things. But first, are you sure you understand just why I'm asking these questions? Sometimes people are suspicious, can't understand why the government, far off in Washington, should send someone away down here to ask questions. Maybe you'd like to ask me some questions before you answer mine?"

"Mrs. Oshinsky says you come to collect the fines."

"Fines?"

"The twenty-five dollars for people, if their children work. You inspector?"

"No," said Miss Egmont, simply, and it surprised Mrs. Kazalski that the accusation did not embarrass her. "There are inspectors," Miss Egmont continued, "and there are fines for employing children; but the bosses, not the workers, pay the fines. Only, my work has nothing to do with fines. The government is making a study of what's good for children and what's bad for children. You see, children are the most valuable things in the world; but it is only lately people have learned that in order to make them healthier and happier, we have to study them, and see how things affect them. The Children's Bureau is finding out how work affects them—how it affects their health and their chances of growing up strong and healthy and happy. What do you think about it? How do you feel about the work your children do, and the other children?"

Mrs. Kazalski had never thought of it. But the question turned her scrutiny back from her visitor to herself. It half flashed through her mind that she had never before thought of anything aside from how to get money for the next day's living; how to keep her children and her house clean; what to cook; whether the oysters would be large or small; how to pick out the wettest can and to work quickly, so that as much water as possible could get in with the oyster-meat, before it was weighed. [Pp. 91–92]

The relief of being able to ventilate in a supportive atmosphere is also depicted.

And when Miss Egmont took up her questioning again, with "How did you happen to leave Baltimore, to come down here?" Mrs. Kazalski found herself wanting to tell the whole story of their hardships. It would be blessed relief to talk about her troubles, to put them into words, to a person quite detached from her life, someone she would never see again. Never had she done this; never had it occurred to her. She had always thought of her burdens as inevitable, inflicted by Providence, goading her to laborious, irksome effort, which offered no reward. She was not a woman to pity herself, but now, as she poured forth her tale, it was as if she had been given the power to stand apart and see herself; and a rush of self-pity, the first she had known, flooded her for the moment—a strange indulgence of pain that was hotter, but softer, then the hard accepting silence of her many months. Yet there was nothing in her voice, no moisture in her eyes, to tell Miss Egmont, who listened with understanding, of her emotion. She had sent the children out of doors, and in a low voice—that her neighbors might not hear—she had begun:

"Things were enough good with us, till the accident. After five months sick, my man dies; and was left in the house only five dollars thirty-eight cents. Katie coughed bad. That night came the row-boss . . . "[Pp. 96–97]

Finally, there is the beginning of hope and the possibility of change from "only a conversation" with a sensitive worker. Mrs. Kazalski went back to her washtub. She could hear Miss Egmont making the same explanation, could hear her neighbor's guarded, reluctant answers. She did not listen to the words, though she could easily have heard them—at first. But after a while her neighbor's voice lowered. Then it occurred to her that perhaps her neighbor had some trouble as real as her own; perhaps—why, surely every woman in the camp had troubles. Most of them were widows, most of them had children to support. And perhaps other women, all over the country! Why, of course, it was right that the government should send someone down to see how things were!

That night she went to bed with a new feeling. It was as if, for the first time in her life, she was fully alive. Not happy, but awake. Sometimes, in her youth—say, fourteen years ago—at a wedding in Galicia, after a peasant dance, she had a feeling akin to this, yet different. Then the dancing made one forget the hard furrows and the heavy plough. Now there was no forgetting, rather a full remembering, a coming alive of her mind. A full remembering of herself, and, therefore, of others. [P. 101]

VALUABLE FEEDBACK

I feel that the self-appraisal that takes place when we do see ourselves, positively and negatively portrayed, within the pages of fiction, is a valuable piece of feedback. I hope that we can laugh when what we see is funny, improve our practice when it is negative, and be proud when we like what we see.

1. Mary Gordon, *Final Payments* (New York: Ballantine Books, 1978, pp. 189–192. Copyright © 1978 Random House, Inc. Reprinted with permission.
2. From *I Never Promised You A Rose Garden* by Hannah Green (Joanne Greenberg). Copyright © 1964 by Hannah

Green. Reprinted by permission of Holt, Rinehart and Winston, Publishers.

3. Viola I. Paradise, "Only a Conversation," *Atlantic Monthly* (January 1923), pp. 81–93. copyright © 1922, by The Atlantic Monthly Company, Boston, Mass. Reprinted with permission.

(SOURCE: Copyright 1981, National Association of Social Workers, Inc. Reprinted with permission from "Social Workers in Fiction: A Brighter Image," Vol. 26, No. 3.)

The unresolved nature of public perceptions of social work is a significant context for its practitioners. The relationship with colleagues is a professional one involving cooperative delivery of service. The relationship with clients, as we have seen, is a helping one. With the public, social work seeks recognition for its status as a profession, sanction from society to develop standards for its members, and resources and funding to carry out its activities.

Given the nature of society's perceptions and expectations, the relationship of social work with laypeople, politicians, and other policy makers can be difficult at best. Social workers have to balance the public belief that they control, reorient, or change those they work with against the profession's goal of enhancing clients' social functioning in line with clients' interests and intentions. Equally difficult is social work's desire to change structures and develop social opportunities to help people. Dealing with members of the public who do not recognize social responsibility for such problems, let alone any societal causes for them, can be frustrating for social workers.

Dealing with the public is operationalized in several specific relationships that members of the social work profession have with elected and appointed representatives of the public, such as politicians and other policymakers, who often exhibit the mixed perceptions about social work that we have discussed. Officials may also see themselves as representing and upholding such beliefs on behalf of their constituents, thereby reinforcing these ideas about social work (Navarro, 1983).

For example, national and state legislation allocates funding for many programs in fields of social work practice. Child welfare, protective services, community programs, mental health, and senior services are a few fields of social work practice that receive substantial public funding. In order to receive such monies, representatives of the social work profession must develop, advocate, lobby, and testify on behalf of policies of concern to members of legislative bodies.

Once legislation has been passed and signed into law, human service bureaucracies develop additional regulatory guidelines and mandates to carry out the social policy established by law. A child welfare law, for example, is translated into regulatory mandates that determine how much funding and under

what conditions an agency will receive it. Again, following appropriate chan-
nels and procedures, social workers work as lobbyists, advocates, and administrators for the development of these regulations. The context for social work
initiatives is the varying perceptions and expectations held by the elected or
appointed representatives of the public. Their attitudes become a major force
in deciding what social work will receive from public officials (Navarro, 1983;
Conlan, 1984).

Many fields of practice receive money from other sources, including the
United Way, the Community Chest, and private philanthropic funds. Social
workers must also advocate for the policies and programs they wish to have
funded to meet the needs of their clients. Social work competes with other professions and interest groups in seeking out such monies. Practitioners advocate
the programs they want and use processes for requesting them as forums in
which to interpret their profession as positively as they can to those who make
decisions.

Within the agencies that employ them, social workers also face the opportunity to develop new programs or seek changes in existing ones. Public agencies
are governed by administrative bureaucracies that are ultimately accountable
to some elected or appointed officials. Private or voluntary organizations have
boards of directors that are responsible for policymaking. Although in both
structures, the administrators and board members may be quite supportive of
social work, it is likely that the practitioner will face a similar task of interpreting to them what social work is and why its activities warrant funding consideration.

The perceptions and expectations of social work held by lay people and
acted on by their elected or appointed representatives form a critical side of
social work's societal context. Their perceptions are complex, ranging from
negative views accompanied by hostile actions through ambivalence to positive
outlooks and (mildly) supportive behaviors. Part of any social worker's practice
context is interpreting to the public and its representatives the benefits society
derives from the profession. These benefits include meeting the needs of clients
within social welfare and social work's fields of practice, promoting the social
functioning of all members of society, and directing the public into recognizing
and meeting its responsibility to help people meet their needs.

It means that social workers must continue to help members of society understand what social work is and why its activities are important to society.
This challenge faces all social workers equally. Both social work and social welfare are emerging as a profession and a social institution, respectively. In
both—the "societies" they face and the institution of social welfare where they
carry out their purpose—social workers are like pioneers. The message of these
pioneers must stress the benefits given to society by social work: Social work
aims to create better conditions and to enhance social functioning for its clients, while educating society to deal with an emerging area of its collective
responsibility (see interviews on pages 89–90).

I AM A SOCIAL WORKER
"Opinions about Social Work"

GRACIELA CASTEX: I always find it interesting that when people ask me what I do, I don't say to them that I am a social worker. When I worked in agencies, I never said that I was a social worker. I always described what I did. People would say, "That sounds so interesting and so wonderful; what a fulfilling kind of job. How do you get to be that?" Then I would say, "I have a social work degree." It seems to me that people in general tend to value the work that social workers do—the interventions, the sensitivity, the knowledge and the skills that we have, the techniques that we use.

I think that these are the kinds of things that the public values. What is not valued as much is the actual name of the discipline. Many people will put value on the work of social workers, not necessarily the label—social work.

BERNICE GOODMAN: It depends on which public you mean. By and large, most people still have a residual attitude about social workers as "goody-two-shoes" or "lady bountifuls" who are interested only in "giving" things away. In this sense we are not a highly rated profession. Two things account for this attitude. First, it was started out by women and on a high or so-called professional, not a grass-roots, level. Social work stands for certain values about people, and these are not often shared by members of the public. Social workers stand for the belief that people are more valuable than profit and that all people have the right to be heard. These are not popular views. On the other hand, another public in another culture would prize these values and the profession that stands for them.

BETTE HARLAN: Currently I am working in Arizona, where a governor said that no one should consider a career working for the state. That assertion applied to social workers, of course. That governor did not see as important the work of social workers to improve the public welfare system and to help people who needed its services. This attitude was reflected in a proposed salary increase that did not match the increase in the cost of living. The governor's attitude, however, in my opinion reflected an earlier one about social work and its value to society. Over the years, I have seen the development of greater understanding and acceptance of social work on the part of the public.

TRACEY JOHNSON: Sometimes, as social workers become involved in helping clients, as they push agencies to take action, as they pressure others to do something about problems, social workers are perceived as troublemakers. Un-intentionally, getting involved in helping people leads to the worker being seen as a threat by agencies and by clients and their families. This perception, how-ever, is part of the social worker's job.

IRMA SERRANO: Although the public, and public officials, may not have a very high opinion of social work, we can change that opinion by educating them about what we can do. We need to sit down with public officials and tell them, "This is what we can do." We are experts on social issues. We have devel-oped valuable knowledge about current social problems and how to help people. A lot of people will find out different definitions or opinions of social work exist when we teach them what we do.

ADELE WEINER: I feel that the current public opinion of social work is rather negative, and I think there are several factors that account for this. Pri-marily, the current political administration has been perpetuating the myth of the welfare client taking advantage of the system and has cut back on funding. Much of the current tax cutbacks have been made at the expense of social wel-fare programs.

Secondly, since social workers are identified with welfare, income mainte-nance programs, they are stigmatized by association with the people they serve. This might help to explain the current movement among professionals from public welfare programs to mental health clinics and private practice where they deal with a different socioeconomic class of clients. Few people under-stand the educational requirements to be a true social worker and often confuse the clerks, income maintenance workers, and other categories of civil service workers with social workers. This is compounded by the fact that the term "so-cial worker" is used generically in many agencies, although the staff member has a degree in psychology, education, or sociology. Social work as a profession needs to continue to push for licensure and restricted use of the term "social worker" to help improve the image of social workers that the public holds.

A third misconception that leads to the negative stereotype of social welfare is the belief that it is somehow "them" and not "us" that are being served. This "them and us" mentality is clearly evident in the government's response to the AIDS crisis. As long as the victims were "throw away people" (i.e., gays and minority I.V. drug users), then government response could be slow and inade-quate. Once people begin to realize that we are all in this together, that many people are simply "one paycheck away" from welfare, that many health, nutri-tion and education programs affect us all, then the public opinion of social work will improve.

CONNECTING SOCIAL WORK AND SOCIETY

Social workers operate within the context of competing and conflicting expectations for the profession and perceptions of what social work can do. They work with professionals and nonprofessionals within their own agency and in other programs that they contact on behalf of their clients. Clients are not unified in their relationships with social workers and differ in their degree of cooperation and their hopes about what will emerge from their contact with social workers. Lay people and politicians may support or attack social work and enhance or undermine professional opportunities. Social workers in their practice must balance and negotiate these various contending factions. Taken together these factions compose one part of the societal context of social work practice. These diverse groups of people may be called the "societies" within which social work practice takes place. Their divergent viewpoints offer numerous paths that may sidetrack you on your search for how social work is valued. Where might their differing opinions take you if you heeded one set only?

> From colleagues you would find out that they could be supportive of social work and that they might quickly come to understand and accept social work as valuable to their practice. But be wary and prepare to explain the benefits social work offers to them and to society.
>
> From clients you would discover that not all of them are willing or able to understand and appreciate social work. Again, in the worker-client relationship, to avoid any ineffective wanderings about, workers must include an explanation of worker expectations and an exploration of any differences in perception held by clients.
>
> From members of the public and its representatives you might hear that social work is not, nor should it be, recognized as a profession. Given the connection of social work to public and private funding sources, careful attention has to be given to public expectations and, if necessary, to achieving a reorientation in the public's attitudes.

Given all the opinions and viewpoints and having thought through your own perceptions, where do you stand? The foregoing discussion may create the image of life on a frontier. Imagine having left your family, working and struggling to settle into a new place, and cooperating with some of your new neighbors in relocating. However, you have lost the support of your family whom you left behind because they do not accept your aim as worthwhile. To them you must explain your aim at the same time you are working to achieve it.

Such is the social worker's role in the context of various "societies." To each group, the worker must interpret and explain professional purpose. From each, the practitioner seeks cooperation. To each, the social worker offers various benefits and rewards. Maintaining an identification with social work given the conflicts of this context can be difficult for persons engaging in practice for the first time. For those already involved in the practice of social work, it should be stressed that the divergent perspectives of colleagues, clients, or laypeople should neither distract you from fulfilling professional purpose nor keep you from maintaining a correct sense of who you are and why you are important. For those engaged in finding social work, a way to evaluate and interpret the worth of the profession is an important part of your endeavor.

For Further Study

1. Make appropriate arrangements and interview a number of people regarding their views about social work. Include social workers, those who work with them, and members of the public.
2. Discuss the degree of responsibility you think society should have in providing help to people so that they can meet their needs and function effectively.
3. To understand the concept of involuntary clients, think about a situation in which you were forced to interact with another person. What feelings did you have? What were your actions in this situation? How comfortable were you?
4. In the social workers' discussion of teamwork in this chapter, which factors seem to lead to a positive or a negative experience? In what ways did each worker create a positive social work presence on the team?
5. According to the social workers' interviews, what are some opinions held by the public about social work? Discuss which of these were somewhat surprising to you.
6. Discuss the nature of the client depicted in Document 3.2.
7. Using material in Document 3.3, compare the two images of social work. Identify and discuss images from other fictional accounts of social workers.

Glossary

TEAM. A group of workers from a variety of disciplines or professions in a given agency or unit who work together in the provision of services to a common client system.

NONPROFESSIONAL. Members of occupations without as extensive a time of training or the degree of responsibility of professionals in the delivery of services to clients. Workers such as receptionists, outreach workers, and aides are nonprofessionals who are critical in helping clients.

NETWORK. The systematic development and maintenance by a social worker of a group of professionals who cooperate in sharing ideas, information, and strategies about a given client population.

COLLEAGUES. All professionals and nonprofessionals who interact with social workers within their agency or area of practice.

CLIENT OR CONSUMER. Terms for people social workers help that are derived from professional usage or from the notion of consumers of social work services.

INVOLUNTARY CLIENTS. Persons who do not themselves seek social work services and may or may not be willing to cooperate with the worker assigned to them.

AGENTS OF CONTROL. Social workers are seen as representatives of the interests and interventions of social institutions and agencies, not of clients.

AGENTS OF CHANGE. The view of social work that focuses practice on creating changes in the environments of clients and is not exclusively concerned with bringing about changes in the clients themselves.

UNIVERSAL COVERAGE. Coverage of social welfare programs extended to include everyone in need and not restricted to certain needs or to only some people who have need.

SOCIAL RESPONSIBILITY. The acceptance by members of society and their representatives that the public must help with people's problems because the operation of social structures create or contribute to such problems.

STIGMA. Negative and punitive attitudes assigned to some recipients of social welfare services by others who believe that those who are in need are somehow less worthy than those who are not.

REGULATORY MANDATES. Guidelines developed by federal and state bureaucracies to implement the social policies contained in specific pieces of legislation.

UNITED WAY OR COMMUNITY CHEST. Major sources of private funding for social welfare agencies and programs.

BOARD OF DIRECTORS. The policymaking and accountability mechanism of private agencies.

"SOCIETIES." The diverse groups of people (clients, colleagues, and laypersons) with whom and for whom social workers practice.

Bibliography

Abramovitz, M., and J. Blau. "Social Benefits as a Right: A Re-examination for the 1980's." *Social Development Issues* 8(3): 50–61, 1984.

Abramson, M. "Collective Responsibility in Inter-Disciplinary Collaboration." *Social Work in Health Care,* 10(1): 35–43, 1984.

Auclaire, P. A. "Public Attitudes Toward Social Welfare Expenditures." *Social Work* 29(2): 139–144, 1984.

Barth, R. P. "Collaboration Between Child Welfare and School Social Workers." *Social Work and Education* 8(1): 32–47, 1985.

Cingolani, J. "Social Conflict Perspective on Work with Involuntary Clients." *Social Work* 29(5): 442–446, 1984.

Conlan, T. J. "The Politics of Federal Block Grants: From Nixon to Reagan." *Political Science Quarterly* 99(2): 247–270, 1984.

Dove, H. G., K. C. Schneider, and D. A. Gitelson. "Identifying Patients Who Need Social Work Services: An Interdisciplinary Analysis." *Social Work* 30(3): 214–218, 1985.

Glasser, Irene. "Social Workers in Fiction." *Social Work* 26(2): 251–253, 1981.

Hasenfeld, Y. "Citizens' Encounters with Welfare State Bureaucracies." *Social Service Review* 59(4): 622–635, 1985.

Mallory, J. "Police–Social Worker Teams Cool Down Family Crises." *Practice Digest* 2(1): 13–15, 1979.

Meyer, Carol H. "Occupational Social Work and the Public Services: Gains and Losses." *Social Work* 30(5): 387, 1985.

Navarro, V. "The Administrator's Health Policies: Four Myths." *Social Policy* 14(2): 20–22, 1983.

Nichols, Beverly B. "Image of Social Workers in Fiction." *Social Work* 24(5): 419–420, 1979.

Schilling, R. F., II, and R. F. Schilling. "Social Work and Medicine: Shared Interests," *Social Work* 32(3): 231–234, 1987.

Taylor-Gooby, P. "Moralism, Self-Interest and Attitudes to Welfare." *Policy and Politics* 11(2): 145–160, 1983.

Toseland, R. W., J. Palmer-Ganeles, and D. Chapman, "Teamwork in Psychiatric Settings." *Social Work* 31(1): 46–52, 1986.

Watt, J. W. "Protective Services Teams: The Social Worker as Liaison." *Health and Social Work* 10(3): 191–198, 1985.

CHAPTER FOUR

Searching for Societal Connections: The Professional Purposes of Social Work

[Social work] purposes proclaim our intent to work on behalf of the client's needs and to deal with the public issues from which they stem. As we pursue these purposes we demonstrate the authenticity of our profession's values, which are promulgated under the auspices of our profession.

Stephen M. Aigner (1984)

CHAPTER OVERVIEW

The direction we promised to take in our search for social work includes the following:

Examining professional purpose in society.
Defining the area of human and social needs dealt with by social work.
Exploring the contexts of practice.

So far in that search we have identified an area of needs that stems from people's functioning in their environments. We have also outlined a corresponding professional role that helps people with the problems they encounter while meeting their needs during social interactions within their environment. The exact nature of needs people have in social functioning and how social work helps people with it remains to be specified.

In this chapter we take the first step in specifying the special function of social work in society by introducing and discussing more carefully the nature of the needs social work meets and its professional purpose in doing so. In Part II this idea of purpose is expanded into a model of practice, and the area of change in human and social needs is throughly explored as is the practice context of "societies" and services.

This set of ideas connects social work and society. The ideas also provide the framework to use in finding social work—regardless of time, population served, or specific person-in-environment problem.

SOCIAL WORK AND SOCIETY

The direction of our search is to look for connections between social work and society. We have already talked about the profession of social work and defined it as helping people with their social functioning. The purpose of social work, its function in society, specifies what the profession has been sanctioned by society to do. The purpose of a profession is one of its most direct connections to society.

The modern professions and how they are organized differ somewhat from their earlier forms. Several generations ago medical doctors differed in the ways they carried out their work. Before that time they were known by different titles. Indeed, in even earlier cultures the approach and the premises of those who helped people to meet their health needs were vastly different from today's medical doctors.

Modern medicine may not wish to claim descent from the medicine man or woman, but the current human *need* for health and health care (and for a corresponding group of people designated by society to provide expertise in this area) are a continuation of health needs that were once met by the shaman.

An examination of the beginnings of the needs area covered by social work and of those who worked to meet such needs, although they may not have been called social workers, continues our pursuit of the connections between social work and society. Such an examination also begins to specify more precisely the purpose of social work in society by getting at the ongoing reason for the current existence of social work and by answering the question: Why must a profession of social work exist in society?

Finding the reason for the existence of social work in society is fundamental in assessing the value of the profession. What social work does for society as a whole, whether or not it is accepted as a "valid" profession, is what gives it worth. Members of different "societies," or social groups, that relate to contemporary social work may argue about its utility and be at odds with one another about how, and how long, social work should operate. The debate, however, needs to be heard in the context of social work's purpose. Various positions on the value of social work to contemporary society should be interpreted in light of the part played by the profession in meeting an ongoing social need (see, for example, Albert, 1985; Billups, 1985; Tripodi, 1985).

Two approaches are used in exploring the history of people's needs in their social functioning and of social work's origins. One approach offers evidence in the form of the early recorded history of the development of social work; the second supplies evidence in a story about the activities of people who acted like, but who were not called, social workers. The use of historical evidence is common in describing social work. The use of anecdotes is also helpful. Both approaches lead us to a recognition of the ongoing nature of the social needs of people and of efforts of workers to help them meet their needs.

HISTORICAL OVERVIEW AND NATURAL HELPERS

During the early part of the twentieth century, in large urban areas of this country, European immigrants and others were faced with staggering problems associated with their relocation. By the end of the nineteenth century, urban areas were undergoing rapid economic and physical development. Although employment and education opportunities were available, the lack of work skills and language skills among many immigrants made these opportunities inaccessible to them. Great stresses were placed on the functioning of these immigrant families because of low wages and poor living conditions. Urban slums developed that were inhabited by a large, oppressed class of impoverished people who had a variety of family, physical, and mental health problems. These changing urban conditions accompanied industrial development throughout the Western world (Gratton, 1985).

Before the twentieth century, two groups, settlement house workers and volunteers in charity organizations, were grappling with the problems that had developed around social functioning in urban areas. The two groups took somewhat different approaches to the needs of the clients (Addams, 1961, Richmond, 1965).

Settlement house workers moved into the affected urban areas, taking up residence there. In their settlement houses, they opened combined residences for the workers and service centers for those who lived in the neighborhood. Settlement house workers focused on helping individuals and small groups to receive socialization and education to adapt to their new social environment. Settlements also provided concrete services and support services such as child care and recreation. The settlement house workers made efforts to create better living conditions, to increase educational opportunities, and to improve employment for those living in the neighborhood. For example, they sought laws to regulate employment conditions and advocated better housing and living conditions. Their efforts sought to socialize immigrants and to address social issues.

The workers in charity organizations operated out of a different agency structure. They dispensed the charitable donations of money and goods given by the prosperous middle class. Those in need of such charity applied for it through the charity organization, which determined need and decided who was worthy to receive their charity. As procedures were developed and implemented to solicit, collect, and distribute funds, volunteers from the middle and upper-middle classes were used as "friendly visitors," part of whose task was to serve as role models for success and to demonstrate appropriate behavior to the poor. The charity organizations focused on a "case," either an individual or a family (Leiby, 1984).

The charity organization workers "professionalized" their job by getting it salaried, by crowding out volunteers, and by establishing training programs for new workers on how to collect and assess data about clients and their needs. The environmental and family factors surrounding the social and economic needs of their clients took on a new importance. Charity workers addressed the financial and social needs of individuals. Gradually the charity organization workers became known as social case workers. Their approach to helping people to function better in society was to individualize each person, treating the person and problem as a case. Thorough investigation of the entire situation, including environmental and individual factors, became their hallmark. However, they did not conceive of environmental change as a major part of their work.

Other agencies that dealt with problems the new urban poor encountered in their social environments also came to use workers similar in function to the charity organizations' social case workers. Agencies such as schools and hospitals added social caseworkers to their staffs. They sought information about the client's social environment, including family, employment, and living conditions. As noted in our discussion of the development of the professional organizations, the associations of these various groups combined and adopted the professional title *social worker*.

These new workers wanted to solve their clients' immediate problems and to assist them in dealing better with their lives. In handling client problems, the workers assisted with adjusting and changing client behavior. The issue of social control as a primary preoccupation of social work has its roots in this era of practice. To get clients to function better in social institutions, their investigations sometimes seemed to border on spying and their interventions on moralizing control efforts. Their response, nonetheless, was to what was at the time defined as needs in the area of people's social functioning.

The settlement house workers also sought to help people operate effectively in their environments so that they could meet their needs. They sought to help the immigrants fit into their new society. They also tried to help the urban poor behave appropriately and as successfully as possible in social institutions. Their efforts at helping people live better lives in society seemed less obviously focused on control and adjustment; settlement workers also made extensive efforts to improve opportunities and to create a new environment for their clients. Both charity and settlement workers dealt with person-environment needs but pursued different purposes in this area of human and social need (Austin, 1985).

This historical overview illustrates changing names and titles for the groups dealing with people's social needs. It also points out an ongoing demand for a group to work in this area of human needs. The workers who emerged to handle these problems were not uniform in their purpose or in their approaches. Conflicting traditions of how to help people function better in society and competing notions of where to focus change efforts emerged. Some workers would change people to meet a changing environment; others would change systems and environmental structures to make them more effective for people.

Those who first used the title *social worker* were not the only group of work-ers who contributed to the social purpose of meeting people's needs in their social functioning. The two philosophies, taken along with other inputs, make up the purposes that became those of contemporary social work. Professional purpose is the reason for the existence of a profession and transcends vari-ations in its organization and operation. Purpose indicates that a profession is of ongoing importance to society.

Now let's turn to another source of information about the origins of social work. Verbal stories about natural helpers who were akin to social workers alert us to activities that preceded formal helping efforts in the area of social func-tioning. Some aspects of the current, more complex purposes of social work emerged from the efforts of these natural helpers.

Many persons from poorer areas of the rural South recount that members of their family or community were social workers in action but not in name. One woman gave as her motivation to become a social worker a story illustrat-ing that her grandmother had been one. At the time the granddaughter told the story, she was about thirty-five years old. She had grown up in a part of the rural South that had lacked any social work educational programs or social work services until the lifetime of her mother. Hence, how could her grand-mother ever have been a social worker—without benefit of education, title, or position? The granddaughter explained that her grandmother had not been called a social worker, nor did she get paid to be one. Members of the commu-nity where her grandmother lived, however, thought of her as the person they would turn to if they had any of the following problems:

Needed money.
Were having problems with their children.
Had a family member who was drinking too much.
Wanted to get in touch with a family member who was far away.
Needed someone to talk to.
Were emotionally depressed.

The grandmother had no extra money, but she knew where those who came to her could go to get some. Members of the community preferred to talk to the grandmother about certain problems than to the community doctor or to their own minister. The grandmother was the one they could relate to, the one who helped them talk, the one who guided them to a solution for their problems.

This anecdote describes a person who functioned remarkably closely to the way we think a contemporary social worker does. It also reveals that commu-nity members in need of help in their social interactions wanted someone to help them who was not necessarily a doctor, minister, or a member of their own family. (See Ballew [1985] for a consideration of contemporary natural helpers.)

Thinking about such natural helpers clarifies the existence of a function or purpose in society to be carried out by a group of designated professionals in this area of human and social need. Natural helpers were sought out by people in some communities. Parallel to this expression of meeting human needs was the emergence, as summarized earlier, of two sets of workers usually considered as the predecessors of today's social work practitioners.

Along with the activities of early social case workers, the helping activities of natural helpers are the antecedents of contemporary social work. The reason for social work to come into existence was the need for a group which could manage, modify, or control how people function or interact within society.

If we think of the emergence of social work along these lines, we can begin to conceive of social work in a broader sense than the trappings of its debatable status as a profession. We see it as a means developed in society to help people with their social functioning. The essence of social work, its utility to society, is in its basic social purpose as it is carried out today and as it was practiced by its predecessor groups.

Searching for societal connections emphasizes a profession's social purpose. In the short span of time covered by the history of social work, we can discover that the title accorded its workers may have changed but that the function or purpose it has in society remains the same. Social work will continue to exist as a needs-meeting mechanism as long as the need covered by its purpose exists in society.

SOCIETAL SANCTIONING OF A NEEDS AREA

As pointed out earlier, the activities of contemporary social workers are not universally valued by members of society. However, social work is essential to all members of society, and the profession has been legitimated by society itself. The social mechanisms that develop in society to enhance its functioning and to ensure its continuation do not necessarily receive the approval of all members of society. Nor do people necessarily have to agree or even be in favor of the ways such mechanisms operate. This is especially true of social work, as explored earlier in our discussion of the expectations of laypeople.

What is most important to keep in mind, however, is that societal recognition of human needs and of ways to deal with them is given when institutions and professions develop to address them. Their emergence and the accompanying degree of public acceptance of their existence indicate their significance to an effectively functioning society. Public consensus improves their operation but does not entirely indicate their worth in society. Being placed on society's agenda, so to speak, by having been institutionalized also affirms the value of social work. The public and scholarly debate about how Western societies either are becoming or have become "welfare states" captures the idea that social welfare and its helping professions have been institutionalized.

In a similar fashion, professions that emerge to meet socially sanctioned needs are also institutionalized and become part of the social fabric. Whether loved or unloved, they too play a necessary role in society. Our previous discussion of settlement house workers, charity organization society volunteers, and natural helpers showed how the profession of social work and its purpose were sanctioned by its institutionalization. That overview of social work's historical development exemplifies the emergence of society's recognition of an area of social and human need and of a professional structure designed to help with problems people have in meeting it. It also showed how their purposes were often at odds. The two groups of workers dealt with people facing the same types of needs. Their differing approaches, however, reflected different aspects of the purpose of social work.

The people they dealt with had similar economic, political, and family problems. The specific causes and nature of their problems varied. Their need was for support, social resources, and individual and community growth and change to deal with the problems they had in meeting their needs. Similar needs were exhibited by other members of an industrial society when it placed demands and consequent stresses on people in its ever more complex and changing structures.

Social work emerged as the profession to assist people *and* society in meeting these needs. Social work's designated purpose is to help people and society in this needs area. In a sense, what social work must deal with are the *human* needs of people faced with problems in managing their societal relationships. The factors that occur in *society* that account for the needs people have and that cause some of the difficulties they encounter in their social environments are also of concern to social work. This is a blend of the needs of people, the needs of society, and the attitudes of the public about needy people and about some of the social changes taking place in society. Social work must confront changes in people and changes in society.

To state it in another way, social work currently deals with a needs area that has emerged on two basic levels in society:

Among people with problems in meeting their social needs.
Within social institutions that are changing and causing people problems.

Furthermore, the needs or problems are of two types and stem from:

Crises faced by people or institutions.
The ongoing development and growth of people and institutions.

Certain aspects of the level of need and type of problem have been accepted by members of society. The crisis-like problems of individuals and society have been grudgingly considered and dealt with; the ongoing need to manage individual and social change has been ignored or denied.

Historically, for both individuals and small groups, society first acknowledged emergency or crisis problems such as those caused by accidents and natural forces. Resources and help were made available by social welfare and social workers as well as others.

What is still emerging and still being institutionalized is the fact that people may require support along with ongoing social resources to guarantee their growth and development. These ongoing resources and the help needed to ensure effective social functioning are provided in part in the family, school, and economy. What is emerging is that the institution of social welfare and the help offered by social work can meet other needs as well.

For social institutions, as for individuals, an area of "social" need has emerged when an institution or social service resource system faces a catastrophic problem or change that poses an immediate problem. If the need for change is crisis-like in proportion, then social workers guide change within the affected part of the institution.

Still not fully institutionalized is acknowledgement of the need for ongoing social change in institutions. Approaches for guiding such needed changes have been only partly realized.

What has emerged is a dual area of human needs *and* societal needs. These human and societal needs are interrelated, and various aspects of them have been institutionalized. Only some of their institutionalized aspects have received public approval. The purposes of social work, as one of the professions helping people in this needs area, reflect the complex interdependence of people's and society's needs. These purposes are part of the emerging societal mechanisms aimed at acknowledging and dealing with problems associated with meeting needs in this area. We return to this topic in the next chapter (see Document 4.1).

DOCUMENT 4.1

Curriculum Policy for the Master's Degree and Baccalaureate Degree Programs in Social Work Education

4.0 SOCIAL WORK PURPOSES

Interrelated Purposes

4.1 The fundamental objects of social work concern are the relationships between individuals and between individuals and social institutions. Historically, social work has contributed to the development of these relationships in such a way as to promote social and economic justice and protect the opportunities for people to live with dignity and freedom.

4.2 Professional practice thus focuses on the transactions between people and their environments that affect their ability to accomplish life tasks, alleviate distress, and realize individual and collective aspirations. Within this general scope of concern, social work, as it practiced in a wide range of settings, has four related purposes:

4.2.1 The promotion, restoration, maintenance, or enhancement of the functioning of individuals, families, households, social groups, organizations, and communities by helping them to prevent distress and utilize resources. These resources may be found in people's intrapersonal or interpersonal capacities or abilities and in social services, institutions, and other opportunities available in the environment.

4.2.2 The planning, development, and implementation of the social policies, services, and programs required to meet basic needs and support the development of capacities and abilities.

4.2.3 The pursuit of such policies, services, and programs through legislative advocacy, lobbying, and other forms of social and political action, including providing expert testimony, participation in local and national coalitions, and gaining public office.

4.2.4 The development and testing of professional knowledge and skills related to these purposes. . . .

(SOURCE: This material was first published in the *Handbook of Accreditation Standards and Procedures,* 1988, and it is reprinted here with permission of The Council of Social Work Education.)

THE PURPOSE OF SOCIAL WORK IN SOCIETY

The purpose of social work has been described in a number of different ways. Each approach aims to answer the following questions:

Which are the problems that people have with their social functioning that are within the realm of social work practice?

What is the nature of the social resources needed to assist people deal with these problems?

How should social workers address these problems?

How should social work alter and develop societal resources that address these problems?

Answers to these overlapping questions add up to the purpose served by social work in society.

During the past decade two similar statements of the purpose of social work have been developed. One appeared in 1977 in *Social Work*, the professional journal of the National Association of Social Workers, and a restatement appeared a few years later (Minahan and Pincus, 1977; "Working Statement," 1981). They state that the promotion or restoration of mutually beneficial interactions between people and society is the purpose of social work. This purpose aims to improve everyone's life. The 1981 statement affirms social work's belief that the environment should provide resources to people that are adequate to meet their aspirations, meet their common needs, and alleviate their distress. People should work for their own well-being and that of others. Justice should mark the interaction among people. The statement identifies individuals, families, groups, communities, and organizations as clients. Clients, others in their environment, or both clients and others may need to change in order to achieve the purpose of social work. To meet this purpose several objectives are listed, such as helping people become more competent, obtaining resources they might need, working for responsive organizations, influencing the relationship between organizations and institutions, and influencing social policy.

This statement emphasizes several important aspects of social work and its purpose. It identifies the important role people's environments play in enabling them to lead healthy, satisfying lives. It designates intervening in the needs area of social functioning as the purpose of the profession. And it defines social functioning as the interactions between people and society. Furthermore, the statement suggests that a range of interventions is used to achieve professional purpose.

A second statement of the purposes of social work appeared in *Educating the Undergraduate Social Worker* (Baer and Federico, 1978, 1979). It also built on earlier ideas about social work's place in helping people in their social functioning. This statement also stresses the interaction among people, resources, and the societal institutions and organizations that make up the social environment. The Baer and Federico statement was based on an earlier work of Pincus and Minahan (1973). The statement by Baer and Federico reads as follows:

> Social work is concerned and involved with the interactions between people and the institutions of society that affect the abilities of people to accomplish life tasks, realize aspirations and values, and alleviate distress. These interactions between people and the social institutions in which people function occur within the context of the larger societal good. Therefore, three major purposes of social work may be identified: (1) to enhance the problem-solving, coping and developmental capacities of people; (2) to promote the effective and humane operation of the systems that provide people with resources and services, and (3) to link people with systems that provide them with resources, services, and opportunities.

This statement also emphasizes the interactions between people and their environment that enable people to live full lives and to achieve their goals, as well as to deal with situations of distress.

These statements of purpose and our earlier discussion of social work as a profession stress that it deals with the interactions of people and society, through social institutions and institutional services, resources, and opportunities. (See Figure 4.1.)

Sometimes this interaction is not effective. The interaction breaks down, so to speak, resulting in inadequate social functioning. People's needs are not met by their social functioning. Any aspect of the interaction may cause this inadequate social functioning. We discuss this at greater length in the next chapter. (See Figure 4.2.)

Social workers become involved in such interactions by using interventions whose aim is to improve whichever aspect is creating difficulties. (See Figure 4.3.)

Social work has a three-part purpose:

Strengthening people's abilities to problem solve, cope, and develop.
Linking people with systems in their environment that provide services, resources, or opportunities to improve their social functioning.
Promoting effective and human operation of service, resource, and opportunity systems.

Using all or part of this three-part purpose, a social worker may focus on the following:

1. Changing people: (See Figure 4.4).
2. Linking people with resources: (See Figure 4.5).
3. Changing the environment of people: (See Figure 4.6).
4. All, or some combination, of the purposes.

These simple diagrams graphically present the purposes of social work. They depict social functioning as the interactions between people and social institutions (and their composite structures) in which people attempt to meet their social needs. When these needs-meeting interactions do not work very well, we label such interactions as problems in people's social functioning. Workers intervene in problematic social functioning, on the basis of their stated purpose to enhance people, to link them with the resources they need to meet their needs, or to strengthen and change the structures of social institutions (see interviews on pages 107–109).

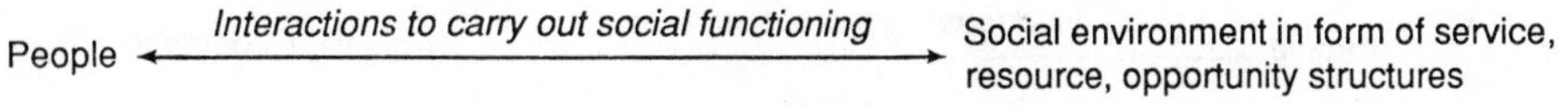

People ←———— *Interactions to carry out social functioning* ————→ Social environment in form of service, resource, opportunity structures

Figure 4.1

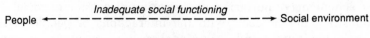

Figure 4.2

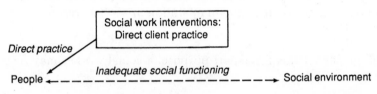

Figure 4.3

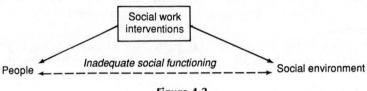

Figure 4.4

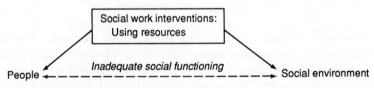

Figure 4.5

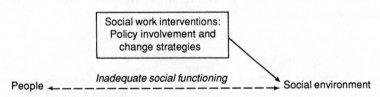

Figure 4.6

I AM A SOCIAL WORKER
"Defining Social Work's Purpose"

GRACIELA CASTEX: I like the definition that talks about linking people with resources. The one that talks about working with vulnerable populations I like less because when it is spelled out that way it seems to exclude people. Just when one mentions vulnerable that way, many say that they are not vulnerable, because they are not Black, are not poor, or are not this or that. We need to realize that all of us can potentially enter situations where social work interventions might be helpful. It does not mean that we were born vulnerable just because we were born into a certain segment of the population, but that it is the experience of life that makes us need the intervention, not because we happen to have been born into a certain segment of the population.

I see everyone as a potential social work client. I think that the delivery of social work services can take place with many different groups at many different times in their lives. Some may not need services until they are old or very ill, which becomes the point of intervention. But everyone may have such a need.

BERNICE GOODMAN: This is my own definition of social work. Social work basically is a female concept of healing that requires a commitment and a caring relationship with others. It is not a competitive position. Healing is an integration of positive forces in a person, small group, or social structure. It seems to me that the whole profession of social work is based on interdisciplinary notions of wholeness and connectedness, which is an institutionalization of the concept of healing. Within each of us is the capacity to be whole, to grow, and to live. Social work is the profession that attempts to promote this capacity in all persons through its interactions with individuals and institutions. As about the only profession indigenous to the United States, it is based in qualitative considerations and a helping process. Social work aims at a natural integration of all aspects of people, including thinking and feeling. Recent efforts to evaluate the profession using a quantitative approach, which is largely based on the male concept of separating thinking and feeling, has paralleled the entry of men into social work. In some ways, this approach does a disservice to the profession because it is inadequate to measure its wholeness.

BETTE HARLAN: I see social work as a profession in which workers function as advocates for and problem solvers with clients. Social workers have a wide range of interventive skills. They are a very necessary member of teams in many settings.

JOE HERNANDEZ: A social worker is someone who provides services, whether concrete or psychosocial. He or she links people to resources. The worker is there to assist people by supporting them, advocating for them, counseling them. Workers use many interventions to meet many needs.

SUSANNA HUESTON: Although I see that social workers provide people with resources and connect people with them and that social workers create change, I believe that for me social work especially helps people to develop. For example, when one little boy I was working with said, "I want to be a pimp when I grow up," I told him that he should learn to be the very best. I didn't exactly encourage him to pursue this fantasy, but I did help him to realize that he had to develop himself to the fullest.

TRACEY JOHNSON: In school I learned definitions of social work. I learned that social workers hooked people up with services, that they were involved in concrete services as well as counseling of a sort. I have worked for several years now with my BSW. My experience leads me to define social work in a more complicated fashion. I see it taking place on many levels and in many agencies. In a way, child care workers are social workers. Administrators, responsible for policy implementation, are also a type of social worker. Outreach workers, who seek clients in the field, appear to be different from those in child care or administration, yet they too are social workers. In a sense, what is similar among these different workers is how they help people plan for and reach new goals in their lives, by considering all kinds of social factors.

If I were to define social workers, I would say that they are a different kind of person, by training and according to their personality. They are more caring, have feelings not only on a superficial level, but care enough about what happens to people to get involved in making changes. They do the types of things, and get involved in helping people, where others are not willing. If social workers identify a problem or concern, they have to get involved beyond what they are immediately doing. They see people's problems in the context of people's total lives, and they intervene accordingly.

Social workers also possess a method of working that is not only nonjudgmental but also based in knowledge of people and their needs. The method is planful and goal-oriented. It works with people to resolve problems.

IRMA SERRANO: Trying to define social work is tough, with each of us having our own definition. Basically the way I see it is that social work is the profession that helps an individual to put together his or her inner feelings and the outside world around them. This definition may sound simple and you usually find it in textbooks, but it actually covers the profession. I don't see social work as clinical or concrete services.

A lot of people believe that social workers "help" people. They believe that a social worker sits in an office, people walk in, and you "help" them. That is a dream, a misconception. Social workers cannot impose their own values or solutions in helping but must respect other people. Social workers help people move on but do not impose their own values. This is a most difficult process in working with other people.

ADELE WEINER: Social work is the profession that helps individuals meet their needs for daily living. Most individuals are able to do this on their own, but a few are faced with problems that preclude their ability to solve problems on their own and must turn for help. What distinguishes social work from some of the other helping professions is its focus on the person-in-the-environment and the ability to use environmental resources to help solve problems. This brokerage function for social workers will become more important as other professions become more specialized and focus only on their own services. This is becoming increasingly evident in medicine, where many practitioners do not know the differences between Medicare and Medicaid, qualifications for services, what services are available, how to get services.

Working in the field of aging, in a society where grown children often live at great distances from their elderly parents, this support and linkage function of social work is extremely important. As the clients' level of functioning may decrease, they will need assistance in performing very basic tasks that we all take for granted. There is really no other profession that can help the community elderly negotiate the many programs and entitlements they need.

The types of skills that social workers develop are applicable to a diversity of settings. While historically social workers functioned in traditional social welfare agencies, currently individuals with social work skills are finding themselves in nontraditional settings. Banks are using social workers in will and trust departments. Law firms are using social workers to do assessments for domestic matters, custody decisions. Unions are using social workers in their health and welfare benefit programs. Doctors in private practice are using social workers to help do assessments, process entitlements, and help clients deal with difficult medical regimes. Private corporations are using social workers in employee assistance programs involving retirement planning, drug and alcohol programs, stress management, and family concerns.

PROFESSIONAL PURPOSE AND THE CONTINUING SEARCH FOR SOCIAL WORK

As you read this, you may be thinking that practicing social work is like a magician's act of balancing contending forces, some critical of and others highly conducive to practice. From our discussion of societies, you have learned that you face conflicting expectations for your professional behavior. The foregoing discussion of purpose indicates that it is composed of contending ideas about intervening in an area of societal and human needs. Learning this can also be unsettling. In one sense, the balancing act is extended beyond the attitudes of people with whom social workers deal in practice to the very reason for the existence of social work. The various expectations for social work, the emerging societal acknowledgment of the needs areas it helps to meet, and the professional purpose required to handle it all have to be juggled.

This magician's act is necessary because the profession of social work is to be the servants of society and the scapegoats of some of society's members at the same time. Society assigns to social work the task of helping people to meet needs in their social functioning. Some members of the public realize that others can't help themselves but resent having to let social workers help such people. If the professionals err in their helping efforts, they take the blame because societal mechanisms must operate to ensure society's survival while meeting the needs of some of its people. Moreover, within the needs area of social functioning both society (as an interacting set of institutions and their composite structures) and society's people (with real and potential needs in this area) compete for help. Social work deals with both sets of interrelated needs. Its purpose to do so makes social work indispensable to society and its people.

In your search for social work and your place in it, professional purpose is quite useful in other ways. It reveals the essence of what your practice may be like. If you have not done so, think about yourself in relation to this ongoing area of need and the purposes of social work. What experiences have you had in helping people with such needs? Is there a tradition in your family of being a "natural helper"? Do you think of yourself as wanting to help people? Do people seek you out for help in dealing with problems in their social interactions? Do you see yourself dealing with some of the structures that make up social institutions? Have you considered the contribution to all of society that is made by social work as it deals with human and social need?

Professional purpose guides your search for social work in yet another way. It provides the framework to make possible your identification of social work in the future and to help others identify social work as the details of its practice change. Your search for social work does not end when you have discovered what people think it is and have found out what it does in society. Your search will continue throughout your (practice) life. Practice entails educating others about social work. Professional purpose helps to lead others to understand social work, and it sensitizes you to identifying and interpreting future changes in it.

For Further Study

1. Which purpose of social work as discussed in this chapter have you most frequently used to identify what social workers do? With which are you most (and least) comfortable?

2. Have you ever known anyone of whom others thought as a "natural help-er"? Or do others think of you as one? Identify the kinds of problems people came to you with for help in resolving, and discuss the type of helping they received. Which purposes of social work do they most match?
3. Identify agencies in your area that have been giving services for the longest time. Select one and study it to determine how its services have developed over time.
4. Compare the definitions of social work and its purpose that were offered by the social workers who were interviewed for this book with those defini-tions discussed in this text.
5. Compare and contrast the purposes of social work offered in Document 4.1 with those outlined in the text.

Glossary

SETTLEMENT HOUSE. During the late nineteenth century, a movement that dealt with urban poverty in which workers settled in immigrant neighborhoods, opening houses or agencies from which they provided services and launched investigations and efforts to reform urban living and working conditions.

CHARITY ORGANIZATION. In the late nineteenth century, an organizational re-sponse to urban poverty that focused on the scientific collection of funds and the professional delivery of goods and services.

FRIENDLY VISITORS. Volunteers who were used by the agencies of a charity organization to serve as role models for the clients served by the agencies.

PERSON-IN-ENVIRONMENT. A term used to characterize the particular focus of the profession of social work on people's interaction within the social struc-tures they use to meet their needs.

NATURAL HELPERS. People who, although lacking professional training, are turned to by their neighbors in poorer and/or rural communities for help with their problems.

WELFARE STATE. The development and institutionalization of social welfare as a social institution in Western countries along with a range of helping profes-sions, social services, and financial programs that are expected to help their citizens meet their needs.

HUMAN AND SOCIAL NEED TO MANAGE CHANGE. The needs area dealt with by social work as it helps society and individuals deal with the difficulties people encounter within their social environments.

PURPOSE OF SOCIAL WORK. A threefold purpose of social work in helping people deal with the problems they encounter during the interaction between them and the structures that make up their social environment: (1) enhancing people's abilities, (2) linking people with resource systems they may need, and (3) promoting the effective and humane operation of such systems.

SOCIAL ENVIRONMENT. The social structures and people who comprise the daily living environments of people.

SOCIAL WORK INTERVENTIONS. The actions of social workers aimed at improving people's social functioning by doing something with them to overcome the cause of their problem through direct client practice, the use of resources, or changing or improving systems of service delivery.

Bibliography

Addams, Jane. *Twenty Years at Hull House.* New York: New American Library, 1961.

Aigner, Stephen M. "The Curriculum Policy: Implications of an Emergent Consensus." *Journal of Education for Social Work* 20(1): 5–14, 1984.

Albert, J. "Social Work and the Public Interest." *Urban and Social Change Review* 18(2): 4–7, 1985.

Austin, D. M. "Historical Perspectives on Contemporary Social Work." *Urban and Social Change Review* 18(2): 16–18, 1985.

Council on Social Work Education. *Handbook of Accreditation Standards and Procedures.* Washington, D.C.: CSWE, revised 1988.

Baer, Betty L., and Ronald C. Federico. *Educating the Baccalaureate Social Worker: Report of the Undergraduate Social Work Curriculum Development Project.* Cambridge, MA: Ballinger, 1978.

——, (eds.). *Educating the Baccalaureate Social Worker: A Curriculum Development Resource Guide.* Cambridge, MA: Ballinger, 1979.

Ballew, Julius R. "Role of Natural Helpers in Preventing Child Abuse and Neglect." *Social Work* 30(1): 37–41, 1985.

Billups, J. O. "Unifying Social Work: Importance of Center-Moving Ideas." *Social Work* 29(2): 173–180, 1985.

Gratton, B. "The Invention of Social Work: Welfare Reform in the Antebellum City." *Urban and Social Change Review* 18(1): 3–8, 1985.

Leiby, James. "Charity Organization Reconsidered," *Social Service Review* 58(4): 523–538, 1984.

Minahan, Anne, and Allen Pincus. "Conceptual Framework for Social Work Practice." *Social Work* 22(5): 347–352, 1977.

Pincus, Allen, and Anne Minahan. *Social Work Practice: Model and Method.* Itasca, IL: F. E. Peacock, 1973.

Richmond, Mary E. *Social Diagnosis.* New York: Free Press, 1965.

Tripodi, Tony. "Comments on 'Where Has the Profession Gone? Where Is It Going?' Social Work: Search for Identity, by Michael Frumkin and Gerald O'Connor," *Urban and Social Change Review* 18(2): 19, 1985.

"Working Statement on the Purpose of Social Work." *Social Work* 26(1): 6, 1981.

PART II

SOCIAL WORK AND SOCIETY

PART OVERVIEW

We are following a three part model as a guide in searching for social work and its societal connections. The model includes:

1. Viewing the purpose of a profession as its essence.
2. Recognizing individual and societal change as an area of human and social need in people's social functioning.
3. Seeing "societies" and services as contexts for practice.

Part II further examines each part of the model.

So far we have examined professional purpose carefully and have introduced the idea of "societies" and social welfare as contexts for practice and that of managing change as an area of human and social need. The basic ideas that make up the practice context have been introduced. We have identified as part of the context of social work practice an emerging social institution in which resources in the form of social programs and services are gathered for use by social workers and other helping professionals. We also have listed a number of fields of social work practice in which social workers apply specialized social welfare resources to specific human problems people encounter in their social environments. In addition, we have explored as a second part of the context of practice a variety of expectations that colleagues, clients, and lay people have for social work.

113

As our guide, the model is designed to help you to locate social work as it presently exists and to aid you in interpreting it correctly for yourself and others in the future. The model points to a core of critical aspects of social work without neglecting the following:

How social work can differ so vastly in detail at different times in history.
Why social work is practiced differently with different clients.
What, including their own diversity, makes different people relate to and evaluate social work so differently.

The next step taken in the chapters of Part II explores thoroughly how individual and societal change constitutes an area of human and social need. We begin with a summary of social science knowledge about human growth and development and about social change. We then explore the significance of interaction with other units of society for human development and the ways concepts of change help to indicate and explain the emergence of problems in people's social functioning.

The ideas of social work's professional purpose and of human and social change as an area of need are used to develop a model of social work practice. The model presents the special responsibility of the profession and moves from purposes to practice interventions. The knowledge base and value system that lend support to practice are also covered.

Finally, the context of social work practice is examined in detail. The idea of social responsibility and how diverse "societies" exhibit particular problems and needs are explored. The nature of existing services that deal with change is covered also. Our earlier caution about words still holds. What do you associate with the following words:

Purpose.
Need.
Society.
Services.
Change.

Do they have meaning and value associations for you other than those used in this text? Do you see it as possible to make change in the structures that make up social institutions? Do you see social institutions as causing problems for the functioning of people who use them to meet their needs? To understand the meanings and values associated with the terms used in this text is to follow its direction; to exclude differences you may have with them is to lose your own interpretation.

CHAPTER FIVE

Managing Change: An Emerging Human and Social Need

I'm gonna make a change,
  for once in my life
It's gonna feel real good.
  gonna make a difference
Gonna make it right . . .

I see the kids in the street.
  with not enough to eat
Who am I to be blind?
  Pretending not to see
  their needs . . .

That's what I want you to
  know
I'm starting with the man in
  the mirror
I'm asking him to change
  his ways
And no message could have
  been any clearer
If you wanna make the world
  a better place . . .

Take a look at yourself, and
  then make a change . . .

Garrett and Ballard (1987)

CHAPTER OVERVIEW

Professional purpose has directed us to the social functioning of people in institutions as the focus of social work practice. The discussion in this chapter offers a way of thinking about organizing some of the human and social needs required for satisfactory social functioning. Factors in individual and social growth and change that lead to problems in people's social functioning are covered. Summarizing concepts from a number of social science disciplines about growth and change indicates that growth itself, as well as change of a more unexpected nature, must be managed by people in order for them to achieve adequate ability to meet their needs in social functioning. These ideas are used to present an emerging needs area—that is, managing individual and social change—and to discuss social work's responsibility for dealing with such needs.

SOCIETAL FUNCTIONING: THE INTERACTIONS OF PEOPLE AND INSTITUTIONS

A human life is lived in a complex process of meeting needs. To live, a person needs food, clothing, and shelter. Not to meet needs leads to problems in living, or even death. In many cultures, however, a human life is incomplete and not lived adequately if needs other than the physical are not met. As noted earlier in this book, among these other needs are love, community interaction, mental health, self-fulfillment, spiritual life, and being treated justly. Meeting these needs contributes to living our emotional, psychological, and spiritual lives adequately (see Document 5.1).

DOCUMENT 5.1

Decent Shelter for All . . .

Secretary-General Javier Pérez de Cuéllar, inaugurating the International Year of Shelter for the Homeless, 1 January 1987

Shelter is a basic human right and necessity. The conditions in which people live determine to a great extent their health, well-being and ability to engage in gainful occupation, to pursue self-improvement through education and recreation and, in consequence, to attain a better standard of living. As an estimated one in five of the inhabitants of our world lack decent shelter, and several million of our fellow human beings lack shelter of any kind, it has been a timely decision to devote 1987 to the aim of providing shelter for the homeless. This is an important undertaking in the larger process of bettering the condition of humanity to which the United Nations has dedicated itself.

The problem of shelter, if unsolved, poses a threat, both immediate and long-term, to the welfare of peoples and the development prospects of the international community as a whole. Homelessness and poor housing conditions, though most appalling in the bursting urban centres of the developing countries, constitute a global problem affecting rich and poor countries alike. The declaration of the Year reflects the determination of Governments to take effective measures, individually and collectively, to combat the threat. Many Governments, international organizations and non-governmental organizations have already adopted new programmes and strategies focusing on the shelter needs of the poor and disadvantaged. These need to be carried forward with vigour and commitment for the achievement of our ultimate goal of decent shelter for all.

In most of the developing countries, we see the twin forces of rapid population growth and increasing urban poverty converging into a crisis which may assume monumental proportions in the coming decades. Only action now, concerted, bold and imaginative, can help relieve the current pressure and avert the future shock.

I would, therefore, appeal to Governments to give the necessary priority to providing shelter and basic services to those who lack them. I would also like to call upon all United Nations agencies and bilateral and multilateral financial institutions to support the efforts of Governments in this regard. I invite the non-governmental organiza-tions, the private sector, professional bodies and the world community to mobilize assistance and support for shelter programmes at the national and local levels.

Let us all bear in mind that a society is judged not so much by the standards attained by its most affluent and privileged members as by the quality of life which it is able to assure for its weakest citizens.

As we move towards the closing years of the twentieth century, we cannot fail to bear in mind that our actions today or our inaction will determine living conditions in the next century.

With the start of the Year of Shelter for the Homeless, we are beginning a journey whose destination is yet distant. Much has been, or is being, accomplished but the need persists glaringly.

(U.N. Chronicle-Public Domain.)

Needs are met in a complex of interactions between the individual and others, the individual and institutions, and the individual and self. Overall, many of our needs-meeting efforts take place in social structures and depend on adequate social functioning. Adequate social functioning, like adequate mental and physical health, contributes to our well-being.

If we are unable to function adequately within social institutions and if we lack competence in carrying out the interactions with others that are necessary to our social functioning, we cannot meet many of our needs. Although adequate social functioning is necessary to meet needs in other areas, social functioning has its own needs. There are needs of an ongoing nature as well as needs that develop when problems arise. In other words, we function or interact in social institutions to meet needs. Social functioning also can be viewed as a need each of us has.

Adequate social functioning is based on ongoing human and social structural growth and development. To achieve such development, everyone must meet basic physical, emotional, and social needs. The ways people meet these needs are the building blocks of their social interactions. As social functioning becomes inadequate, problems emerge in people's needs-meeting efforts. Then additional needs must be met in order to restore their social functioning and to meet their regular needs in institutions.

There are several layers of need associated with people's social functioning, as there are with all areas of human need. People have ongoing needs in each area and needs that arise only when problems occur. In the area of social functioning, there is also the need to accept that change may occur and that people must be prepared to face and to manage change.

In the area of social functioning, there have been two emphases for social work. One has been on helping to meet needs as problems arise, as well as helping people and institutions to become stronger.

A second, although weaker, emphasis has been on maintaining adequate social functioning by managing the factors of change that threaten social functioning. Preventing breakdown, maintaining good social functioning, and reestablishing social functioning are traditional social work goals stemming from the work of the settlement houses and charity organizations. The approach to social functioning in this chapter focuses on defining managing change as a need. Examining the effect of growth and change on social functioning prepares for defining change as a human and social need.

THE EFFECT OF GROWTH AND CHANGE ON SOCIAL FUNCTIONING

In earlier parts of this book, reference has been made to social workers helping people with their social functioning and with meeting some of their needs. Examples include the following:

> Children without parents.
> The frail elderly.
> Alcoholics.
> Abused children.
> The hungry.
> Homeless people.
> The mentally ill.
> Impoverished communities.

We have graphically presented such problems in social functioning in Figure 5.1. With such impaired social functioning, the interactions between people and their social environment leads to failure in meeting needs and living a full life.

Inadequate social functioning
People ←— — — — — — — — — — — — — — — — —→ Social environment

Figure 5.1

Can we state what the specific need is for adequate social functioning? What causes inadequate social functioning? How do we identify common aspects of the needs people have in their social functioning? What, if anything, in terms of need do these problems or concerns have in common, and how do such problems develop?

Using our examples, we might list specific needs as:

The life of the child without parenting is incomplete and requires a child-rearing unit for ongoing socialization and support, without which the future of the child will be marked by inadequate social functioning. The homebound frail elderly, who may be without loved ones or neighbors to help them, cannot long meet even their physical needs, let alone their psychological ones. They will continue to deteriorate in the area of social functioning. The life of alcoholics is consumed by their addictions, which create inadequate social functioning in their family unit, at their place of employment, and in structures of other social institutions. The life of an abused child may be distorted physically and emotionally. Such children need family, love, care, and security. The lives of the hungry and the homeless are painful examples of inadequately met physical needs. The life of the mentally ill is such as to require restoring interactions with many social units. The life of an impoverished community is characterized by the inadequate meeting of basic needs in areas such as health, shelter, food, and justice.

A variety of changes—in individuals and in institutions—account for the emergence of many of the problems and needs listed earlier. There are changes in expectations, changes in social structures, changes that amount to a loss (Roskin, 1982), changes that come from the processes of human growth (Vander Kolk and Bright, 1983). Moreover, certain changes are necessary to restore the social functioning in each case presented.

The child needs parents; the elderly, care-giving and support; the alcoholic, rehabilitation and new ways of coping; the hungry, food; the homeless, shelter; the mentally ill, psychological and emotional change; and impoverished communities, new social structures and opportunities. Deviation from expected patterns in individual lives and in social structures causes problems in social functioning. Addressing these changes will alleviate problems and restore people's functioning. Managing change also means that the affected people must face the meaning for their lives posed by these problematic and restorative changes. Whether the problems stem from processes of psychological and social development, from unexpected changes in people's lives, or from the structures of social institutions where people interact and obtain resources to meet their needs, all people have to manage change in their lives.

People who need to learn how to manage or overcome changes in their lives sometimes need support while learning to do so. At other times, they need help in altering social structures so that the structures better meet their need. Social workers address such problems and develop resources to help people confront the necessary change. Resources are such useful items as services, support, or money for meeting needs and restoring functioning. As doctors restore physical health by intervening in the course and causes of illness and disease that disrupt ongoing physical functioning, social workers restore social functioning by helping to manage human and social changes that contribute to the disruption of adequate social functioning. In other words, people have a need to manage the growth and changes that contribute to or detract from their social functioning. Some must learn new living and interactional skills, others need resources while they meet their needs or overcome the problems facing them, and still others need to manage the environmental causes contributing to their inadequate social functioning. Others need help in managing their psychological growth and development. To address these types of changes, social workers develop parenting classes, help children to learn to deal with divorced parents, teach children to say "no" to drugs, and help the elderly prepare for retirement.

This definition of managing change as a human and social need in the area of social functioning brings together under a single heading a variety of problems and needs people face in contemporary living. All people must function adequately in their social interactions, and many are faced with some type of disruptive or needed change in their lives. Many of this latter group are able to handle and face the changes they confront. In addition, all people must be able to deal with this sense of change itself as a need. Managing change as a need is similar to a need for food, shleter, and clothing; for community and companionship; for security and safety. In this way, change is a basic need for all people because it is essential to the social functioning of everyone in a complex, changing, post-industrial society (see Document 5.2).

DOCUMENT 5.2

Martin Luther King III
William Greider

He is thirty years old now and an elected politician. Martin Luther King III—"Marty" to his friends—is one of the seven commissioners of Fulton County, Georgia, which encompasses the city of Atlanta. Soft-spoken and self-effacing, Marty King clearly lacks, as he would be first to admit, the legendary dynamism and leadership of his father. But in his own quietly effective way, he could be moving toward playing a national political role someday.

Marty was born in Montgomery, Alabama, the second of four children and the first son of Martin Luther King Jr. and Coretta Scott King. He grew up in Atlanta, near the Ebenezer Baptist Church, where his father and grandfather preached. He was graduated from Atlanta's Morehouse College—his father's alma mater—majoring in political science and history. For several years he worked on voter-registration campaigns, lobbied for legislation to make his father's birthday a national holiday and served on diplomatic missions to African and other third-world countries . . .

[I]n 1966, Daddy had started to attack Lyndon Johnson on the war in Vietnam. Lyndon Johnson was a good man. Even though he was a Southern conservative, Lyndon Johnson passed more civil-rights legislation than any other president in history. Johnson really knew how to maneuver politically. He got the Civil Rights Bill passed, signed it, then the Voting Rights Act and then other legislation.

And then Daddy comes out in 1966 and attacks his stance on the war. Well, that made people feel like he was not grateful for what Lyndon Johnson had done. But that's not really what the major issue was, because everything is over economics. When Daddy talked about Vietnam, he didn't just talk about it from a moral standpoint; he talked about it from an economic standpoint. It was interesting that in Vietnam we were able to design bombs to bomb villages yet our bombs never bombed any of the poppy fields. So he

was getting on to an economic issue, a corrupt economic issue. And that's when people started saying, "Well, hmmm, he's talking about turf."

In late 1967 he called for a poor people's campaign, and he talked about redistributing the wealth and resources of this land. That's what he was killed about—redistributing the wealth and resources. And if anybody could've organized the masses to say, "We want this wealth redistributed," he could have. So the powers that be said, "Well, he's got to be removed." That's my understanding of what happened.

On his economic ideas, I believe he was saying, "Teach a man to fish, and he's fed for a lifetime." We gotta teach people how to provide food, clothing and shelter for themselves. What that means is that the wealth has gotta be redistributed to some degree. It's absurd, he said, to have so many millionaires in America who've got so much and at the same time to have so many poor.

So there needs to be some balance— that's what he was saying. And he had the ability to unify masses of people— not just black people but white people too. He started to bring in whites in 1965, and white ministers started supporting the civil-rights effort. When they started seeing his leadership of the masses—the moral leadership, the spiritual leadership he could provide as a preacher—they said, "This guy is dangerous." . . .

I see myself as hopefully being able to enhance the dream that Martin Luther King Jr. had. Although we say dreams never come true, the dream that he talked about can be a realistic dream. It obviously is not gonna happen today, this week, next week, next month or even five years from now. It may not even happen in my lifetime. It may be a hundred years. But it is a dream that can happen . . .

That dream essentially says that freedom and justice and equality can be real for all mankind, and that we will one day begin to judge people based on their merits and qualifications, not by their color . . .

Some of us, especially in the black community, thought that after we acquired citizenship in 1964, with the Civil Rights Bill, and the right to vote in 1965 and fair housing in 1968, that our battle was over. But it tells us that the battle is not over. . . .

The Fifties and Sixties were decades of action by masses of young people and students. Blacks and whites demonstrated together in the Sixties. Then in 1968, when the nation lost Martin Luther King Jr. and Robert Kennedy, it kind of took the activist energy out of the entire nation. If Robert Kennedy had become president, with the ideas that this man had, there's no telling where this nation would be today. The Seventies were more of a recovery decade, recovery from the upheavals and assassinations of the Sixties. And in the Eighties we became more complacent and began to focus on individual concerns.

My father used to say that life at its best is three-dimensional. Those three dimensions were length, breadth and height. The length of life is not how long you live but how you prepare yourself for your own personal objectives. If it means getting your doctorate degree, or if it means working every day establishing a savings account for you and your family—your own personal development, nothing else. The breadth of life is the outward reach to others, like we did with Ethiopia back in 1984. And the height of life is the continuous reach to God, developing your personal relationship with God and spreading the word.

Now, in this decade we got stuck in a length mode—personal development. You've got yours, I've got mine. Our schools teach us to be competitive. But the competition is not necessarily healthy. We're taught how to make a living for ourselves. We're not really taught how to live, how to live amongst each other. . . .

Usually what happens when a crisis occurs is that people turn to each other. In the Depression, people helped each other out as much as could be. But now people are not turning to each other. I mean, Martin Luther King Jr. talked about the highest level of love, the kind of love that seeks nothing in return, that is totally unconditional. It's not based on anything other than the fact that you know that your existence is tied to the existence of your brother or sister, be he black, white, native American, Hispanic, Asian, et cetera. We don't espouse those values, that kind of love, anymore. . . .

Today we have over 7000 black elected officials, and I'm glad to be amongst them. Even though it's still less than one or two percent of the total number, that's progress. I think Daddy would be happy about that. He might even be tickled. . . .

He would probably be proud of the fact that a black American can seriously run for president of the United States. I think he would really be very proud. . . .

(SOURCE: "The Rolling Stone Interview," by William Greider from Rolling Stone, April 7, 1988. By Straight Arrow Publishers, Inc. © 1988. All rights reserved. Reprinted by permission.)

People and institutions have a need to develop the ability for the following:

Confronting change.
Planning for change.
Avoiding change.
Managing necessary growth and change.
Redirecting change.

The need for change may be caused by disruption in regular, ongoing functioning. Examples of such disruptions are family breakups, economic dislocations, and emotional breakdowns. Disruption may also come from a lack in growth or development that leads to inadequate social functioning, including inadequate parenting, absence of business development in a community, and physical limitations. These are a few examples of the need to manage change that is explained by exploring social science knowledge about human growth and change.

SUMMARIZING KNOWLEDGE ABOUT HUMAN GROWTH AND SOCIAL CHANGE

Various academic disciplines such as biology, psychology, and sociology contribute concepts about how growth and change affect the social functioning of people. This includes changes in the operation of organizations and other structures that influence the social functioning of people. Individual changes arise from ongoing growth and development as well as from disruptions in this process. The ability of people to meet their needs is determined by aspects of their development in a number of areas of growth, which together make up the total life and the functioning of a person. The development of a person takes places in stages or phases in areas such as:

Moral understanding.
Physical health.
Psychological well-being.
Cognitive growth.

Attainments in these various areas interact and are interdependent. Some of this personal growth contributes to meeting the needs of people in their social interactions. People grow and develop in each area in different ways and at different rates. Some develop fully, others less so in some or all areas, and the rate of growth affects their social functioning. To be independent and to interact adequately enough in social institutions to meet personal needs or to provide for the needs of others, a certain overall level of development is required. Each area may differ for adults and for children, and the interaction among them creates different specifics about pursuing needs to manage their growth and change.

When changes occur, people need to manage the necessary changes in themselves or institutions. They need to control and manage their own growth and development as well as to confront the effects of environmental change on their lives.

What level of development is required in each of these areas for adequate social functioning? What disruptions in social interactions or pressures from institutions necessitate changes on the part of people to improve their social functioning? What losses or changes in human development lead to problems in social functioning?

The person who has been physically limited from early childhood may have dealt with the need to manage his or her special way of functioning so that it does not affect self-concept or social functioning (Weinberg, 1982). Persons who are older when they are confronted with a change from physical mobility to a state of physical limitation need to learn to manage the specifics of their physical change and to deal with the impact of this change on themselves and their social functioning. What does everyone need to learn in order to be able to understand and accept the place of change in our lives?

We diagrammed adequate social functioning in Figure 5.2.

In the areas of people's growth, development, and change, there are several types of changes. To interact effectively with institutions in their social environment, people must have developed moral standards, psychological selfhood and emotional self-confidence, physical mobility and health, and the ability to relate to and accept others. Without adequate or ongoing growth, lack of change may block social functioning. Changes in their level of social functioning can also come from losses or deterioration of growth in one or more areas. In addition,

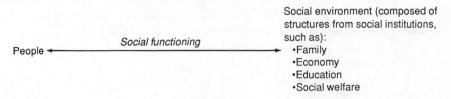

Figure 5.2

social change has several other important effects. Changes that disrupt the social functioning of people take place in social institutions, such as the economy,
education, social welfare, or the family, and they may prevent people from continuing to meet their needs in these social institutions.

In the area of moral development, people grow through several phases.
They begin without a sense of ethical standards that incorporate fair treatment
of self and others in social interactions. Then they move through a stage of
mechanistic ideas of right and wrong, and finally some come to incorporate
standards of fair play and a sense of justice in their treatment of others and in
their social relationships (Gilligan, 1977; Kohlberg, 1981). We expect children
to need guidance, support, and education in moral development. Many adults
also have not developed fully in this area and need help in managing necessary
changes.

Expected or typical physical development ranges from the relative physical
dependence of an infant through the prowess of late adolescence and early
adulthood to the lessened physical abilities that accompany middle and older
age. At each stage, people who fail to achieve the expected level of physical
growth must deal with its impact on their social functioning and with what
their failure to achieve expected growth may mean to them. The adolescent
who matures early, or late, and the older person who ages more slowly are
examples of the need to manage change in physical development and to face
unexpected life situations.

Psychologically, growth in personality and mental health development
leads to increases in awareness and the use of selfhood. Infants initially are
unable to differentiate self from others. A growing sense of trust in and separation from others gradually occurs, followed by an internal integration of ego
that creates psychological independence and integrity. Psychologists conceive
of life stages and associated tasks from birth through death. Each stage contains
growth and contributes to further psychological development. The label of a
dependent child or immature adult captures the idea of inadequate change from
one stage to the next. Mental illness represents psychological development that
has failed or an integrated personality that has been destroyed. In either case,
people are unable to use effectively their psychological self in social interactions.

Cognitively, a person also must grow and develop in order to achieve adequate social functioning. People need to achieve a certain level of problem-
solving ability to assist in social functioning. They move through cognitive
stages from the literal or concrete to the abstract. Failure to achieve an expected
level affects how effectively and creatively people use themselves in their social
interactions. Losses of cognitive abilities among some elderly people, for example, pose a problem for their independence, planning, and security.

Along with these examples of human growth and change, the notion of
coping indicates how people must make changes in expected moral, physical,
psychological, or cognitive behaviors to accommodate inadequacies in their

lives. They develop new ways and approaches, some of which are judged unacceptable by the conventions of others, in order to live their lives and meet their needs.

These growth processes contribute to the ability to interact in society. People need to meet and to manage the changes arising from expected and unexpected growth and development. Some people must deal with their need to change, to grow, and to develop in order to function better within society. All of us must learn to face up to the possibility that we will need to change one or more aspects of our lives at one time or another.

The phrase, "getting on with your life," captures the idea of adequate social functioning. Some people need to learn how to manage growth in themselves and changes in their environment as it affects them. Some people, as they grow and develop, learn how to manage and face change in their lives so that they can "get on with it"; others need help in learning these skills.

Changes that people face and that affect their social functioning may not come from ongoing changes in or loss of their achieved growth and development. Instead, it may stem from changes that are external to them. For example, a person facing a divorce, the elderly person with reduced income who must move to a retirement home, the victim of a crime, or farmers who are going bankrupt need to manage the effects of change on their lives. This includes dealing with what change means for their image, their security, and for their sense of self.

Many external factors disrupt people's social functioning and lead to a need to manage these changes and to restore their social functioning. Changes in the ways social structures operate or are organized affect how effectively people meet their needs within these structures. Concepts about growth and change in systems help to identify their effect on people's social functioning. Because social workers deal with issues facing people in their social functioning, knowing how changes will affect the interaction between people and social institutions is essential knowledge for fulfilling professional purpose.

Changes in family structure, from the extended family to the nuclear family, for example, have strongly affected the social functioning of parents, as has the fact that there are now more families in which both parents work. Both these changes have created the need for social structures to support the rearing of children. Couples need to be able to manage and face the consequences for their lives of these institutional changes. Organizations serving families have also had to face the consequences of these economic and family changes. Organizations such as schools, community centers, businesses, and day-care centers have changed to meet these needs.

In addition, the family faces other changes. There has been a rise in spousal and child abuse within families, which has affected the socialization of children and led to inadequate development in their lives and subsequent problems in social functioning. Changing social roles for men and women have led to differences in images of masculinity and femininity and in child-rearing patterns.

Sometimes the operation of social institutions and structures also blocks the growth and development of people, changing them in ways so that they cannot interact adequately enough in society to ensure themselves a complete life. The operation of these structures oppresses people. These operations need to be changed while helping the people who are affected to overcome ways in which the operations of systems have thwarted their own human growth and social functioning.

For example, if the civil rights of people are not protected in political systems, the avenues to protection, security, opportunities, and resources are blocked and social functioning is impaired. Various groups of people need to change the systems that deny them their civil rights. The federal system has extended protection against civil discrimination to Blacks, other minority groups of color, and women. Municipalities have granted similar protections while denying them to lesbians and gays. Without such protections, the development of all aspects of a person's life is made much more difficult.

In the economy, structural unemployment means basic changes in business and industrial production or distribution of such significance that large groups of people are left without employment or the resources to transfer their skills elsewhere. The recent crisis in automobile production affected thousands of automobile production workers, their families, and people in related businesses. Other industrial and economic changes, such as the growth of service and information industries, have presented employees and managers with fundamental questions about how to manage such growth and change. Not only do they face loss of income; they also face loss of image and psychological or emotional security provided by their jobs (*Public Welfare*, 1983).

A given organization, in the economy or in another social institution, may change its structure and operations. For example, individual businesses faced with shifts within a given industry may have to change their product, relocate, or perish. If the operation or production of a business changes, so must management and employees. Ecological considerations and foreign competition have created such changes in business organizations. New service and entertainment patterns also change and create organizations.

Whole classes of people, however, are left out of the functioning of political and economic institutions. Such groups suffer a variety of forms of oppression. Oppression is connected to factors such as institutional prejudice and discrimination. Higher rates of unemployment and fewer years of formal schooling completed among young black males is an example of such institutional prejudice and resulting oppression. Institutions operate in ways that exclude or severely limit the participation in them of people from certain groups. The development of oppressed people may be blocked psychologically, socially, economically, educationally, and even morally. The moral growth and development of those who carry out the oppression in such institutions is also adversely affected.

Other groups of people adapt, relocate, or migrate. Such people must address the causes that underlie the change as well as handling the changes posed by their new environment. We noted earlier that the problems faced by early twentieth-century immigrants to this country were dealt with in part by social work's predecessor groups. In this century, the Depression era migration of farming people from Arkansas, Missouri, and Oklahoma to the western United States is an example of a large-scale relocation caused by economic and geographic changes. In more recent times, immigrants have arrived in this country in large numbers from Asia, Mexico, Central America, South America, and the Carribean. These peoples face a staggering number of changes in many areas of their lives. (See McGrath, 1983, for examples.)

For children and parents, the educational changes of the past twenty years represent fundamental shifts and pose the need for families to change. Day-care services, prekindergarten programs, Head Start programs, and a broadened use of kindergarten education have lowered the age at which children begin formal training. Children are affected in their ongoing growth and development, and parents face changes in their parenting roles. Curriculum revisions at the elementary and secondary levels interact with changes in the makeup of the public school population. Lessening public support and threats that federal funding will be decreased have altered methods of teaching, affecting student and parental attitudes about and confidence in what schools provide for them.

Changes in the social welfare institution have been far-reaching also in their effect on the social functioning of people. Budget cuts at the federal level mean the loss of programs from which many people receive support and resources to enchance their functioning in society.

These are only a few ways in which social institutions such as the family, economy, politics, education, and social welfare treat people and affect their social functioning. What does this mean for social work?

SOCIAL WORK PURPOSE AND THE HUMAN AND SOCIAL NEED TO MANAGE CHANGE

Knowledge about the effect of human and social change on people's social functioning and about their need to manage change relates directly to the purpose of social work, the purpose of which is to help meet people's need to manage change as it affects their social functioning. This effect and the meaning it has for social work are shown in the flowchart shown in Figure 5.3. Social work helps people manage change in themselves, helps people locate and use resources needed to attend to necessary changes, or helps people change social structures to enable people to function better within them.

The converse of change is stability, continuity, or sameness. We live in a world that does not value and frequently denigrates change. It bemoans changes in family, in education, in mores. Changes are seen as great threats that should somehow be stopped. As individuals, members of American society are socialized to resist or even fear change. They are not taught to anticipate

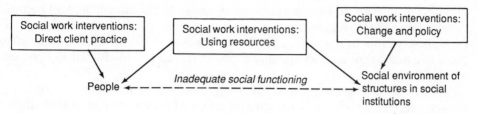

| Social work interventions: Direct client practice | Social work interventions: Using resources | Social work interventions: Change and policy |

People ◀ – – – – – – – *Inadequate social functioning* – – – – – – ▶ Social environment of structures in social institutions

Figure 5.3

or face change in themselves or in social institutions as an ongoing and natural part of their lives.

Social workers have been socialized in similar ways, but must carry out the mandate of professional purpose that can be interpreted as helping people to manage change and to bring about change. Social workers do not always see themselves as guiding change, although with their clients they must face the consequences of change (see interviews on page 131).

For social workers there exist many concepts and ideas from social science that recognize change and its management as a basic part of our lives. Our

---

I AM A SOCIAL WORKER
"The Meaning of 'Change' for My Practice"

BERNICE GOODMAN: My whole concept of practice is based on a concept of change, that change is necessary for life. Unless change occurs in your environment, in social structures, in the world around you, then you die.

IRMA SERRANO: As social workers, we are trying to change the world, but many of us do not want to believe that we can contribute much to those changes. That is very difficult because if we don't realize that there is something that each of us can do to create change, then we are not very clear about our part in change. One debate in the profession I don't like is the "clinical" versus the "social." That is a debate that has been very detrimental in our profession. People who do not consider that social problems are worthy of their professional consideration claim to be social workers. We are training too many to be clinical workers but not social workers. We have to look at social work and at what it changes in a broader sense than the changes of an individual in clinical practice.

previous discussion of how psychological, physical, moral, social, and mental growth takes place recognizes that a variety of changes is an ongoing part of each person's life. In one sense, the theories that growth and development take place in a number of stages see life as change that can be anticipated and guided or modified.

What remains to be covered are some ideas about the need people have consciously and deliberately to manage, use, or control change in their lives. Social work, in its practice, uses ways of helping people and social structures to complete growth processes, to replace existing psychological or cognitive approaches to living that have been destroyed by changes, to rehabilitate parts of people's lives in relation to human or social change, or to take care of people who have been partly or completely damaged by change.

Some ideas, however, reflect the acknowledgment, confrontation, and guidance of change. Consider the following:

Prevention
Social reform
Reeducation or resocialization
Rehabilitation
Planning

Think about some of the problems about social functioning discussed earlier in this chapter. For the abused child, the parents need to be reeducated or resocialized as adults and equipped with new parenting skills. The frail elderly and others in their environment also need to learn new ideas and approaches to life. Part of the rehabilitation of alcoholics is relearning a sober lifestyle. Displaced workers and adult immigrants also face the need to learn not only new skills but sometimes radically different lifestyles. In dealing with the mentally ill and their families, helping often involves teaching them new coping and relationship skills or offering them care.

For the impoverished community, planning indicates ways to manage and direct the changes it needs. As an idea and a discipline, planning would have people identify social problems, collect data about them, and develop ways to solve them. Planning is based on the notion that changes and their consequences can be anticipated and dealt with by rational means. Economic, city, and social planning are examples.

Organizing as a method of helping communities also captures the idea of managing change by altering the oppressive or resource-allocating operations of social structures. Those affected by needed changes in their environment are brought together to work on and solve the problem by using their resources or by forcing a targeted social structure to change. Community members and the community itself grow in social functioning and in the influence they have in their interactions with public and private power structures.

The concept of prevention includes ideas about preparing for and dealing with change. To prevent is to anticipate, prepare for, and be ready to deal with an event. Prevention aims to reduce the development of problems in social functioning before they occur or to reduce the scope of their consequences if they do occur. Programs for the prevention of juvenile delinquency, for example, try to reduce the development and effects of factors that change the behavior of adolescents from law-abiding to delinquent.

Social reform indicates ideas about social change and how to manage it. Earlier we noted that part of the efforts of settlement house workers was to reform society and its institutions. Other examples include penal reform, child labor reform, and civil rights reform.

Some of the ideas presented in this discussion are developed more fully in the next chapter, which discusses a model of practice. That model is based on the existence of a body of knowledge supporting the notion that people and society need to manage change. It also includes the belief that social work can draw on ideas about how to redirect human growth and social change in their efforts to help people deal with their problems in social functioning.

FEELINGS ABOUT CHANGE

Where are we now in our search for the relationship of social work to society? We have identified its professional purpose in society as helping people with their social functioning, focusing on the interactions between people and the structures and people that make up social institutions. In this chapter, we have discussed people's need to manage changes in themselves, in others, and in institutions. These changes affect their ability to function adequately enough in society to carry out needs-meeting activities.

To be adequate in its needs-meeting activities, social functioning itself has a range of needs. People meet some of these needs through their interactions in the structures of such social institutions as family, education, politics, the economy, and social welfare. To do so requires development in people's moral, physical, psychological, and cognitive selves. With adequate, stage-appropriate growth, people are able to use themselves to interact in society and to obtain and use services, resources, relationships, and opportunities to live satisfying lives. When faced with changes in self, others, or social institutions that cause problems in their social functioning, people must overcome the problem by facing and managing the change and its consequences for themselves and their environment.

As purpose provided us with the reason for social work's existence in society, so helping to meet people's need to manage change reinforces the social utility already assigned to the profession. It also reaffirms the complex, multifaceted nature of social work.

We likened the juggling of the expectations of "societies" and professional purpose to a magician's act. The needs area we have just discussed is yet another potential avenue for diversity and difference. The problems people face in their social functioning can be subsumed under the rubric of change, but the details of these problems differ greatly. We said that the need to manage change is universal, yet the needs-meeting aspects of people's interactions with their environments are vast and diverse. Another significant and universal aspect of the changes that affect social functioning is the feelings people have.

People change. Institutions change. You change. And social work changes. To be a social worker, you need to face how you feel about change and try to understand its impact on others. Consider the changes you have faced in your life.

In what ways, if any, was your physical, psychological, or other growth and development different from what was expected? How did others treat you? How did you feel?

Have you ever faced a situation in which you did not know how to act and take care of yourself? Was it because you had not learned how to act or had forgotten how to act? How did you deal with this inadequacy? How did you feel?

Have you ever faced an abrupt change such as the loss of a loved one? How did you feel? How did you handle the loss and your feelings?

Can you recall the changes in your growth and development as an adolescent? If so, how did you feel? How did you manage? Did you need help from parents or peers?

Have you ever had to deal with change in an institution? Was your district or community school integrated? Did an industry fail or change to such an extent that you or someone who provided for you lost a job? How did you feel?

And how has any of these changes in your life affected your functioning in social institutions? Did you become depressed or fearful? Did you drop out of school or lose friends? Did your trust in family or loved ones waiver?

These questions are posed for a reason. People who face problems in their ability to meet their needs face the risk of loss in some aspect of their life, or even the loss of life itself. These problems pose threats to people and generate strong feelings.

The focus in managing change is not just on taking care of the problem posed by the change, nor is it just on helping people to learn and grow in ways that may make them stronger and more capable in their social interactions. A strong component of helping people to manage change is supporting people while they confront how they feel about what the change has done or will do to their life. This confrontation is at the core of people's need to manage change because in confronting their feelings about change people take their first step in meeting this need.

For Further Study

1. Discuss some personal changes you have faced in your life. Include those you faced because of physical and psychological growth, those stemming

from family change, and disruptions or unexpected changes in the patterns of your life. What did you do to manage them and your feelings about them?

2. Read back issues of your local newspaper(s) to identify several changes that have taken place in social or economic structures over the past five years. Examples would be a plant closing or other business change. How did these changes affect people and the community? If possible, contact someone involved in the situation to get his or her response to what happened.

3. In what ways, if any, has your life been affected by the changing social roles of men and women?

4. Talk to someone who has been involved for a long time in the Black Civil Rights movement or Women's Liberation. Discuss with that person her or his views on social change and what her or his involvement has meant.

5. Discuss the various ways Martin Luther King III (Document 5.2) identifies change as an issue for society and as an individual need.

Glossary

ADEQUATE SOCIAL FUNCTIONING. The goal of social work interventions that aims at helping people achieve ongoing growth and development to meet all their basic needs through their social interactions in the structures of various social institutions.

RESOURCES. Useful items such as money, services, and other social supports used by social workers to help restore adequate social functioning.

CHANGE AS A HUMAN AND SOCIAL NEED. The need all people have to manage the growth and changes that contribute to or detract from their adequate social functioning.

INADEQUATE OR IMPAIRED SOCIAL FUNCTIONING. When the interactions between people and aspects of their social environment are inadequate, leading to problems or difficulties such as hunger, alcoholism, homelessness, or abusive interpersonal relationships.

STAGES OF GROWTH AND DEVELOPMENT. A human being's physical, moral, psychological, social, and cognitive life conceptualized as preceding through predictable stages according to age.

COPING. One response to change in which people manage their lives by developing new approaches and ways of functioning, that may or may not be acceptable to others.

MIGRATION. The movement of groups of people within or across national boundaries, presenting them with numerous life changes.

OPPRESSION. Patterns of operating in social structures that block or limit the participation of certain groups of people in society and in the distribution of its resources, leading to inadequate or impaired social functioning on their part.

PREVENTION. A social work approach to change that attempts to prepare people for change, to anticipate its consequences, or to stop it from occurring.

PLANNING. Both an idea and a discipline that solves problems by researching, managing, and directing changes in social structures for the benefit of entire communities.

ORGANIZING. An approach to social work that works with communities to enable them to confront or guide change in the operations of social structures.

REEDUCATION OR RESOCIALIZATION. To recreate or restore some aspect of a person's functioning after it has been disrupted by physical, emotional, or social change.

Bibliography

Garrett, Siedah, and Glen Ballard. "Man in the Mirror," from the album *Bad*, by Michael Jackson, MJJ Productions, 1987.

Germain, Carol. "Time, Social Change, and Social Work." *Social Work in Health Care* 9(2): 15–23, 1984.

Gilligan, C. "In a Different Voice: Women's Conceptions of Self and of Morality." *Harvard Educational Review* 47(4): 481–517, 1977.

Greider, William. "The Rolling Stone Interview: Martin Luther King III." *Rolling Stone* 523:63–69, April 7, 1988.

Kohlberg, Lawrence. *The Philosophy of Moral Development.* New York: Harper & Row, 1981.

McGrath, J. E. (Ed.). "Social Issues and Social Change: Some Views from the Past." *Journal of Social Issues* 39(4): entire issue, Winter 1983.

"Opinion: Saving the Industrial Heartland." *Public Welfare* 41(3): 5–9, 1983.

Pérez de Cuéllar, Javier. "Decent Shelter for All," *UN Chronicle* 24(3): editorial page, 1987.

Roskin, M. "Coping with Life Changes—A Preventive Social Work Approach." *American Journal of Community Psychology* 10(3): 331–340, 1982.

VanderKolk, C. J., and B. C. Bright. "Albinism: A Survey of Attitudes and Behavior." *Journal of Visual Impairment and Blindness* 77(2): 49–51, 1983.

Weinberg, N. "Growing Up Physically Disabled: Factors in the Evaluation of Disability." *Rehabilitation Counseling Bulletin* 25(4): 219–227, 1982.

CHAPTER SIX

Delivering on Purpose: A Model of Social Work Practice

The practice nature of the social work profession has led persistently to a search for . . . models that might not only contribute to a diagnostic understanding of societal problems, but also yield treatment strategies for intervention. . . . How we define a situation determines what we actually do in practice. . . . Current frameworks . . . claim that they satisfy the profession's search to understand the person-environment relationship. . . . A variety of models has been proposed for social work practice. . . . The life model's approach to practice is based on the assumption that "all forms of life strive toward a goodness-of-fit with their environments. . . ." The life model of practice assumes basically, that people and environments together constitute a transacting system. . . . The conflict model, on the other hand, provides an alternative interpretation; that "imbalance" . . . not equilibrium . . . [is] characteristic. . . .

Ketayun H. Gould (1987)

CHAPTER OVERVIEW

The objective of this chapter is to provide you with a framework to use in identifying social work practice. It is not to teach you how to practice or to provide you with a detailed account of specific practice methods. The model emphasizes some of the major elements of generalist practice that relate to social work's societal connections.

Problem-solving steps are used in the generalist method of social work practice to achieve the professional purposes of enhancing people, linking them with resources, and making social structures more effective and just (O'Neil, 1984). These steps include the following:

Engaging the client in a relationship.
Data collection, problem identification, and assessment.
Setting goals and planning interventions.
Implementing and evaluating the intervention plan.
Disengagement from the relationship.

Necessary to effective problem solving is an adequate knowledge base about the problems people have in social functioning and ways of helping people with them.

In this chapter, the definition of professional purpose and some of the knowledge about people's need to manage change, along with ideas about values, assessment, intervention, and practice relationships, are incorporated into a model of social work practice. The model furthers our search for social work's societal connections and provides a framework to define and explore practice. The model uses the notion of purpose and the need to identify the direction of practice. It also outlines values about people and policy that are associated with this direction, offers ideas about system interactions for use as a knowledge base in practice assessments and interventions, and explores the nature of practice relationships as a series of "limited partnerships." An opportunity is provided for you to examine some of the characteristics that make people likely candidates to become the type of practitioner who can deliver on social work's purpose.

FROM PURPOSE TO PRACTICE

As discussed earlier, all professions are characterized by values, a specialized knowledge base, and skills, among other factors. For the profession of social work, its purpose determines each of these. In addition, any model of practice that is part of an effort to introduce its readers to social work's connections to society best serves that goal if it is based on professional purpose. The flowchart on page 139, although it does not indicate the complex, interactional nature of its parts, shows their connection to professional purpose.

The three-part purpose of social work that helps people to manage change as it affects their social functioning has been thoroughly explored in preceding chapters. The direction given to practice by the emphasis on change, purpose, and need has also been indicated.

As people function in society to meet their needs, problems arise in the interactions between them and the various structures of the social institutions that make up their social environment. Some of these problems originate with change in people and institutions, whether unintended, expected, or needed. Social work practice is directed toward change, in helping people to manage it in their social lives and in changing social structures. To change people and social institutions and the interactions between them is the basic direction practice takes (Pincus and Minahan, 1973). (See Figure 6.1.)

Because social work practice moves workers in the direction of change, strong value positions are associated with the profession. Social work as a profession focuses on how people should grow and develop, how they should be treated if they need help in their social relationships, and what responsibility the social environment has to provide resources for meeting needs and offering opportunities to people. These values, associated with purpose and need, be-

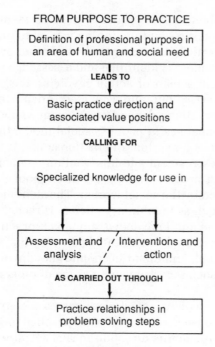

Figure 6.1

come an integral part of practice interventions and policymaking. They also help to determine the nature of practice relationships.

The value positions of social work emphasize maintaining the independence and self-determination of people and helping society to assume responsibility for supporting people, for building effective and humane structures, and for treating people fairly in their social interactions. The direction of social work practice also means that social work value positions may conflict with those of other members of society and create controversy for professionals as they advocate for policy and programs to support these positions.

Social work's specialized knowledge base also supports this emphasis on change. This knowledge base emphasizes understanding the interaction between people and other human systems and between people and social structures. Systems concepts, ego psychology, knowledge of social welfare opportunities and resources, the idea of human diversity, role theory, and some of the knowledge about change discussed in Chapter 5 are especially relevant for understanding and assessing such interactions.

This knowledge is employed primarily by social workers in two of the five or six parts of the problem-solving process. In assessment or problem analysis, knowledge about people's social functioning is used to understand what is taking place in the interaction between people and other systems. Working with the client system, a problem is identified and assessed, a goal for problem solution is determined, and a plan of action involving the client, worker, and/or others is developed, carried out, and evaluated. Adequate problem assessment and appropriate interventions depend on relevant knowledge and interpretations of what creates changes in people's social interactions. The key to problem resolution is a focus on system interactions.

In addition to its assessment and intervention components, the other steps of the problem-solving process are applied throughout the life of the practice relationship established by the social worker. The steps are interdependent and modified by factors such as involuntary clients. Directed by purpose and need and supported by value and knowledge, any given practice relationship of social workers can be described as a "limited partnership." Practice relationships are limited by time, goal, and client need, and they involve professional problem solving between social workers and a range of others, centered on but not limited to clients.

As purpose identifies how social work serves society, so purpose and the needs areas it aims to meet direct social work practice toward the controversial areas of change. To pursue this direction means social work must take strong value positions. The professional values associated with helping people with their need to manage change have a dual nature: to safeguard public confidence and consumer interests and to support the direction of professional purpose.

SOCIAL WORK VALUE POSITIONS

Values are strongly associated with the profession, its purposes, and the needs areas it covers. These value positions are fundamental to maintaining change as the direction of practice and for assuring clients and the public of the delivery of the profession's purpose. Understanding the meaning of professional values may be approached in different ways. For example, we already have discussed values as one attribute in identifying a profession. In that usage, professional values are thought of as a set of ethical principles that guide the behavior of practitioners (Constable, 1983). They guard against misuse of professional knowledge or skills and protect consumers from other forms of exploitation by professionals from whom members of society expect help. In our previous discussion, we noted some of the social work values that spell out the way workers ought to treat their clients.

Another way of seeking out professional values is to view them as value positions taken by the social work profession on issues and ideas that develop from the nature and public treatment of social work's clientele and from the arena of its practice. Some of these value positions are also found in the Code of Ethics of the National Association of Social Workers. (See *International Social Work*, 1985, for another example.)

Our emphasis on *looking for* social work's connections to society and not just *looking at* social work as a conventional profession permits us to find these value positions and the importance to social work in taking such stances. The contexts of practice—societies and social welfare—and the human and social need to manage change produce for social work critical issues of justice and social policy. The issues arise out of social work's involvement in assessing and working to solve problems in people's social functioning.

Social functioning, human need, society, change, and the words used to define them have many value and meaning associations. Earlier, we discussed how multidirectional these and similar words and terms are and the necessity to think through one's own opinions and beliefs about them. The need to take such stances on these values is also true for the profession of social work. Because the profession takes such stances and given the range of values and meanings associated with many aspects of its practice, controversy over these positions and conflict with members of the public and its representatives are likely.

People with problems, individual motivations, social justice, social problems, social change, social welfare, and even social work are terms that are charged with meanings and values. Social work value positions are choices taken on several overlapping issues that are related to helping people with their social functioning, including the following:

> The relation between people and society regarding the causes of problems.
>
> The needs diverse people have in order to function adequately in society.
>
> The decision as to whether or not social and political changes are necessary.
>
> Ways to extend just and fair treatment, even to people who have problems.
>
> Individual motivation to succeed versus the availability of social resources to help people achieve.

For example, in talking about the problems people have in their social functioning, popular wisdom places value on individual responsibility for success and failure. Not people's problems but personal failure; not social functioning but individual success. These are the more typical words associated with positions about how people should interact with society and its institutions.

According to this view, society's part in the needs-meeting interactions with people is thought of as neutral or even nonexistent: Society should not bother with, or be bothered by, the problems people have in meeting their needs. Society and its structures, if considered at all, are thought of as perfect enough in their functioning to have no processes that could create significant problems for people. Ample opportunities are fairly provided to everyone and society is not responsible for their needs-meeting efforts. Failure to meet needs stems from inadequate motivation on the part of the people involved.

Social work takes a different position on these issues. Human diversity, political and social change, social justice, people's right to participate in decisions affecting their lives, society's responsibility for resources, and problems caused by structural factors represent some of social work's value positions on these issues.

Social work values all people and views each person and the group of which they are a part as valuable. Not only clients but their environment or their interactions with these environments are seen as likely sources of the causes of problems. This social work stance on problem causation emphasizes the ways environmental factors may create conditions that lead to the inadequate social functioning of people. Because the people with whom social workers deal are so different, social workers value human diversity as a source of strength in social functioning. Social workers value the strength inherent in different lifestyles and in people's differing approaches to meeting their needs. Valuing human diversity is not widely found in public opinion and action or in institutional operations.

Social work values political and social change as well as individual change. Because of social work's focus on how problems are created in changes that affect the interaction between people and structures of social institutions, the profession takes the stance that political and social change is necessary. This value is not universally applied to social structures. Social workers value involvement in policymaking and political activity to protect the human rights of all people (see Documents 6.1 and 6.2).

DOCUMENT 6.1

NABSW Code of Ethics

In America today, no Black person, except the selfish or irrational, can claim neutrality in the quest for Black liberation nor fail to consider the implications of the events taking place in our society. Given the necessity for committing ourselves to the struggle for freedom, we as Black Americans

practicing in the field of social welfare set forth this statement of ideals and guiding principles.

If a sense of community awareness is a precondition to humanitarian acts, then we as Black social workers must use our knowledge of the Black community, our commitments to its self-determination and our helping skills for the benefit of Black people as we marshal our expertise to improve the quality of life of Black people. Our activities will be guided by our Black consciousness, our determination to protect the security of the Black community and to serve as advocates to relieve suffering of Black people by any means necessary.

Therefore, as Black social workers we commit ourselves, collectively, to the interests of our Black brethren and as individuals subscribe to the following statements:

I regard as my primary obligation the welfare of the Black individual, Black family and Black community and will engage in action for improving social conditions.

I give precedence to this mission over my personal interests.

I adopt the concept of a Black extended family and embrace all Black people as my brothers and sisters, making no distinction between their destiny and my own.

I hold myself responsible for the quality and extent of service I perform and the quality and extent of service performed by the agency or organization in which I am employed, as it relates to the Black community.

I accept the responsibility to protect the Black community against unethical and hypocritical practice by any individuals or organizations engaged in social welfare activities.

I stand ready to supplement my paid or professional advocacy with voluntary service in the Black public interest.

I will consciously use my skills, and my whole being, as an instrument for social change, with particular attention directed to the establishment of Black social institutions.

(SOURCE: NASBW Code of Ethics
Annual Report-Fair Use.)

DOCUMENT 6.2

NASW Code of Ethics
Summary of Major Principles

I. THE SOCIAL WORKER'S CONDUCT AND COMPORTMENT AS A SOCIAL WORKER

    A. *Propriety.* The social worker should maintain high standards of personal conduct in the capacity or identity as social worker.

    B. *Competence and Professional Development.* The social worker should strive to become and remain proficient in professional practice and the performance of professional functions.

C. *Service.* The social worker should regard as primary the service obligation of the social work profession.

D. *Integrity.* The social worker should act in accordance with the highest standards of professional integrity.

E. *Scholarship and Research.* The social worker engaged in study and research should be guided by the conventions of scholarly inquiry.

II. THE SOCIAL WORKER'S ETHICAL RESPONSIBILITY TO CLIENTS

F. *Primacy of Clients' Interests.* The social worker's primary responsibility is to clients.

G. *Rights and Prerogatives of Clients.* The social worker should make every effort to foster maximum self-determination on the part of clients.

H. *Confidentiality and Privacy.* The social worker should respect the privacy of clients and hold in confidence all information obtained in the course of professional service.

I. *Fees.* When setting fees, the social worker should ensure that they are fair, reasonable, considerate, and commensurate with the service performed and with due regard for the clients' ability to pay.

III. THE SOCIAL WORKER'S

ETHICAL RESPONSIBILITY TO COLLEAGUES

J. *Respect, Fairness, and Courtesy.* The social worker should treat colleagues with respect, courtesy, fairness, and good faith.

K. *Dealing with Colleagues' Clients.* The social worker has the responsibility to relate to the clients of colleagues with full professional consideration.

IV. THE SOCIAL WORKER'S ETHICAL RESPONSIBIILTY TO EMPLOYERS AND EMPLOYING ORGANIZATIONS

L. *Commitments to Employing Organizations.* The social worker should adhere to commitments made to the employing organizations.

V. THE SOCIAL WORKER'S ETHICAL RESPONSIILITY TO THE SOCIAL WORK PROFESSION

M. *Maintaining the Integrity of the Profession.* The social worker should uphold and advance the values, ethics, knowledge, and mission of the profession.

N. *Community Service.* The Social Worker should assist the profession in making social services available to the general public.

O. *Development of Knowledge.* The social worker should take responsibility for identifying, developing, and fully utilizing knowledge for professional practice.

VI. THE SOCIAL WORKER'S ETHICAL RESPONSIBILITY TO SOCIETY

P. *Promoting the General Welfare.* The social worker should promote the general welfare of society.

(SOURCE: NASW Code of Ethics-Fair Use.)

Social work's value on human diversity and its position on problem causation parallels its strong stance on social justice. Not only opposing oppressive practices such as racism, sexism, ageism, and homophobia but taking policy actions to reduce and replace them is a value position that guides practice. Lip service is given by nearly all members of society to the fair and just treatment of everyone. In the action it takes, social work speaks loudly on this issue (*International Social Work,* 1985).

Because of the value they place on people and their emphasis on interactions with the environment as a principal contributor to people's problems, social workers' value positions hold that clients should be in charge of resolving problems in their lives. Referred to as *client self-determination,* this stance includes client participation in working on and planning for changes in themselves as well as in their environments. According to social work, the person side of the "person in interaction with environment" equation has the right to determine how he or she wants to be treated in solving problems, and that person must be permitted to have input into the decisions that affect his or her life, including planning to change social structures. Unfortunately, persons other than social workers see social work clients as being without the right to decide their own futures.

The importance for practice of these value positions is twofold. One is their importance as input to the policymaking of the public and the profession. These value positions often place social work in conflict with public representatives in the arenas of public policymaking. To take positions on these issues leads to controversy; not to take stances means failure to be the practitioner called for by social work's professional purpose.

Second, social work value positions help workers to know how to handle the "juggling acts" required in balancing the difference between professional purpose and public expectations. Public difference with social work arises less from disagreement with purpose than from conflicts over value positions. Social workers assertively use the profession's value base to support their part in the public debate over helping people to manage their needs in the area of social functioning. (See Alexander, 1985, for an illustration of this idea, and see interviews on pages 146–149.)

KNOWLEDGE FOR SOCIAL WORK PRACTICE

In our discussion of professional purpose, we introduced social work interventions and implied that they stem from knowing the nature and cause of

I AM A SOCIAL WORKER
"How I Use Values in My Practice"

GRACIELA CASTEX: I think that one of the most painful experiences that I ever had in social work came when I worked at the hospital in Miami. I worked on the thirteenth floor. I got in the elevator, a crowded elevator, and very loudly two medical interns were talking. One said, "I wish that damned woman in 1310 would die already, she's a pain in the ____." At that point, a woman who was standing next to me said, "That is my mother." We completed our ride down to the first floor, which took about forty hours. The elevator was dead quiet. We got down there, she got a security person to lock us in the elevator, she called a hospital administrator, and right then and there we had to give depositions.

I ended up having to go to court to testify about what these two physicians had discussed. They were kicked out of medical school. I always tell that particular vignette when I talk to my students about confidentiality. You just don't do that as a professional; you don't talk like that.

I learned very early what you do ethically; I learned very early what confidentiality is and the ramifications for you as a professional as well as for the individual client system involved.

If the daughter had not been there and I had heard their comments, I can only reflect on what I would have done based on other times I have been confronted with injustices. I would have spoken up—what else I don't know. At other times, when some other ethical issue was involved, I've said things and acted. Social workers are responsible to take actions based on the profession's values.

BERNICE GOODMAN: Social work is based on the recognition that the individual and society are intrinsically connected. Social work is in the business of insisting that the value of a person's wholeness not only be recognized but be respected and incorporated into the operations of this society's institutions. Social work sees the intrinsic connection of the individual to the group, and vice versa, and views the basic health of each individual as necessary to the total growth of society. Social workers do not ignore the ill health of anyone, because it affects all of us. Because social structures teach values to the young, social work must ensure that its positions on the worth and dignity of each person becomes an ongoing part of the socialization of children. It seems to me that the use of drugs, teen suicide, and child abuse represent the dominance of a set of values that support profit at any cost and that as a consequence lead people to value themselves negatively. If we can help young people to care about themselves, and by extension, about others, then the larger problem of social and environmental destruction will also be addressed. In my practice I use the dynamics on which relationships are formed to help people see themselves as uniquely important and as possessing positive elements. Based on that concept I am constantly helping people sort out their self-perception in positive ways. In a sense I try to get them to value their own self-actualization. I work with people of color, with lesbians, and with gay men who have been told repeatedly that they are of no value. My practice brings to them the value social work places on all people. My practice is an expression of the value that there is inherent worth in all people. I help people define and value themselves.

BETTE HARLAN: I try to reflect in my practice the social work ethic that the primary responsibility of the worker is to the client. I insist upon confidentiality in dealing with my clients. I also support the right of clients to informed consent, which goes beyond having clients sign a consent form to making certain they are informed about and understand what they are signing. I also think that those of us who work with the hospitalized mentally ill have a responsibility to society not to release those who might pose a threat to anyone, including self. This value is not always thought of in the same way by all members of the team with which I work. Of course, values in practice come across relative to nondiscrimination issues. This becomes a practice dimension when clients are diagnosed differentially according to sex or ethnic background.

JOE HERNANDEZ: Social workers, first of all, have to value people and their differences. To me this is a critical area. Workers have to be aware of whom they are going to work with, their cultures and the ways they are diverse. In a sense, social workers should value the values of those they work with.

Professional values, like confidentiality, sometimes seems to be set aside in practice. For example, in covering the caseloads of those workers who were absent, privileged material was shared with me in order for me to meet case goals. Also, sometimes social workers seem to violate, in their relations with one another, basic professional values such as self-determination and respect for the individual. Much of the mistrust and undermining that takes place in worker-worker relationships would not be tolerated with client-worker relationships. Unfortunately, I've observed supervisors come across as judgmental when the line worker they are dealing with is from a different cultural background.

SUSANNA HUESTON: When I work with children, in terms of confidentiality, I tell them that regardless of the issue, I reserve the right to tell someone— my supervisor or their parents. I let the children know prior to sharing it with someone else that I intend to do so. When a child says, "Ms. Hueston, I have something to tell you that you can't tell anyone else," I reply, "Don't tell me." I learned a long time ago that a child's growth and development may depend on parental involvement.

TRACEY JOHNSON: Because of people's basic humanity, everyone's worth and dignity should be respected. Social workers should believe in people's dignity and help others do the same. It is also important to value your feelings and those of others and to be honest with yourself and with others. Social workers need to value self-awareness in themselves. In working with people, social workers should not be judgmental, should not just jump in and tell people what they should do. Social workers need to understand people's choices. Social workers should not let how they see things interfere with the decisions of their clients. They should set aside their own biases in a given situation. It is difficult to be nonjudgmental. For example, what is clear to me may not be so to someone else. You have to live with someone else's idea.

IRMÁ SERRANO: Social workers cannot impose their own values about helping, about needs, or about solutions. They must respect people.

ADELE WEINER: Interestingly enough, I believe that I subscribed to the values of social work prior to my choice of it as a career. When I was a child growing up, my parents had been involved in social service organizations and I had been introduced to volunteer work at an early age. My mother helped to set up one of the first E.O.O. Head Start Programs. I myself had been involved in Girl Scouts and had been involved in many public service projects. Somehow, I had always felt that it was my responsibility to help other individuals who were less fortunate than I. This was not charity but, rather, the responsibility of all citizens.

As a college student in the 1970s, I was exposed to a number of issues that made me think about the role of advocacy and citizenry in shaping public policy. My school has very active student groups involved in advocating rights for blacks, women and gays/lesbians. Thus, it seemed to me that part of my education process helped me to look at individuals who had been oppressed.

By the time I got to social work school, I held a set of beliefs that was congruent with the profession, but I can truly say that I lacked expertise and knowledge to implement them. Since I did not have an undergraduate degree in social work, I was required to go through a two-year MSW program. I learned a great amount about program and policy issues and practice. The analytical skills that I had developed in psychology research served me well as I learned to assess situations and develop plans for intervention. My interpersonal skills benefited from my concern about people, but I did have to learn how to use this concern in a constructive manner. Professional interviewing and relationship skills can be taught and learned in very concrete ways. As I learned basic skills, I could build on them to develop more sophisticated skills.

As a social work educator, I believe that many of the skills that social workers use can be taught. It is the values that create difficulty. I hope that by the time a student has selected social work as a career choice, he or she has done some self-analysis and discovered that this profession is congruent with their own personal values. The "gatekeeper" function of the social work educator is to help students to discover whether this is a good career choice for themselves. When this process has not happened prior to embarking on a social work course of study, students may go through a painful process only to discover that they have made a poor career choice. The role of the educator is to help individuals who are ill-suited for the profession to make other choices for themselves.

---

people's problems in their interactions within society. These interactions carry out the purpose of social work. The idea of systems further specifies the various types of interactions that might take place between people and other social units. Systems ideas (or perspective) picture the variety of interactions and also help to introduce how social workers assess people and institutions and develop ways to handle problematic interactions.

The flowchart in Chapter 5 shows the general nature of people's interactions with social institutions (see Figure 6.2). Focusing on social functioning as well as all interactions among parts of a system is shown in Figure 6.3.

A few ideas about systems are employed in these flowcharts. A system is composed of parts interacting in a somewhat predictable fashion to achieve a goal. A boundary, abstract or tangible, determines which parts or subsystems are involved in the interaction. The interacting parts create a balance, or mode of operations, of sorts. The balance, based on the interactions of the system's various parts, serves the goals of maintaining the system, replenishing its energy or resources, and (if it is an open system) interacting with other systems.

In our charts, although the person may be seen as a complete or independent human system and social institutions as complex and independent social systems, both person and institution may also be viewed as a subsystem within the boundaries of the person's social functioning. Their interaction, comprising people's social functioning, is akin to a system's balance. Social functioning may be adequate and meet people's needs, thereby achieving their goals, or it

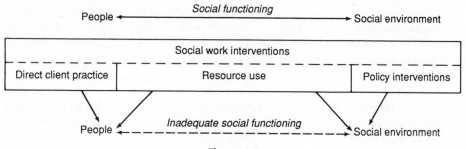

Figure 6.2

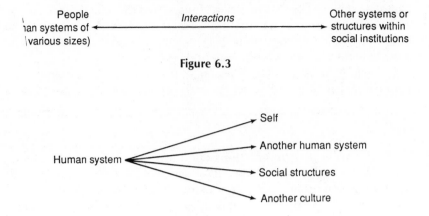

Figure 6.3

Figure 6.4

may be inadequate and not meet people's needs. If it is inadequate, it will be maintained as part of the system balance of the person-social structure interaction. Movement from adequate to inadequate, or inadequate to adequate, represents change in the system. This change, as indicated earlier, may come from alterations in the parts of their interactions. Changes may help people or cause them problems in their social functioning.

There are a number of interactions of a system-like nature that people may have with self, other human systems, or structures of social institutions. Individuals interact with other people within social structures or within cultures other than their own. The interactions of one human system is diagrammed in Figure 6.4. All or some of these interactions may be adequate, whereas others may be inadequate.

Concepts from a variety of disciplines help to explain adequate or problematic interactions (Compton and Galaway, 1979; Pincus and Minahan, 1973). These concepts summarize the totality of a given human system's functioning within its social environment. Concepts from developmental psychology and human relations explain the interaction with self and between individuals; social psychology, among groups; role theory and knowledge of social welfare resources, the interaction between people and certain institutions; and the theme of human diversity, the relationship among people of different cultural or ethnic backgrounds. The various interactions, as explained by social science concepts, can be seen in Figure 6.5.

Another way of viewing these various system interactions of people in their social environment and the type of knowledge helpful in learning how they take place would focus on type of interaction and knowledge used to interpret it, as shown in the following list:

1. Human   to   self   uses   developmental psychology's stages.
   system

2. Human   to   human   uses   ego psychology's idea of person.
   system   system
   (person)   (person)

3. Human   to   human   uses   role expectations, such as worker
   system   system   and client.
   (position)   (position)

4. Human   to   social   uses   ego psychology, role, goal directed
   system   system   behavior, resources, human
                                      diversity.

5. Human   to   cultural   uses   human diversity.
   system   system

See Imre (1984) for illustrations of further types of knowledge.

This approach to using social science concepts to explain the environmental interaction of various sizes of human systems sees individuals as a psychological person or performing a social role. Individuals interact with social systems and cultures. The complex interaction within a multi-person system's environment and within its major subsystems is diagrammed in Figure 6.6.

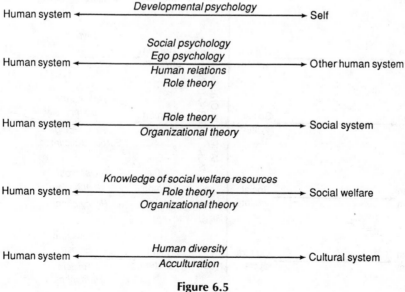

Figure 6.5

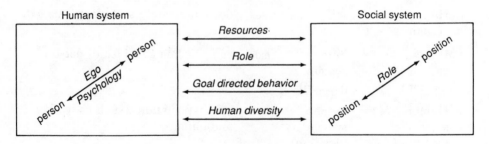

Figure 6.6

We have already explored how human growth in a number of developmental areas and operations of and change within structures of social institutions account for basic interactions, or the social functioning, of people in society. We have also noted that change—unexpected, unintended, or needed—creates problems in people's social functioning. Examples of problems in each area of a human system's functioning is illustrated in Figure 6.7.

Social workers use knowledge to specify inadequacies in people's social functioning as problems caused by changes in interactions between a human system and other systems in its environment. This leads to the development of

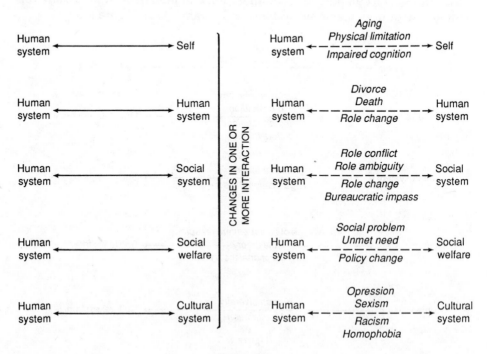

Figure 6.7

professional problem assessment and intervention. One of the keys used in so-cial work problem assessment is the focus on interactions within systems. People's interactions become the key to assessing social functioning and main-taining a social work value perspective on people and problem causation. (See also Lewis, 1984, who adds an ethical component to assessment.)

For example, the interaction between this country's so-called majority cul-ture and members of minority groups of color has been racist. One source or cause of the problem is the racist practices coming from the majority culture's social systems, resulting in inadequate social functioning for members of other groups. Similarly, the majority culture and its social structures interact with women in a sexist fashion and with lesbians and gays by means of homophobic reactions (Devore and Schlesinger, 1981). Opression of a whole group of people isolates them, cutting off interaction with other social systems. The develop-ment of ghettos in urban areas and job or educational discrimination isolate people in this manner.

Other examples of changes in interaction would be ending one or more interactions in a human system. For a married couple, the possibility of divorce and the reasons for it are part of a series of changes associated with an ending relationship. Other interactions that may end include that of employment either through retirement or job loss.

Social problems exemplify a disruption in the interaction between a group of people and social institutions when they fail to fulfill an expected role. Un-wed parents and spousal abuse are examples of disrupted interactions within the institution of the family. Conceiving of problems in social functioning as caused by shifts within the complex interactions a person or larger human sys-tem maintains with a number of other systems in their social environment per-mits going beyond explaining these problems exclusively in psychological terms. Growth and development, social psychology, role theory, human diver-sity and culture, and organizational theory lend ideas to a social worker's un-derstanding of social functioning within this framework (see interviews on pages 154–155).

The nature of problem identification and assessment in the problem-solving process, along with its attendant goal setting, determines the type of interac-tions used by social workers. Knowledge of human behavior and the social envi-ronment, as outlined in the preceding discussion of system interaction with other systems, is used in assessment and in developing and carrying out inter-ventions.

We have already noted that interventions must focus on changing people, their social environments, or aspects of their interactions with other systems. From our discussion of change, several of the approaches used in managing it serve to introduce some basic social work interventions or methods. Ap-proaches such as supporting, educating, developing policy, planning, organiz-ing, shaping agencies, and counseling people on issues of growth and develop-ment have been identified as useful in managing change. In addition, social

I AM A SOCIAL WORKER
"The Importance of a Knowledge Base in My Practice"

GRACIELA CASTEX: When I first worked as a BSW in a psychiatric center, I was assigned Spanish-speaking clients because I could speak Spanish. Again, when I worked in a hospital in Miami after getting my MSW, I was assigned Spanish-speaking clients. There was a difference, however, because my experience and education had increased my knowledge. As a BSW, I had a solid knowledge base, but the caseload at times presented problems that were beyond it. Later I knew more about providing services and how that connected with what else was going on in the hospital or agency. I did not feel so isolated by inexperience or a newness of knowledge in providing services.

BERNICE GOODMAN: Social work requires a knowledge of a variety of disciplines—anthropology, sociology, and psychology among others. Social work knowledge starts with the notion that many, many ideas are important to working with people and understanding people and society. The implication of this concept is enormous, both in terms of understanding people and in terms of knowing so much about people and society. For social work it is the understanding that the dynamic is of greatest importance that leads to the profession's development and use of a knowledge base. Using knowledge as the basis of working with people helps the worker avoid getting caught up in the "stories" of people and focus on the dynamics of their relationships with others and with institutions. It also helps workers focus on problems and solutions as being in the dynamics of the situation. I use this sense of a knowledge base to open up people's lives, not shrink them to the confines of a given theory.

BETTE HARLAN: Believing that a knowledge base is helpful in working with clients is a value to me. I keep working on it. I also insist that my workers or field education students have and work on developing a solid knowledge base. I need knowledge of people in order to make assessments of client situations. I also need knowledge of legal systems, policies, and procedures. As a supervisor, I also teach my workers the new knowledge that I come across. In the mental health field, it is necessary to continously update one's knowledge base. It is necessary to keep up in order to make a contribution to the work of the team. Without a good knowledge base, one can't be a good team player. In a way, it is necessary to have a good knowledge base in order to defend social work against those who would attempt to denigrate it.

JOE HERNANDEZ: For me, knowing about the culture of the client population is critical. Knowing how they think, what they value, who is important in their family system are all valuable for the practitioner.

SUSANNA HUESTON: At this point in my development in social work, my knowledge base is supported by my experience. I always recall what my father said when we were growing up, "You can have all the books you want, but if you don't have common sense, then all the books are useless." So, in many ways I see social work as a combination of knowledge, experience, and common sense. I use specific social work knowledge of human dynamics along with my common sense. I rely on experience, keeping in focus that my aim is to enable a child to function within a given school situation. Depending on the problem—be it a family problem or some expected difficulty in adolescent development—I rely on the practice experience I've gathered in the past thirteen or fourteen years to supplement my knowledge of behavior.

TRACEY JOHNSON: In the several jobs I've had as a BSW, I've worked with many people who had a college degree but not in social work. They certainly could do the job as described. They lacked, however, the social worker's perspective on human behavior and a knowledge of how people function and of social problems. The other workers made decisions not based on how people behave, on their needs, or on how to work together with clients to create and carry out plans. I came to respect greatly my social work knowledge of how to work with people.

IRMA SERRANO: In my first job after I got my MSW, I learned a great deal because when you first finish school you don't know very much. I think this was especially so in working in psychiatry with children. My knowledge base was not complete about the normal developmental stages of children, about their behavior. I also had to learn more about techniques of working with children. I had classes in child and human development, of course, but what I needed to know was what to do with a child once he or she was in my office. You had to develop ways to observe children and their behavior and to record that. What I had was a basis, but I needed to know and learn more skills.

---

workers create self-help and support groups or consult with colleagues and organizations. These general types of interventions are modified by the need of the particular problem in social functioning and the nature of the changed interaction leading to it.

One approach to organizing ways to locate and identify social work interventions is to develop examples that are useful for achieving each of the purposes of social work. For example, enhancing people's problem-solving, coping, and developmental capacities includes the following:

Supporting individuals.
Developing support groups.
Teaching new behavior.
Counseling around change.
Role playing.
Behavior modification.
Confronting.
Working with families.

Linking people to resources so they may meet their needs includes the following interventions:

Advocating for a client.
Coordinating cases.
Identifying opportunities and services.
Developing resource linkages.
Referring to other systems.
Following up.
Creating contacts and networks.
Developing resource files.
Managing information.
Acting like a broker.

Making more effective and just systems that deliver resources and opportunities to people and that develop organizational and social policies can include the following types of interventions:

Organizing.
Planning.
Developing policy.
Changing organizations.
Advocating for classes of people.
Creating alliances and networks.
Administering programs.
Lobbying and testifying.
Taking action on legislation.
Developing funding proposals.
Developing public relations.
Educating the public.
Mobilizing professional associations.

Developing social change organizations.

Reorienting social work and other professions to value change.

Such interventions may be thought of as direct client practice, information and referral, and indirect client practice. *Direct client practice* involves face-to-face contact with the client system, whatever its size. It can be an individual, a small group, a family, or a commuity. The efforts aim at changing the client, primarily with worker-directed efforts. Information and referral involve the worker in managing information and contacts about concrete resources and opportunities people need either to manage change or to meet their needs while handling a problem. *Indirect practice* includes less contact with a client system on a face-to-face basis. It includes managing and developing programs, services, and policies that deal with social structures and their resources. Direct work with people, other than clients, is involved. The same range and kinds of interventions are connected to these types of practice and roughly parallel those exemplifying the purpose of social work.

Basically, interventions are the actions or efforts at change created and put into operation by social workers and their clients. Interventions may involve worker, client, and others. Their goal is to overcome the problem caused by changing interactions within the client's social environment. Interventions, then, are the actions of social workers to help people manage changes that affect their social functioning. Problems in interactions among human systems use enhancing or resource-linking interventions. Problematic interactions among human systems and social or cultural systems may involve all types of interventions (see interviews on pages 157–158).

I AM A SOCIAL WORKER
"Interventions I Use"

GRACIELA CASTEX: Throughout my practice career, in many instances I have created a whole new way of delivering services, a new way of intervening. It focused on creating ways to service a population whose culture and life differed from those who had been using agency services before. It meant creating new policies and a new practice.

BERNICE GOODMAN: Although I do not disagree that social workers are somehow the instrument of change, the users of interventions, I view social work as a process in which the worker engages with clients and others. I start with the knowledge that the client has both the problem and the solutions. I use the tool of the interactional process of thinking and feeling. In that interactional process, change takes place. I try not to come across as having the answers but as interacting with people to help them to make choices about how to live their lives.

BETTE HARLAN: Crisis intervention is important to all members of the team at the hospital where I work. Crisis intervention has to be used with superiors and colleagues, as well as with patients and their relatives. Other interventions include cognitive restructuring, confrontation tactics, reality therapy, and from a social systems approach, basic problem solving.

JOE HERNANDEZ: As a direct service worker with persons with AIDS, I delivered concrete and clinical services. I counseled, confronted, supported, advocated for, and found resources for my clients.

SUSANNA HUESTON: In the school, I use crisis intervention, limited counseling, and referrals. I also do a great deal of work with the families of students. I use a lot of external resources. In a sense, I am involved in developing agency policy.

TRACEY JOHNSON: As a line worker, I have monitored agencies and their policies, been a teacher, acted like a caregiver or nurturer, provided protective services, and been an advocate.

IRMA SERRANO: I am a coordinator of children's programs and involved in professional associations. I write grants, create programs, get money, and reassess community and client needs. As an active member of NASW, I have served on committees and provided leadership as president of the New York City Chapter of NASW.

ADELE WEINER: Once a person begins to work in the field of social work, it becomes apparent very quickly that one must be concerned about policy and policy development. First, one must be able to read and analytically analyze policy statements (e.g., state, local, and agency) in order to turn them into concrete procedures that can be operationalized. Much of the time, these statements are stated in jargon and are ambiguous enough to develop into numerous procedures. In order to help clients get what they need, the worker needs "to find the loopholes in the system and shove the clients through them."

Second, as one becomes aware of the inequalities in the system and the needs of clients, workers will become concerned about the development of policy. Clients can often be organized to work on their own behalf. For example, the residents in a nursing home (a fairly debilitated population) were able to develop a writing campaign among themselves and with their families to have input on a citywide policy on bedholds when a patient went into a hospital.

PRACTICE RELATIONSHIPS AS LIMITED PARTNERSHIPS

As purpose determines the basic direction of social work practice and its value position and knowledge base, so professional purpose also determines the nature of practice relationships. Practice relationships occur among workers and clients, workers and colleagues, and workers and decision makers in the social structures that affect people's social functioning. The nature of practice relationships can be described by two sets of factors:

> What the participants personally bring to them and what the place where they occur contributes.
> Why they develop as "limited partnerships."

See Specht's (1985) discussion of professional interaction for another typology.

When a social worker deals with clients or works with others on a client's problems, personal characteristics and the expectations of the participants are instrumental to the development of an effective practice relationship. The worker's professional relationships are the basis for carrying out the steps of the problem-solving process. Important ingredients, as discussed earlier, are worker, colleague, and client expectations about social work. Expectations set the tone, determine how participants will act toward one another, and shape communication. The personal characteristics of all parties contribute to or detract from the creation of an effective relationship. Differences in background are especially important, as are strengths and weaknesses in communication. As we discuss fully later, diversity is a critical element in social work practice. Moreover, locating the relationship in an office unfamiliar to a client or in a more neutral setting to which a client or colleague may already have a connection sets up differences in the professional relationship.

Because social workers move in the direction of change in their practice and because their values about people and clients focus on participation and self-determination, practice relationships are akin to "limited partnerships." The value of clients' self-determination, giving them the right to determine their own life goals, leads to the development of a worker-client partnership. It is limited by time, degree of intensity, and problems to be handled.

The relationship takes form as a decision-making partnership based in a contract. The decision-making partners explore problems, and they propose options along with the exploration of problems. They mutually determine the best way to achieve what the client needs. In generalist practice, the partnership focuses on using the problem-solving process to determine how best to meet client needs by enhancing their social functioning, linking them to needed resources, or changing systems. Each of the basic parts of the problem-solving process—engagement, data collection and problem assessment, goal setting and planning, intervention, evaluation, and termination—takes place within this partnership that is focused on mutual analysis and action. To the extent possible, each client is actively involved throughout the life of the practice relationship.

This idea of partnership also holds true for the relationships social workers maintain with colleagues. The team-like nature of collegial contacts has already been discussed. Team members act like partners, with their attention limited to solving the probelm(s) of their shared client.

Social workers are also engaged in limited partnerships with other persons, in addition to clients and colleagues, in their efforts to change systems. Social workers create partnership-like alliances with other interested parties in their efforts to develop and change the policies and practices of social structures. These alliances, discussed earlier as networks, work on program development, lobbying efforts, and pressure-group tactics.

Practitioner relationships, as derived from professional purpose, can be seen as a series of limited partnerships, as follows:

1. Mutual decision making with clients for problem analysis and action.
2. Teamwork and networking with colleagues for problem solution, referrals, and resource linkages.
3. Networking and alliance building with colleagues, clients, and others to confront decision makers about changing policy and making service delivery systems more effective and just.

The notion of a series of limited partnerships moves us away from identifying social work relationships as exclusively of an interpersonal, problem-solving nature. Professional purpose is served by a range of limited interpersonal, collegial, advocacy, or group relationships in which a social worker acts somewhat like a partner of the other participants.

A PRACTITIONER TO FIT SOCIAL WORK'S PURPOSE

The last, and quite significant, component of this text's model of social work practice is the nature of the person who carries out social work's purpose, upholds its value positions, and uses its knowledge base and practice skills in helping people. If we recruited the *ideal* person for this model of social work practice, what characteristics would we want that person to have?

Some of these characteristics have been implied in the questions posed in earlier chapters about your opinions on profession and change, your attitudes and feelings about the diverging expectations of social work, and how you would respond to juggling some of the different ideas and value positions that are held about social work. This chapter suggests several more characteristics through its discussion of the basic direction of practice, the value positions and knowledge base, and the nature of professional relationships (see Document 6.3).

Social work's purpose takes practitioners in the direction of helping to manage change, and as noted earlier, into an area of need that is less well under-

---

DOCUMENT 6.3

A Mother Fights City's Red Tape
for Her Family: Welfare Agencies Come
Under Fire at Hearing

Josh Barbanel

A social worker at a City Hall hearing yesterday told a tale of indifference and blundering by New York City agencies as she struggled to reunite a former drug addict with her five children, who had been in the city's foster-care system for as long as eight years.

The social worker, Lenore Berlingieri, spoke at a session led by Senator Daniel Patrick Moynihan, Democrat of New York, and City Council President Andrew J. Stein. It was called to examine city services for troubled families.

After going through a drug-rehabilitation program, the mother appeared early last year before a Family Court judge, who told her that all she would need to rejoin her children was an apartment of her own.

But what followed, said Mrs. Berlingieri, of Little Flower Children's Services, was an odyssey through the welfare and housing bureaucracies.

'YOU NEED THE RIGHT PERSON'

Because the mother, Baronda McBroom, was not living with her family—the city was paying thousands of dollars a month to care for her children—she did not qualify for special priority for housing offered to homeless families.

When a judge ordered the Housing Authority to give Miss McBroom priority for an apartment, a representative of the agency told her and Mrs. Berlingieri, "You need the right person to push the right button," the social worker recalled.

When the city finally found a large apartment for her to rent in Harlem—under pressure from the staff of Mr. Stein and the City Ombudsman—it had exposed wiring, and Consolidated Edison refused to turn on the gas, according to Mrs. Berlingieri.

Miss McBroom, who was at the hearing, said she had finally moved into the apartment and hoped to get her family back in a few weeks. She said she was 34 years old, had children ranging in age from 7 to 18, and hoped to complete a course in word processing soon.

The Human Resources Administrator, William Grinker, pointed to signs of progress and discussed new programs—for example, to prevent homelessness by preventing the evictions of families—being started.

BEYOND 'DEPENDENT BEHAVIOR'

From Mr. Moynihan to Mr. Grinker, there was a sense of pessimism throughout the hearing, a doubt that services could be greatly expanded.

When one critic urged Mr. Moynihan to look beyond "dependent behavior"—high school dropouts, unwed mothers and the like—to underlying causes, Mr. Moynihan interrupted.

After touring welfare centers in the city, the Senator said, he found that "the capacity to provide services is so small" and that poor people must be more responsible for their lives.

Challenged repeatedly by Mr. Moynihan about lagging efforts to collect child-support payments from absent fathers—a major theme of Mr. Moynihan's attention to welfare—Mr. Grinker said collections were expected to go up, from $25 million a year to $38 million next year.

Mrs. Berlingieri recalled that in trying to help reunite Miss McBroom with her children, she once spent three days straight, nine hours a day, in a welfare office trying to obtain rent money for the city-owned apartment.

The apartment, when she first saw it, had no wiring at all, according to the social worker. Later, the city ran a temporary wire in through a window. The front door to the building had no lock.

A spokesman for the Department of Housing Preservation and Development, Lynn Guggenheimer, confirmed that the building had wiring problems and that it was being completely rewired.

At the Housing Authority, Val Coleman said that the authority followed "the most scrupulous rules of fairness in choosing who gets in" and that if the family had problems, it was because of a waiting list of 200,000 families.

(Copyright © 1987 by The New York Times Company. Reprinted by permission.)

---

stood or acknowledged by those with whom social workers practice. To handle working with people in this area, our ideal worker would need to be *patient* with people as they try to come to terms with and accept the nature of their problems in social functioning and as they realize the part played by change in creating problems for themselves and for other systems in their social environment. Patience is also required in facing decision makers who take positions on human and social issues that are counter to those of the profession.

To face the inherent conflict and controversy generated by the value positions of the profession, the ideal worker must also be capable of *standing firm on convictions*. This characteristic means that workers have to understand and accept the value positions of the profession, incorporate them into their own set of convictions about how the world should be, and know that they will not waiver in their commitment to these positions. Acceptance of professional values means that a social worker should not back down on or go along with a racist, sexist, or homophobic position. Workers must empower themselves and their clients (Pinderhughes, 1983).

A characteristic that goes along with the ability to develop and act on a strong commitment to social work value positions is being *assertive* (Kurtz and Dickinson, 1981). We have stressed throughout this text that social work, although recognized by society's sanctioning of the needs areas it covers and having been institutionalized within social welfare as the profession to handle it, nonetheless faces controversy from several segments of society over its image.

Given the failure of public representatives to accept social work's positions and thereby to validate the profession, social workers have to be assertive in educating the public as well as in bringing about needed structural and policy changes (Albert, 1983). Practitioners also need to be assertive in interpreting and supporting the rights and needs of their clients. Faced with this prospect in their practice, workers also have to be highly tolerant of potential conflict and the likelihood of little public support.

Social workers also have to be *tolerant of ambiguity* because of the nature of some of the problems people have in their social functioning. Like some of the more complicated psychological or medical problems, multiple causation complicates difficulties in social functioning. Hence, assessment is difficult and solutions to them are less than clear-cut.

For such problems, interventions are equally difficult. Therefore, workers must be *creative* in their practice. Recipe-like practice approaches cannot be applied in routine fashion. Social workers have to be inventive, resourceful, and willing to think hard and long to come up with workable goals and appropriate interventions for the particular mix of needs, problems, changes, and causation in a given client system's functioning. To think of practice interventions as being limited by conceptions stemming from casework, group work, or community organizing methods is too simplistic for the complex problems social workers handle for their clients.

Implied in being creative are *hard-working* professionals who are willing to undertake efforts to change social structures as well as to change people (Brawley, 1985). Unlike the professional who is trained to deal only with individuals or a small group, the generalist practitioner must also analyze and resolve environmental changes that affect people's social functioning.

In dealing with changes in people's lives, our ideal social workers have to be *sensitive to people's feelings* about such changes, and they must *place value on human diversity* as ethnically, physically, and socially different people face these changes. Social workers face clients who are ill-prepared to manage changes in their lives and whose interactions with other systems have too frequently robbed them of the abilities, opportunities, and resources they need to meet their needs on their own terms in their social environments. Made different in many ways, people possess strengths to use in solving their own problems. Social workers must be sensitive to their feelings and to the differences that make them potentially stronger.

Social workers must juggle many expectations. Professional purpose expects both people and institutions to be strengthened, whereas the expectations of the public are in conflict about what they want of the profession. Controversy is inherent in the profession's value positions, the developing nature of its knowledge base, and its practice skills. Therefore, our ideal practitioner must be *secure in self*. This sense of security is based in awareness of personal strengths and resources and a basic confidence to face clients and others as they carry out professional purpose. Practitioners must be able to manage the growth and change that will enable them to continue to be competent. They need to know enough about themselves to face this task of making changes in their professional practice. Social workers have their own self-doubts. They are not perfect. They do not always have the answers. They must seek out support and help themselves. Some social workers do not always act in the best interests of their clients, and the professional associations have mechanisms to handle this.

To keep abreast of changing knowledge about people, new knowledge of emerging problems, and increases in knowledge about practice skills, our ideal practitioners must be *lifelong learners*. In an emerging area of human and social need within a young profession, practitioners need to grow along with their profession's knowledge base.

All these characteristics are best supported by people who do not have to function according to conventional work patterns and rewards. Although workers often face quite traditional approaches in social agencies, our ideal professional must be *unconventional* about problems. Social workers often handle unconventional problems, and the people they help are not always accorded the same treatment as conventional members of society receive. And the conventional rewards of status, money, prestige, and respect accorded to conventional professions have not been completely forthcoming for social work. Our ideal practitioner must not place too great an emphasis on conventional symbols of professional status (see Arches, 1985, for a related discussion). For social workers, a high salary and the highest degree of professional respect and recognition, even from colleagues, is not an automatic or frequent reward for practice well done. The rewards come from other sources, including the worker's own feelings about accomplishment and achievement in service to others.

Our list of characteristics of the ideal practitioner is not intended to be exhaustive. It outlines some of the factors required of practitioners by the model of practice discussed in this chapter. That model calls for practitioners to whom the following descriptions apply:

Patient.
Firm in their convictions.
Assertive.
Tolerant of ambiguity, conflict, and change.
Creative.
Hard-working.

Lifelong learners.
Willing to work for institutional change.
Sensitive to feelings.
Supportive of human diversity.
Secure in self.
Not guided by conventional status symbols.

Practitioners with these characteristics are "professionals" in their practice behaviors. Earlier, we noted that some of the meanings and values usually associated with the term *professional* are well-paid, courteous, knowledgeable, and caring in relationships. The image derived from our earlier discussion is of an educated, decent, skilled, competent, polite, concerned, and trustworthy person who is well rewarded by society.

The description of professionalism presented here also indicates how people would like to be treated by a professional and what professionals might expect in return. Social workers display professionalism in this sense as well as being educated, skilled, and competent according to our earlier discussions. They also must display some less acceptable professional characteristics, such as assertion and taking controversial actions.

In our earlier discussion of professions and practitioner behavior, you were asked to compare ideas about those topics with your own. Make the same sort of comparison with this set of ideal practitioner characteristics and where you see yourself in relation to them. How tolerant of ambiguity, how willing to confront change, how assertive, or how needful of conventional status symbols are you? What is your fit with the characteristics of an ideal practitioner? Which would you modify or avoid?

For Further Study

1. Identify a problem situation you have faced in your life and discuss how you resolved it. Apply the steps of the problem-solving process to this situation. In what ways, if any, would the problem-solving approach have changed your course of action?
2. With which social work value positions are you most, and least, comfortable? Explain why you selected these positions.
3. Diagram the interaction between you (or your family) and your (family's) social environment.
4. Refer to the lists and definitions of social work interventions in this chapter. With which are you most, and least, comfortable? Which ones on the list did you expect, and not expect, to find as a social work intervention?
5. The social workers interviewed offer a variety of definitions of values. Compare and contrast their definitions. What do they add to the discussion of value positions in this chapter?

6. Discuss the different approaches to the definition and use of a practice knowledge base offered in the social workers' statements.
7. Using Documents 6.1 and 6.2 compare and contrast the Codes of the National Association of Black Social Workers and of the National Association of Social Workers.
8. Which of the characteristics of an ideal social worker were displayed by the social worker discussed in Document 6.3?

Glossary

GENERALIST METHOD OF PRACTICE.   The practice approach that uses problem-solving steps to achieve the purposes of the profession in helping individuals, small groups, and communities.

PROBLEM-SOLVING STEPS.   As used in the generalist method, a series of interacting steps through which the worker engages with the client system, collects data about and assesses the problem situation, sets goals and develops a plan of action, implements and evaluates the plan, and terminates or disengages from the helping relationship.

SOCIAL WORK VALUE POSITIONS.   The purpose and practice efforts used by social work to support strong positions on how people should grow and develop, how they should be treated in society and within social welfare agencies, and the degree of responsibility society should have in helping people.

KNOWLEDGE BASE.   Knowledge about human behavior and the social environment drawn from a variety of disciplines and used by social workers to assess and intervene in problem situations.

LIMITED PARTNERSHIPS.   The professional decision-making relationships between workers and clients and workers and others that are limited by time, goals, client need, and the nature of agencies and services.

SOCIAL RESPONSIBILITY.   The responsibility of society for its operations that create or contribute to people's problems and that makes society accountable for helping people in difficult situations.

HUMAN DIVERSITY.   The differences people present according to their ethnic, cultural, gender, class, or physical backgrounds.

SOCIAL CHANGE.   Involvement in policymaking and in political activity to strengthen and/or alter social structures.

SOCIAL JUSTICE.   The creation of a society that values and supports all people without racist, sexist, homophobic, ageist, or class-conscious practices.

CLIENT SELF-DETERMINATION.   Client participation in working on and planning for changes in their lives and environments.

SYSTEM THEORY.   The parts within a designated boundary that interact in a more or less predictable fashion to achieve a goal.

RACIST, SEXIST, HOMOPHOBIC, AGEIST, OR CLASS-CONSCIOUS PRACTICES. The oppressive, discriminatory, and isolating interactions between members of the majority culture and members of minority groups and between majority social structures and members of minority groups.

SOCIAL WORK INTERVENTIONS. The actions or change efforts undertaken by social workers and their clients to restore the client system's social interactions or social functioning to a satisfactory level by strengthening people, changing their social environment, or linking them with needed resources.

DIRECT CLIENT PRACTICE. Face-to-face client system contact to address the system's problems by supporting and strengthening the client.

INFORMATION AND REFERRAL. Worker efforts to manage information and contacts about resources and opportunities needed by the client system.

INDIRECT PRACTICE. A practice with less face-to-face contact with clients and with more contact with others in the management and development of change efforts directed at the environmental and social welfare system.

IDEAL PRACTITIONER. A practitioner having the set of personal characteristics most likely to enable her or him to deliver on professional purpose in practice.

Bibliography

Abramson, M. "The Autonomy-Paternalism Dilemma in Social Work Practice." *Social Casework: The Journal of Contemporary Social Work* 66(7): 387–393, 1985.

Albert, R. "Social Work Advocacy in the Regulatory Process." *Social Casework: The Journal of Contemporary Social Work* 64(8): 473–481, 1983.

Alexander, C. A. "Contradictions of Contemporary Society and Social Work Ethics." *International Social Work* 28(3): 1–8, 1985.

Arches, J. "Don't Burn, Organize: A Structural Analysis of Burnout in the Human Services." *Catalyst: A Socialist Journal of the Social Services* 5(17/18): 15–20, 1985.

Brawley, E. A. "Making a Difference: An Action-Oriented Approach to Social Policy for Undergraduate Social Work Students." *Arete* 10(1): 50–55, 1985.

Devore, Wynette, and Elfie Schlesinger. *Ethnic Sensitive Practice.* St. Louis: Mosby, 1981.

Compton, Beulah Roberts, and Burt Galaway. *Social Work Processes.* Rev. ed. Homewood, IL: Dorsey Press, 1979.

Constable, R. T. "Values, Religion and Social Work Practice." *Social Thought* 9(4): 29–43, 1983.

Gould, Ketayun H. "Life Model Versus Conflict Model: A Feminist Perspective." *Social Work* 32(4): 346–351, 1987.

Imre, R. W. "The Nature of Knowledge in Social Work." *Social Work* 29(1): 41–45, 1984.

"International Code of Ethics for the Professional Social Worker." *International Social Work* 28(3): 9–11, 1985.

Kurtz, G., and N. S. Dickinson. "Assertive Skills for Social Workers." *Journal of Continuing Social Work Education* 1(4):7–10, 26–27, 1981.

Lewis, H. "Ethical Assessment." *Social Casework* 65(4): 203–211, 1984.

National Association of Black Social Workers. "Code of Ethics," *Annual Report*. New York: NABSW, 1979.

National Association of Social Workers. *Code of Ethics*. Washington, DC, 1980.

O'Neil, Maria Joan. *The General Method of Social Work Practice*. Englewood Cliffs, NJ: Prentice-Hall, 1984.

Pincus, Allen, and Anne Minahan. *Social Work Practice: Model and Method*. Itasca, IL: Peacock Publishers, 1973.

Pinderhughes, E. B. "Empowerment for Our Clients and for Ourselves." *Social Casework* 64(6): 331–338, 1983.

Specht, H. "Managing Professional Interpersonal Interactions." *Social Work* 30(3); 225–330, 1985.

CHAPTER SEVEN

Contexts for Practice

As a boy I came to your shores,
Oh! What dreams I had;
  I heard so much of the bread and wine
That flows from your rivers.

As a man I've worked my fingers to
the bone.
My wife and children have left me now,
  For I cannot provide for them.

As an Old Man I will swim back home
To my island of paradise;
  Even if I do this in the cloudiness
of my mind.

James Arana (undated)

The social worker should encourage informed participation by the public in shaping policies and institutions.

NASW Code of Ethics (1980)

CHAPTER OVERVIEW

This chapter focuses on social work practice, as do the other chapters in Part II. Chapters 5 and 6 explored the human and social need to manage change and presented a model of practice. The direction of practice that moves workers toward change is derived both from purpose and from the human and social needs areas served by social work. This chapter examines the contexts of social work practice and explores how their interaction with purpose and need creates contemporary practice while maintaining the integrity of the profession.

As introduced earlier, the context of practice in which social work takes place is twofold. One context is the societies within which, for whom, and sometimes against whom social workers practice. The second context is the services, including the opportunities, resources, and social services available to practitioners. Such services largely come from the institution of social welfare and are critical to helping people restore their social functioning. Both contexts grow and change and interact with professional purpose to create a practice that is responsive to new problems and services and that is also faithful to purpose.

This chapter explores how the contexts of practice are like crucibles in which social work practice is shaped and reshaped. These contexts account for differences and changes in practice. Therefore, the interaction of each context with professional purpose must be guided by practitioners to assure the integrity of the profession.

Social workers must learn about and use the power of human diversity to strengthen people and better deliver on professional purpose. Professionals must also lead members of the public into assuming responsibility for their part in people's problematic social functioning and to create the resources and protection people need.

In other words, social workers in their practice continuously strive for the following:

Strengthening societal responsibility in the context of social welfare services.

Valuing human diversity as it defines the context of societies.

To understand these contexts and their interaction with purpose, this chapter explores society's agenda to deal with change and how that agenda affects practice. The power of human diversity is explored as well as the ways purpose, societies, and social welfare services interact. The responsibility of social work to shape itself within the contexts of societies and services expands on the discussion of their interaction.

In our initial discussion about our journey to discover social work, it was noted that a means has to be developed to help readers to identify precisely the latest developments in social work practice without losing sight of the basic nature of the profession. The interaction among purpose, societies, and services that is guided by social work practitioners accounts for the changing and updating of practice. It provides a way of looking at social work and its practice over time without losing sight of the essence of social work.

How to become involved in guiding the interactions with the contexts of practice concludes the chapter's discussion. An opportunity is provided for you to examine how to prepare yourself for these practice contexts.

SOCIETAL AGENDA FOR DEALING WITH CHANGE

Few professions are charged with telling members of society that:

Society is responsible for causing problems which interfere with the functioning of individuals as well as society itself.

Citizens must assume responsibility to provide significant resources for
a social institution that many people would prefer not to use.

Citizens are responsible for protecting and supporting the right of
fair treatment for those who need help in their social functioning.

The purpose of social work would have practitioners remind the public of these
interrelated responsibilities. Furthermore, social workers must make members
of society understand and acknowledge society's responsibility in these areas.
In a sense, social work is the conscience of society.

It is part of professional purpose and direction in practice to help society
manage change and the effect of change on people's functioning. The impact
of the public and its representatives on the shape of social welfare services
directly affects social work practice. Social workers, along with their clients,
need to cease being passive recipients of the public's social welfare allocations
and become more active as shapers of the programs and structures that comprise the institution of social welfare.

The nature of what society holds as its responsibility in this institution is
to be found in the way the structures and programs of social welfare are established and operated. Society's agenda to deal with change is contained in its
sense of responsibility for helping with people's social functioning. Social responsibility is measured by determining which people are eligible for help,
which needs are to be covered, how problem causation is viewed, and how
people are to be treated in social welfare structures. The response of society
to helping people meet the human and social needs they have in their social
functioning has taken several forms and has been assigned to several social
institutions. Moreover, the needs and problems people present have changed
considerably (see Document 7.1).

DOCUMENT 7.1

The Safety Net Catches Children, If
They're White

Daniel Patrick Moynihan

In his final State of the Union Address in January, President Reagan
said, "Some years ago, the federal government declared war on poverty, and
poverty won."

It happens I was present in the Rose
Garden at mid-morning of Aug. 20,
1964, on the occasion when President
Johnson signed the Economic Opportunity Act of 1964. At no point in his
remarks that day did he use the term
"war on poverty," but that usage be-

came common and Reagan surely reflects a widespread judgment that as a nation we failed in that great undertaking.

About one American in six was poor in 1964; about one in six is poor today. This seemingly intractable proportion is the result of two quite opposite movements.

In 1964, poverty was essentially a problem of the aged. More than a quarter of the aged were poor. But programs enacted under Johnson and Richard M. Nixon greatly reduced poverty among the elderly to the point—still not an acceptable one—where 12.4 percent of those 65 and over live below poverty level. By contrast, all of a sudden we look up to find there are more poor Americans today than a quarter century ago, and that the poorest group in our population is children.

How has this come about? At one level the answer is simple. It is, as Samuel H. Preston, president of the Population Association of America put it, "the earthquake that shuddered through the American family in the past 20 years."

As the census has just reported, in 1986, nearly one in every four children—23.5 percent—live with only one parent, 2.5 times the proportion in 1960. The vast majority—89 percent—of these 14.8 million children live with their mothers. Estimates of the number of children who will live with a single parent at some point during childhood are yet more striking. The Bureau of the Census predicts that 61 percent of children born in 1987 will live for some time with only one biological parent before they reach the age of 18. Inevitably, large numbers of these children require some form of public assistance.

Further, in providing such assistance, we have created an extraordinary institutional bias against minority children.

The Social Security Act has two provisions for the care of children in single-parent families. The first is Aid to Families with Dependent Children, enacted into law as part of the original 1935 Social Security Act. The second is Survivors Insurance, added to the act in 1939. The characteristics of the two populations served by these programs are quite different. The majority of the children receiving SI benefits are white. The majority of the children receiving AFDC are black or Latino. Since 1970 we have increased the real benefits received by children under SI by 53 percent. We have cut the benefits of AFDC children by 13 percent. The U.S. government, the American people, now provide a child receiving SI benefits almost three times what we provide a child on AFDC.

Those who say we don't care about children in our country should note that since 1970s, the average provision for children under SI has been rising five times as fast as average family income. We do care about some children. Majority children. It is minority children—not only but mostly—who are left behind.

Why this institutional bias?

I believe we know why. Welfare has become a stigmatized program. Children dependent on it—as many as one child in three before reaching 18—are stigmatized as well.

The Family Security Act, our legislation that has 56 co-sponsors and is now under consideration by the Senate, is designed to get rid of that stigma by emphasizing the collection of court-ordered child support payments and the education and training adults need to get off welfare. There has been a great deal of talk about both, but the federal government has really never backed either. Once that stigma is gone, or diminished, states will once again feel the moral obligation to maintain and even increase AFDC payments to dependent children. They are free to do so now. They do not. We want to change this.

Let me declare my own conviction apart from the provisions of our bill: AFDC should be a national program with national benefits that keep pace with inflation, in exactly the same way that Survivors Insurance is a national program with national benefits. Had the Family Assistance Plan, which I helped fashion for President Nixon, been enacted, we would now have such

a program. Had President Carter's Program for Better Jobs and Income, which I supported in the Senate, been enacted, we would have such a program. Both proposals fell before a coalition of those who thought the benefits were too great and those who thought them too little. But that is history. Today, our federal budget deficit is such that there is no possibility whatsoever of establishing national AFDC benefit standards.

We can have welfare reform this year. But welfare reform must become the art of the possible or it will become a diversion of the essentially unserious.

(SOURCE: "The Safety Net Catches Children, If They're White," by Daniel Patrick Moynihan. April 5, 1988, Shreveport Journal. Reprinted by permission of Los Angeles Times.)

Whether or not the so-called capable members of society should help and protect those deemed to be incapable is a fundamental issue in social responsibility and social justice. Its resolution determines who will be helped, which needs will be met, and what manner of treatment people will be accorded while receiving help. How a society resolves this and related issues becomes the measure of the responsibility it will assume in helping people.

Understanding social responsibility begins with identifying what society defines as a need and with deciding what needs society will meet. Historically, meeting the so-called basic needs of food, clothing, and shelter of those who were unable to do so for themselves has been partly assumed by varying social structures. Sometimes governments have been assigned responsibility by society to meet basic needs for some of their people. This was so in the Roman Empire and is the arrangement in contemporary Western Societies. At other times slavery, as in ancient Greece and pre–Civil War America, provided for these needs. In medieval Europe and early modern England, formal religious institutions were the providers. In the contemporary United States of America, the level of government that should assume responsibility is at issue (Gruber, 1983).

In meeting these basic needs, society's responsibility has been viewed in the past as help at a minimum level that is offered to a very few people. Contemporary Western societies, on the other hand, have extended the list of needs for which they will assume responsibility to include other areas. Recall the needs spelled out in our earlier discussions. They go beyond physical needs to include psychological, emotional, and social needs. Contemporary societies also have concentrated their need-meeting efforts in the institution of social welfare.

Deciding who is eligible to receive help from society and what constitutes help is another aspect of social responsibility. For example, should unmarried teens be helped with parenting, education, or other needs? Some societies have limited their responsibility by not recognizing the needs of some people and by mistreating or not protecting those it decides to help. Many centuries ago, some people banished or killed those they thought might prove unfit to function within society. Not only the physically limited, as in Sparta, but female babies or the elderly were left unprotected in areas outside their own communities where they would either die from exposure or be killed. Among other peoples, those who were different in sexual orientation were marked for special treatment. Although homosexual males were given special recognition by certain North American Indian tribes as possessing spiritual insight and hence deserving of the community's support, in Victorian England they were held to be so incapable of responsible social functioning that they were banished or persecuted. Other persons who had been jailed for poverty in England from its early industrial period were shipped off to its colonies in North America and Australia.

In contemporary Western societies, the struggle continues to enlarge social responsibility by making some needs-meeting efforts universal in the institution of social welfare, along with increasing the needs areas covered. Few services apply to everyone in the United States. As the number of needs that are covered expands, the total number of people helped by society increases.

Thus, which needs will be covered and who will be found eligible to receive help in meeting those needs are both key ingredients in a society's movement toward assuming responsibility for providing people with needed services and resources (see McQuade, 1983, for a treatment of today's poor). As noted in the human and social needs area of managing change, all people may at some time require help with the following:

Psychological, emotional, and physical growth and development.
Relationships with other people.
Interaction within structures of social institutions.
Functioning within cultures other than their own.

We also noted that the needs area of managing change is an emerging one and is beginning to be institutionalized in social welfare. Its emergence indicates that society is accepting being responsible to help more and more people with more and more needs.

Another part of societal responsibility for dealing with change and people's social functioning is the manner of treatment accorded people who are eligible for help in social welfare services. In medieval Europe, poor people suffered public humiliation along with the receipt of their "charitable" handouts. At the beginning of the Industrial Revolution in England, jails and almshouses were filled with people who had been impoverished and oppressed by economic change and dislocations. Contemporary America has created the discriminatory and stigmatizing procedures of food stamps, welfare bureaucracies, and public assistance as ways of controlling and/or helping a class of poor people whose plight stems in part from the operations of social institutions (Schram and Turbetts, 1983). On the other hand, without stigma, society provides the middle class with educational loans, farm subsidies, and deductions of some of their home mortgage loan payments from their taxable income (see Washawsky, 1985, for other supports for the affluent).

Persons treated less well reflect an acceptance that society can operationalize its responsibility for help by denying just treatment to some peple. Such responses also indicate that our society displays inconsistent patterns in assuming the responsibility to protect the dignity of the people it helps. Underlying this pattern is a society that assumes little or no responsibility for its part in causing the problematic interactions that take place between people and their social environment. Mistreating some people, society says, is permissible because those people have created their own problems. The people who create their own troubles, according to this sense of social responsibility, do not deserve respect and fair treatment as they go about receiving help from society.

Social work purpose maintains that society should help to enhance and restore people's abilities to function in their social environment, develop and provide adequate resources for people to do so, and develop and operate its service structures in an effective and just fashion. In some ways, part of the contemporary sense of social responsibility is not fully consistent with these purposes. The profession's ideas about which people, which needs, and what kind of treatment indicate that society should assume greater responsibility for all people and needs and for adequate protection and fair treatment.

Many needs and many people are covered by social welfare services. The emergence of social work and social welfare are positive. The development of service structures in line with social work's outlook must be developed further. Developing adequate services that treat all people fairly in social welfare indicates future work for the profession (see interviews on pages 176 and 177).

HOW MANY "SOCIETIES"? UNCOVERING THE POWER OF DIVERSITY

From the preceding discussion, one might assume that the purposes of social work, the practice model derived from it, and society's responsibility to provide services and to take care of people fairly in its efforts to help them with their social functioning are determined by and for a single "society." More accu-

I AM A SOCIAL WORKER
"Social Responsibility"

GRACIELA CASTEX: In practicing with Cuban refugees, I began to think about whether or not the community was responsible for the needs of people. I saw that there were large numbers of people pouring into the Miami area who did not have their needs being addressed by the community. The community had to begin to respond to their needs because their numbers were just incredible.

BERNICE GOODMAN: I think that the point at which society cuts itself off from any person is the point at which it starts to die. In some ways, society has been unresponsive. Institutional change is very slow, and in some ways society cannot absorb the use of technology in positive ways as rapidly as it must in order to be responsible.

BETTE HARLAN: The society in which I currently work appears to show little responsibility for those most in need of care—children, the elderly, those with illness. The elections of the past few years seem to have put into office self-serving individuals who lack a commitment to caring for those who need our attention.

TRACEY JOHNSON: On my first job in recreation, I tried to get the department to do something about kids who came to the program without food. The program's staff said the kids' lack of food was not the program's business. I disagreed. All of us are responsible when we see people in need. I am. Agencies are. Society is. Social workers have to have a sense of social responsibility and display it for others and help others take action also.

IRMA SERRANO: We should be proud of the profession, although I do not think we have been using the profession in the right way. We talk about a lot of social problems. Although we are not going to cure the ills of the world, social work has to have more say into that. We have to realize that we should not debate being "clinical" or "social" but realize that together the two make us professional.

   Social work has to help society realize its responsibility and can do so by educating the public and by getting involved politically. Social workers also have to help program funders, service administrators, and others realize how to develop the responsibility of recipients. We have to help everyone be clear about when the help stops. We should be responsible for people's problems and for the consequences for them of the programs we develop. Dealing with social problems and programs almost as consultants to agencies and others should be a part of social work.

ADELE WEINER: Social responsibility is synonymous with social work. Part of the responsibility of being a social worker involves the humane delivery of services and the development of programs that will benefit all of society. Historically, social workers have been at the forefront of many movements to improve society.

rately, these aspects of social work derive from and must be assessed in the context of a variety of subgroups in society.

Sociologists may refer to an all-encompassing society composed of a variety of socioeconomic classes, political scientists to a pluralistic society, anthropologists to subcultures, and social workers to human diversity (Berger and Federico, 1985). This book's title refers to society in the sociological sense but applies social work's meaning of diversity to the "societies" with which social workers practice. In the social work sense of human diversity, those who need help and those who define and/or offer help in the United States consist of many "societies," defined by a complexity of cultural, structural, physical, class, and other characteristics. These "societies" function within a common set of social structures, but they may go about their interaction with those structures in diverse ways and can be accorded different treatment by them.

To social workers, human diversity among their clients and others they interact with stems from the following:

Biological differences.
Psychological and emotional variations.
Physical variations.
Sexual orientations.
Cultural patterns.
Interactions between people and social structures that favor some and oppress others.

Characteristics from one or more of these sources of human diversity are associated with groupings of people who come to be labeled according to these traits. Different by virtue of its identifying characteristics, the group is treated as a unit in social welfare and in other institutions (Castex, 1986). "Societies" are groups that are made different from other groups by a specific trait, they are identified by the trait, and their members receive approximately the same treatment in social welfare and other social institutions (see Document 7.2).

DOCUMENT 7.2

Yankees, and Purple-Hull Peas
Wiley W. Hilburn Jr.

He wasn't a bad guy—not at all. It was just that he sort of put us on edge. When he entered the conversation, everything went quiet, like when somebody starts quoting the Bible in the middle of an argument.

Later, one of the charter members of the Good Old Boys (GOB) figured out why this fellow didn't fit into the fellowship. "Well, he's a Yankee," our GOB said.

Mystery solved then and there. Everybody nodded and we went on to another subject. The issue was decided, but you have to understand that no malice was involved in it.

In fact, the "Yankee" was accepted after that—all his peculiarities explained by geography and genes. If his opinions were delivered unsweetened by Southern tact, "Well, he's a Yankee."

It didn't matter that this "Yankee" turned out to be from Arizona; that Arizona wasn't even admitted as a state until 1912, 47 years after Appomattox.

In North Louisiana, everybody born outside the confines of the Confederacy is a Yankee; Arizonans and Midwesterners and Iranians are Yankees. Border state people are borderline subversive.

Indeed, you really need a grandpa or at least an uncle born in Fort Necessity, Boeuf Prairie, Ringgold or somewhere in Claiborne Parish to instantly qualify for GOB status.

Otherwise, it takes a while to get a permanent booth at the Huddle House in Ruston or a pew in the back three rows of the town's First Presbyterian Church.

But once it's discovered that somebody is a Yankee, then everything is not only understood, but usually forgiven—even being abrupt, an absolute no-no among native Southerners.

Did this sort of odd guy snap at you then?

"Well, he's a Yankee."

Forgive him, fellows, he knoweth not what he says.

Of course, even Yankees can't be forgiven for everything—like not eating purple-hull peas. It happened while I was still living with my family on Marbury Drive in Ruston.

A new family moved in next door. They were Air Force, with AF-ROTC at Louisiana Tech, from the Midwest or somewhere. Yankees. But we were getting along OK until Daddy came home from visiting them late one afternoon, his face angry.

"They don't eat peas," Daddy said.

In North Louisiana, it *is* subversive not to eat peas. At my house, we ate peas, tomatoes, boiled okra and fried ham every night. Everything but the ham came out of Daddy's back-yard garden, and the peas could occasionally be left off the menu, then to be re- placed only by butterbeans.

But the Yankees next door didn't eat peas.

We all felt a surge of hostility toward them.

Still Mother, always nice, was ready to forgive. "Well, Wiley, they are Yan- kees," she told my daddy.

But Daddy had more incriminating evidence against the aliens next door.

"They told me that where they come from, they feed peas to the hogs," Daddy told us.

They feed peas to the hogs?

It was too much to forgive. We were all mad then.

"They don't have a television, either," Daddy said, resting his case.

We never said much to the Yankees next door after that. In fact, even our dog got into fights with their dog.

Soon the Air Force moved these folks away, and we said good riddance. The next couple was AF, too, and also from the Midwest. But they ate peas and owned a television. We got along fine.

(SOURCE: "Yankees, and Purple-Hull Peas," Wiley W. Hilburn, Jr. September 13, 1987, Shreveport- Bossier Times. Reprinted by permission of publisher.)

Men and women differ biologically and accordingly are seen as two differ- ent groups of people, with distinctive outlooks and interests. Physical character- istics, such as differences in skin color and/or facial features, has led to the identification of other groups. American Blacks, North American Indians, and so-called white people are representative groups. Age is another physical char- acteristic; we have come to identify people as senior citizens, youth, middle- aged, or infants. In addition, people's physical growth patterns create other groups. The physically limited, with lessened mobility, and the mentally re- tarded, with limited cognitive development, are set apart from others.

People are also viewed as different according to cultural or ethnic group- ings. Members of various "Hispanic" cultures are an example. People are simi- larly separated into socioeconomic classes. Poor people, who earn less in an economy that does little to accommodate them, are seen as different from the middle class. Another set of divisions is made along the lines of sexual orienta- tion. Lesbian women and gay men are grouped separately and apart from non- lesbian women and nongay men.

Sometimes groups identified according to such characteristics have over- lapping members. Or more than one characteristic may determine membership. Finally, contributing to the idea of diverse groups is the value placed on them by social institutions, attitudes, and norms. Some groups are valued less than others. For example:

Blacks less than nonblacks.
Lesbian women and gay men less than "straight people."
Women less than men.

Such devaluation means that when they deal with social structures members of these groups receive less or are blocked in meeting their needs. This creates underdeveloped and oppressed people, such as an urban underclass or closeted lesbians and gays.

All these variations lead to humans who create different but adequate patterns of functioning within their social environment. These differences are demonstrated in their interactions with other systems in their social environment as they go about meeting their needs. For example, straight women and men meet their need for intimacy, loving, and emotional support by mating, marrying, and rearing children. Lesbian women and gay men also meet these needs but through couples and friend networks (see Hidalgo, Peterson, and Woodman, 1985). All people have a need for intimacy, loving, and support as a strong base for their social interactions, but many individuals create different patterns of meeting these needs. In helping diverse people gain adequate social functioning, social workers must correctly understand what pattern has been disrupted and in what ways it might be restored or replaced. For example, the reasons for the end of a relationship among straight people, lesbian women, or gay men may not reflect the same kinds of changing interactions within their social environments. Nor may they need the same factors to deal with the changes posed by the end of the relationship (Sancier, 1984).

In dealing with diverse groups as clients, social workers must focus on the various ways people function adequately in society and how they handle interactions within their own world and social environment (DeHoyos, DeHoyos, and Anderson, 1986; Norton, 1978). Problematic social functioning has to be seen in relation to the ways diverse groups demonstrate adequate needs-meeting behavior in their own realm of living. The assessment of problems and their causation must be based on a thorough understanding of expected or adequate interactions in diverse human systems. It is diagrammed in Figure 7.1. Problematic interactions among various subsystems within a social environment can be seen in Figure 7.2.

For the social worker, the problem is *not* that the person they work with is any of the following:

A female single parent.
Physically limited.

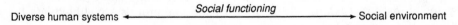

Figure 7.1

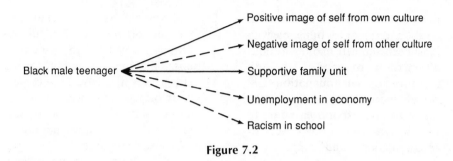

Figure 7.2

Lesbian or gay.
Black.
Hispanic.
White, middle-class, male.
Poor.
Mentally retarded.

The problems social workers must handle are their inadequacies in the social functioning of the members of various groups. The inadequacies stem from changes in the interaction between themselves and other systems in their social environment. The other systems are quite likely to have *caused* the inadequate social functioning of people from diverse groups or to have contributed to it through their treatment of them (see Document 7.3).

DOCUMENT 7.3

Curriculum Policy for the Master's Degree and Baccalaureate Degree Programs in Social Work Education

SPECIAL POPULATIONS

7.3 The social work profession, by virtue of its system of ethics, its traditional value commitments, and its long history of work in the whole range of human services, is committed to preparing students to understand and appreciate cultural and social diversity. The profession has also been concerned about the consequences of oppression.

7.4 Programs of social work education must provide content related to oppression and to the experiences, needs, and responses of people who have subjected to institution- alized forms of oppression. Both the professional foundation and the advanced concentration curric- ula must give explicit attention to the patterns and consequences of discrimination and oppression, providing both theoretical and practice content about groups that continue to be subjected to oppres- sion and those that are emerging into new social roles with greater freedom and visibility.

7.5 The curriculum must provide con- tent on ethnic minorities of color and women. It should include con- tent on other special population groups relevant to the program's mission or location and, in particu- lar, groups that have been consist- ently affected by social, economic and legal bias or oppression. Such groups include, but are not limited to, those distinguished by age, reli- gion, disablement, sexual orienta- tion, and culture.

(SOURCE: This material was first published in the *Handbook of Accreditation, Standards and Procedures,* 1988, and it is reprinted here with the permission of the Council on Social Work Education.)

Indeed these systems may define adequacy from the perspective of a differ- ent "society." It is necessary to stress this point because diversity has not been valued by the operations of social structures and norms in society. The contri- butions of different classes, ethnic groups, cultures, or other diverse groups have not been noted or appreciated because those passing judgment or setting standards are themselves often different. The problems people display are too frequently seen as caused by what the people are. Their successes are perceived as coming in spite of what they are.

In addition to viewing problems in social functioning as coming from changing and problematic system interactions, not from people labeled inade- quate because of their difference, social workers must also be able to perceive the strengths within human diversity (see Lorenzo and Adler, 1984; Olmstead, 1983; Sancier, 1982, for illustrations). The strengths possessed by diverse groups come from their special ways of functioning in society and from how they conceive of problems, resources, and helping (Green, 1984). In this way, one significance of "societies" for social work and for locating the connection of the profession to society is that different people have differing perceptions about and approaches to dealing with the following:

Problems and their causes.
Ways of seeking and using help.
Developing relevant resources to handle their problems.

For example, social workers recognize that among some so-called Hispanic cultures, problems that professionals might label as pyschiatric are believed by members of these cultures as having "spiritual" causes. Solutions and resources to deal with them are available within their communities. (See Green, 1984, for suggestions how practitioners might incorporate the contributions or strengths of diverse groups into their practice.)

Indigenous resources, stemming from diverse groups themselves, are often seen as the key to social work helping. For example, many Black families, although faced with overwhelming economic and social oppression, personal and institutional racism, and political and geographic isolation, continue nonetheless to help and support members of their kinship system (Stack, 1974). Social workers respect and use the power offered by this means of social functioning.

Friendship and community support among lesbian women serves a similar purpose. Among other groups, such friendship-based networks are often quite significant as a source of support and as creators of services and resources (Wilson, 1983). These types of social functioning constitute the power of diversity.

Social workers have been responsible for bringing the power of such variations in social functioning into their practice (Olmstead, 1983). Social workers operate within the context of these "societies." As indicated in our preceding discussion, the institution of social welfare and the sense of social responsibility to deal with the needs area of change, along with social workers' interactions with societies, leads to an ever-changing practice complexion. Social workers face the responsibility of understanding how diversity leads to different patterns of social functioning and of using the strengths of diverse people in handling their problematic social functioning. They must also educate members of society, especially those who believe that differences are to be ignored or denigrated, to be responsive to needs associated with people's social functioning and to respect and incorporate the power of diversity into creating social welfare services. The institution of social welfare cannot reflect the perspective of a single group; it must respond to all societies that define and use it (see interviews on pages 184–186).

THE INTERACTION AMONG PURPOSE, "SOCIETIES," AND SERVICES

The differing patterns of people's social functioning and the shifting acknowledgment by the public of its social responsibility for allocating resources to the institution of social welfare are critical contexts of professional practice that strongly affect the appearance of practice. New service populations and practice approaches emerge as social work interacts with these practice contexts. Purpose demands that social workers enhance people, link them with resources, and modify and strengthen the social structures that serve people. What different societies need and what the public offers to them through social welfare are often quite different.

I AM A SOCIAL WORKER
"Special Populations"

GRACIELA CASTEX: For Hispanics, I think that the strengths of the population are not tapped by traditional social services. Many times workers want to impose a way of doing things, a way of resolving issues on people. Workers say this is how you do it, even if it doesn't quite fit. Again, I think with Hispanics, as with any other group, we cannot force a square into a circle. We've got to have the kind of services that match the clients and what their needs are. This is true, whether it be understanding the family composition better, understanding traditional folk thinking, or understanding community resources.

One way to do this is to consider, in a nontraditional way, that community resources are formal in nature, as opposed to being informal. Many times churches and *botanicas* (stores that sell items related to spiritual needs) are seen as informal resources. At least for the Hispanic population, some of these resources have to be looked at as primary resources, not secondary resources.

For example, many times traditionally when people do not have food we give them food stamps to go to the grocery store and purchase food. That concept of a formal resource, the food stamp and how to use it, is not totally accepted by those who use it. This nonacceptance was true for many of the migrant Hispanic populations. On the other hand, to go to the church and get food from a food closet was acceptable. So, in my opinion, give the food stamps to the church to buy food and have the church give food to people. In other words, the so-called informal community resource system, the church, is treated as a primary part of the formal resource system, the food stamp program. The church is given the formal respect of using it as a service delivery mechanism. The church, within the primary experience of some people, becomes part of formal service delivery structures. In this way we could use community strengths.

Another example is when we talk about strengthening people but don't know what that really means for a particular population. When we talk of developing Hispanic populations by moving them from one level of the economic strata to another level, one of the traditional values is that one saves money and you save the money in a bank. This is a way in which traditional American society developed itself, by having people put money in the bank and the bank invests it in major developments. Many Hispanics don't put their money in banks because in their experience it does not lead to personal or social gain. They say I am not going to put it in the bank, I'd rather have a party to celebrate my child's Xth birthday, which will strengthen the family in another kind of way. That money going into a party will do all kinds of things for that family, for that individual, for that community, that putting money in the bank would never do. Again, it's looking at issues in an exciting new way—not looking at how you budget, put X% of your money in the bank. That approach doesn't necessarily enhance the family, although it might build up their bank account a little bit. It would never do to the family or bring in the kind of status and the kind of positiveness that spending the money on a ritual will bring to the family.

BERNICE GOODMAN: The notion that so-called special populations have strengths is wonderful, and I can tell you about them. I've worked with many, many lesbians and gay men, with women of color. Their capacity to survive in a hostile environment is testimony to their strength. In my work over the years, I have had much exposure to the special strengths of these populations. They are able to reject the negative images of themselves the hostile environment would have them believe and do not feel negative and guilty. They possess the capacity not only to survive but to function and be productive and to hold onto their own self-perceptions. There is a wonderful fabric of humanity, and we all need to recognize that difference is essential to its life, to the survival of life. Of course, not all members of these populations hold this image of themselves. But the number who do is remarkable. As lesbians and gays come out, their strength lies in not giving up the notion that their difference is special and wonderful. Those who are different should not try to be the same as others because it is essential to life that there be difference.

JOE HERNANDEZ: In my practice, cultural factors properly understood could strengthen practitioner relationships. For example, when first-generation Puerto Ricans are addressed by a professional, such as an MD or a lawyer, the Puerto Rican does not necessarily maintain eye contact. They may even look down. This behavior on their part does not mean that they are not listening. It means that they are showing respect to the professional because to them lowering one's eyes indicates respect for those in authority. Knowing what such lack of eye contact means avoids an erroneous assessment that they were inattentive.

In the Puerto Rican culture, the family is the basic strength. It is like the heart of the people—brothers, cousins, everyone. Even if everyone lives independently, in a time of crisis they come together emotionally. They put aside any differences they may have had and for the time of the problem work together. In a sense, because of their supportive attitude, a problem for a member of the family brings them back together.

TRACEY JOHNSON: I've worked with kids and with the retarded, two client groups who are usually not thought of as having any strengths, having little to contribute to solving their problems. Regardless of this, however, because they are people they bring their own worth and dignity to the helping relationship. Knowing this, and treating them accordingly, unleashes strengths.

ADELE WEINER: Over the years it seems that I have worked with two particular special populations: the elderly and Jewish Community Center work. My
work with the elderly has included being the director of social services of a
nursing home, a member of the board of dierectors of an agency specializing
in advocacy and ombudsman services for the elderly, widows' groups in Jewish
Community Centers, and currently, the coordinator of an Elder Abuse Awareness and Education Project. As a social work educator, I have taught a number
of gerontology courses. The elderly are a unique population to work with because they bring to the practice situation a lifetime of knowledge and experience. Often, in the nursing home, they were able to come up with creative and
workable solutions to practical everyday problems. For example, one resident
who had been a carpenter was able to help (verbally only) the maintenance staff
build a screen door that opened in both directions for wheelchairs. The director
of the advocacy and ombudsman agency was a retired woman in her seventies.
Following a flood in the community, she had applied for grants to set up this
agency to help the elderly and had continued to direct and find funding for the
agency for ten years.

I have been involved in Jewish communal services on a part-time basis since
the age of sixteen. Historically, this approach to services involves meeting the
needs of a special population in a traditional settlement house setting. Over the
years, the programs have shifted to meet community needs and serve a diversity
of clients. When I began working in the field, the focus on most children's and
adolescents' programs was on recreation and citizenship. Now day care, after-
school care, and programs to supplement school services (e.g., remedial reading, tutoring, career counseling) are offered. Family life education and groups
for singles, single parents, and widows offer support services to help people
cope with the normal problems of modern life.

Social workers must reconcile this difference (see Gardner, 1984; Hughes,
1983; and Steiner, Briggs and Gross, 1984, for professional implications). Again,
as with purpose and the human and social needs area of change, social workers
are called on to balance and take a stand on conflicting interests (Patti, 1984).
To maintain its professional integrity and to bring about a balance that favors
client need, social work purpose guides worker interactions within these practice contexts. Viewing the interaction among purpose, societies, and social welfare services from this perspective helps us to keep the essence of social work
in sight while taking a look at the latest practice developments. It is also a way
of continuing to "find" social work as it changes in the future.

As noted previously, diverse clients have many ways of functioning in their
social environments, and they hold many conceptions about identifying and
handling their problems. As social workers attempt to enhance the coping, developmental, and problem-solving capacities of the diverse people they work

with, the profession is enriched by the ideas diverse people bring to social work relationships.

Faced with valuing diversity in their practice, social workers could not help people grow if they were to use preconceived ideas about how people function and what they need. It is an idealization of clients to see them as verbal, cooperative people who bring a psychological orientation about problem causation to practice relationships and who are willing to work systematically on problems. This idealized view is being replaced in practice by the reality of clients who may be none of these. The belief that potential clients are too limited or problem-laden to deal with confronting the effect of structural issues on their lives is also being abandoned in practice.

On the other hand, the strengthening of social work's purpose to enhance people by valuing the strengths represented in their diverse manner of functioning is receiving only moderate support from society's current sense of its responsibility for social welfare services. In the past fifty years, the emergence of a so-called welfare state in the United States has meant the institution of programs and professions aimed at bettering the lives of all kinds of people who formerly were excluded from being helped in social welfare. As noted, from meeting the basic needs of the most impoverished, the concern of social welfare has expanded to include some of the psychological, emotional, physical, and other needs of diverse people.

Recently, however, there has been a backing away from this expanded sense of social responsibility. Budget cuts, excused by leaving only enough resources to help the very neediest, symbolize a different conception of which people and for what needs society should be responsible. The shift, it must be stressed, was in amount and type of commitment to social welfare. Social work faces a struggle in reestablishing the scope of social responsibility that once was represented by social welfare funding for services to enhance diverse people. (See Withorn, 1982, for approaches to deal with changes in welfare.)

Social work also has the purpose of linking diverse people with resources. During the past decade, cuts in federal social welfare have meant the loss of social services, opportunities, and resources. Although the lost resources have been made up partly by state, local, and private funds, the overall impact has been a significant reduction in some of the conventional resources relied on by social workers (Dobelstein, 1985; Zimmerman, 1983).

At the same time, the power of diversity offers an alternative way of viewing and using social resources. The diverse societies with which social workers intervene are seen as sources of information about resources, as well as a place to turn to in creating resources. Examples were noted in our preceding discussion. The type and nature of indigenous resources that exist among diverse groups, however, should become models of social welfare services for social workers to present to decision makers in social welfare. Social workers must guide the interaction among the diversity of needs and societal responsibility for funding social welfare services in line with professional purpose.

The strengths and resources found among diverse groups must be extended and strengthened through social welfare. In meeting its purpose of linking people to resources and creating just and effective delivery systems, the power of diversity becomes a model for changing services, not a substitute for the responsibility of society to provide extensive and fair social welfare structures.

Before the 1980s, efforts to change social welfare structures and other social institutions were promoted by several initiatives. The so-called war on poverty (the Johnson administration's efforts to make drastic reductions in the number of poor people by creating new social welfare structures and increasing social opportunities) was an effort at social change. Efforts at making public officials more accountable and monitoring the functioning of bureaucracies were also hallmarks of the past two decades. At the same time, professional associations, such as the National Association of Social Workers, became active in influencing public policymaking. The NASW and other lobbying groups attempted to get their policy positions regarding human rights and social services embodied in national and state legislation.

Except for social work policy efforts, the public has retreated from efforts to achieve social change and social justice. The past few years have seen a winding down of these efforts and public criticism of their usefulness. Social work, however, is commited to developing the social structures that help people with their social functioning to become more just and effective. This commitment necessitates the changing of social structures. To attain change, social workers must create alliances. Alliances are needed with people who are skilled in and committed to social change.

Groups of Blacks, Hispanics, women, lesbians and gays, and the elderly who have experienced varying degrees of success in change efforts could be such allies. Their leaders are potential allies in reestablishing the strong sense of social responsibility for social welfare and recreating efforts to make social structures more effective and humane.

"Societies" challenge social work practice to change and to be relevant to their needs. As social work responds, its purpose to enhance people is strengthened. Valuing diversity also leads to the identification of indigenous resources that become models for changing social service structures. Diverse peoples can become allies of social work in their efforts to create responsive services. Although evidence exists that the number of people and types of need covered by social welfare have increased over the past several decades, the resolve represented by these increases in services has weakened during the 1980s. Social workers are shaping a practice to respond to the twin inputs of social welfare and "societies."

SHAPING A PRACTICE TO DEAL WITH PEOPLE AND POLICY

From the interaction among purpose, diverse societies, and social welfare services, social workers shape contemporary practice that deals with people and policy. Several facets of such practice were noted in the preceding discussion.

From these we can conclude that social work practitioners have a responsibility to perform the following functions:

Identify and help practitioners use the strengths and resources of diverse populations in their problem assessment and interventions.

Educate the public to its responsibilities to provide resources for people's social functioning and to protect their ability to grow and develop in their interactions within social structures.

Develop a strong policy orientation.

As a collectivity, practitioners know a great deal about people, their problems in social functioning, and details about indigenous and social welfare resources that are useful in helping people. An individual practitioner, however, may know little about the needs of a new problem and be uncertain how to manage the changes it poses for people's social functioning. To bring together those who know and those who need to know, professional social work associations provide opportunities for professional growth and development in the form of workshops and conferences. It is through these vehicles that the latest developments in social work practice are shared.

For example, the relatively new problems of runaways and suicide among suburban teens pose new threats to the social functioning of some young people. In a similar fashion, the latest addictive drugs affect members of these same groups of young people. Social workers learn from other social workers how to deal with those problems.

Similarly, the development of contacts in a resource network helps social workers to know about and keep in touch with social welfare services and resources that are needed to deal with such problems. For social work practice to grow and develop and to shape itself in the context of diverse societies, all practitioners face the responsibility to learn about and teach their colleagues new practice developments and knowledge (Kravetz, 1982; Lowe and Cavanaugh, 1984).

Paralleling the responsibility to educate one another about the diverse people and problems they face, social workers must also educate members of the public about the strengths and the varying needs possessed by diverse people. In addition to maintaining professional purpose, social workers must educate and sensitize members of the public and their elected representatives about the responsibilities of society to provide the resources necessary to help people meet their needs to manage human and social change.

Relatively little is done in an organized fashion by the profession to promote social work's conception of social responsibility. The things that are done include scattered testimony at public hearings, the public relations and image-building efforts of the NASW, and those parts of the NASW Code of Ethics that ask members to work for the general welfare by educating and involving themselves and the public in policy development.

Policy can be thought of as guidelines or rules produced by a system, such as a nation, community, family, or individual, to allocate resources and rights to people. Examples of policies are found in federal and state laws, bureaucratic regulations, family rules, and the personal policy or practices of individuals (Pierce, 1984). Related to educating the public about a new, more inclusive sense of social responsibility is the need for social work practice to assume a strong policy orientation in practice. Public debates about funding and developing social welfare programs provide social work practitioners with an opportunity to publicize the profession's conception of social responsibility and its approach to helping. Policy is made at a number of levels and determines which people will have their needs met. Policy also determines the resources that people will receive and how they will be treated. Social workers influence the policymaking efforts of individual colleagues, small groups, local communities, welfare bureaucracies, and public legislators. Policy involvement is the clearest way for social work to control the direction of its interactions with the practice context of social welfare services. Hence, policy involvement is critical to shaping practice that is true to professional purpose.

Keeping abreast of a changing practice and keeping it focused on purpose maintains the integrity of the profession. Developing knowledge useful for social work practice and sharing it with other members of the profession is a key responsibility of all practitioners. Similarly, all social workers strive to instill within public debates the profession's sense of social responsibility and to keep change on the public agenda by being active in the policymaking processes that create social welfare programs. In this way, social workers shape their practice in response to purpose and help to create a society that is responsive to need, regardless of who is displaying the need.

PREPARING YOURSELF FOR THE CONTEXTS OF PRACTICE

Practice contexts shape, and are shaped by, social work. The two contexts affect practice significantly. The effect of diverse societies on problems, goals, services, and helping relationships interacts with professional purpose and interventions. The tension created by the input of diversity furthers change in practice and heightens the responsibility of practitioners not only to incorporate diversity into their practice but to use knowledge of it in their management of change.

Social work's responsibility to manage needed changes in society *and* in social welfare programs and services becomes a second powerful crucible that shapes social work practice. The interaction between social work practice and what social welfare programs and services offer to people become input to altering society's agenda for dealing with change. Society changes social welfare, and these changes affect social work practice. In turn, it is the responsibility of social work to change society and of social welfare to meet human need. This interaction is also a key element in the growth and development of the profession of social work.

Together, these two practice contexts confront you with challenges and opportunities. Staying on top of these contexts of practice calls for the following qualities:

Becoming sensitive to and developing knowledge about diverse people.
Developing skills in working along with diverse people.
Examining your sense of social responsibility.
Learning skills about and getting involved in efforts to change policy.
Developing lifelong learning habits.

Knowledge of diverse people has many sources. Think about how the group of which you are a member differs from other distinct groups, and reflect on how your treatment and status compare to those of the other groups. Also examine any employment or voluntary service experiences you have had with people whose group characteristics differ from yours.

Formal education can teach you about diversity. The psychology of women, the sociology and economics of poverty, and the social structure and anthropology of varying ethnic and cultural groups are examples of such knowledge (see Davenport and Davenport, 1984, and Kravetz, 1982, for two examples). In addition, however, you need to extend your learning beyond the policies and knowledge of traditional disciplines.

Contemporary disciplines are moving away from their earlier biases: the ethnocentrism of anthropologists; the status-quo, socioeconomic class bias of sociologists; and the sexism and homophobia of psychologists. In escaping from these biases, useful studies of diverse people have emerged. These later efforts guide the building of social work's knowledge about human diversity.

To begin your own process of learning about diversity, an examination of your attitudes about diverse groups of people is important (see DuBray, 1985, and Lockhart, 1981, for examples). It is a truism to say that everyone is racist, sexist, or homophobic, therefore, and that examination of your own "-isms" is useful. However, you need to go beyond that to examine the ways in which you believe members of these various groups are strong capable people (Fox, 1983; Weiner, 1988).

For example, in what ways could the Black family be a model for resource development? What are the contributions of lesbians and gay men to society? Can you list the economic and political leaders of several Hispanic cultures? If you can think of few or even no strengths of diverse groups, then you can begin to appreciate how a similar mind set has permeated the studies of social scientists about diverse people. Disciplines focus more on looking at difference as deviance or as fodder for acculturation than at the achievements of diverse people and how they accomplished them.

To avoid perpetuating the built-in negative mind set about diversity that accounts for too much of the existing research, begin to develop your own skills in learning about people who are different from you. Students should learn how to use skills that develop knowledge about diversity from the perspective of the different group itself. This requires applying skills in collecting social science data to the requirements for identifying and assessing social work problems. One example is the use of the ethnographic interview and of community guides to learn about groups that differ from your own (Green, 1984).

This approach calls for social workers to plan and conduct interviews with members of diverse groups in such a way that the social worker becomes the learner. Information about problem identification, members of the group, indigenous resources, and approaches to relating to professionals would first be learned by the social worker from the client. That information would become part of the data to use in developing a plan of action. In addition, the identification and use of community members who are familiar with the group would be sought out for learning purposes.

It is important to begin to examine your own beliefs about social responsibility and justice (Roff, Adams, and Klemmack, 1984). Do you believe that the institution of social welfare should meet needs universally and in an indepth fashion? Or do you believe that it is more appropriate to limit needs coverage and the people served? Do you believe that certain people have been mistreated in their interactions with the social structures that make up some of the subsystems in their social environment? Do you think that the rest of us should compensate them for those injustices? Do members of minorities of color, straight women, and lesbian women and gay men deserve special assistance in meeting their needs in the area of social functioning? Should everyone expect some form of assistance in sorting out the changes that affect their interactions within their social environment? What do you think people have to need or do to earn society's assistance?

Learning how to handle the policy involvement that is required of social workers is critical to dealing with the services context of practice. Merely knowing about conceptions of social responsibility and justice are not enough. Knowledge also has to be developed that will permit you to guide the development of social responsibility and the allocation of resources to social welfare services in line with the purposes of social work. Again, formal learning in sociology, economics, and political science is useful background. Specific knowledge about how policy is made by individuals, social organizations, all levels of government, and bureaucracies that regulate social welfare is also needed. Experiences observing or working in the policymaking of community funding groups or of legislative bodies provide valuable insights.

All the efforts discussed would lose value in practice if your knowledge of "societies" and services were to end with the acquisition of a degree in social work. You need to learn how to continue learning and how to teach others. The practice contexts of diverse societies and social welfare services become crucibles in which social workers shape a changing practice that adheres to professional purposes. To keep abreast of new knowledge about people, practice, and policy you need to develop lifelong learning skills and to make them part of your professional routine.

For Further Study

1. Discuss ways in which the purposes of social work conflict with aspects of the contemporary sense of social responsibility displayed in the United States.
2. Think about yourself in relation to the notion of "societies" covered in this chapter. With which groups are you most and least comfortable? Conduct library research on the group with which you are least comfortable to determine the power or strength to be derived from its differences.
3. Diagram the social functioning of two different groups within their own environments and ways in which problematic interactions between them and other systems are caused by the other systems.
4. Examine the history of different "societies" (such as Blacks or women) regarding how they have used their own resources and alliances with others to bring about change.
5. Conduct an interview with a social worker to determine in what ways the twin inputs of social welfare services and "societies" have shaped that person's practice.
6. Contact a local branch or a state chapter of NASW to determine what professional development opportunities it offered, what public education efforts it made, and what policy initiatives it undertook during the past year.
7. Discuss the ways in which the social workers of that branch or chapter address the issue of social responsibility.
8. Discuss ideas about special populations and their strengths that were added to your knowledge of these populations by the statements of the social workers.
9. Discuss the degree of social responsibility the author's evaluation of children's income maintenance programs offers in Document 7.1.

Glossary

SOCIAL RESPONSIBILITY.   Actions and programs offered by the public that indicate which people with what needs will be helped and what type of treatment they will be accorded in receiving help.

UNIVERSAL SERVICES.   The responsibility assumed by society for ensuring that everyone is helped in a given needs area.

STIGMA.   Efforts to mark by punitive or discriminatory actions certain recipients of public help.

"SOCIETIES." The complex interaction of factors of culture, ehtnicity, race, gender, sexual orientation, age, and socioeconomic class that create the diverse groups of people with whom social workers practice or those who define and/ or create helping programs and structures.

PROBLEMS. As seen by social workers, the problems that arise not from what people are but from changes in or inadequate interactions between people and some aspect of their social environment.

INDIGENOUS RESOURCES. Although not always recognized as such by non-group members, sources of strength or tangible assistance that can be found within different "societies" and that can provide the basis for new types of social welfare services.

IDEALIZED VIEW OF CLIENTS. The failure to see clients as coming from a variety of "societies," leading to a misperception that they are verbal, willing, and psychological in their orientation to problem causation.

WELFARE STATE. The institutionalization of a broad range of public social services to help diverse people with their needs.

WAR ON POVERTY. The Johnson administration's efforts to reduce the number of people in poverty by creating new service structures and helping methods.

PROFESSIONAL GROWTH AND DEVELOPMENT. Opportunities and activities used by individual practitioners to keep up with new problems and programs that affect the people with whom they work.

POLICY. Guidelines or rules produced by a range of systems, such as a nation, community, family, or individual that allocates resources and rights to people.

Bibliography

Arana, James. Unpublished poem, undated.

Berger, Robert L., and Ronald C. Federico. 2nd ed. *Human Behavior: A Perspective for the Helping Professions*. White Plains, NY: Longman, 1985.

Castex, Graciela. "The Role of the State in Defining 'Hispanic' Populations." New York State Social Work Education Association Conference, Syracuse, NY, November 14, 1986.

Council on Social Work Education. *Handbook of Accreditation Standards and Procedures*. Washington, D.C.: CSWE, revised 1988.

Davenport, J., III, and J. A. Davenport. "Theoretical Perspectives on Rural/Urban Differences." *Human Services in the Rural Environment* 9(1): 4–9, 1984.

DeHoyos, G., A. DeHoyos, and C. B. Anderson. "Sociocultural Dislocation: Beyond the Dual Perspective." *Social Work* 31(1): 61–67, 1986.

Dobelstein, A. W. "The Bifurcation of Social Work and Social Welfare: The Political Development of Social Services." *Urban and Social Change Review* 18(1): 9–12, 1985.

DuBray, W. H. "American Indian Values: Critical Factor in Casework." *Social Casework* 66(1): 30–37, 1985.

Fox, J. R. "Affective Learning in Racism Courses with an Experiential Component." *Journal of Education for Social Work* 19(3): 69–76, 1983.

Gardner, S. J. "The Future of Human Services: Building New Constituencies." *Public Welfare* 42(1): 38–41, 1984.

Green, James. *Cultural Awareness in the Human Services.* Englewood Cliffs, NJ: Prentice-Hall, 1984.

Gruger, M. L. "The Intractable Triangle: The Welfare State, Federalism and the Administrative Muddle." *Administration in Social Work* 7(3/4): 163–177, 1983.

Hidalgo, Hilda, Travis Peterson, and Natalie Woodman (Eds.). *Lesbian and Gay Issues: A Resource Manual for Social Workers.* Silver Spring, MD: National Association of Social Workers, 1985.

Hughes, J. J. "Organized Social Work and the Welfare State." *Social Thought* 9(2): 47–55, 1983.

Kravetz, D. "An Overview of Content on Women for the Social Work Curriculum." *Journal of Education for Social Work* 18(2): 47–49, 1982.

Lockart, B. "Historic Distrust and the Counseling of American Indians and Alaska Natives." *White Cloud Journal* 2(3): 31–34, 1981.

Lorenzo, M. K., and D. A. Adler. "Mental Health Services for Chinese in a Community Health Center." *Social Casework* 65(10): 600–614, 1984.

Lowe, G. R., and M. P. Cavanaugh. "Intercultural Contact as a Dimension of Social Work Curriculum and Education." *Social Development Issues* 8(3): 182–192, 1984.

McQuade, S. "Human Service Cutbacks and the Mental Health of the Poor." *Social Casework* 64(8): 497–499, 1983.

National Association of Social Workers. *Code of Ethics.* Washington, DC: 1980.

Norton, Dolores. *The Dual Perspective.* New York: Council on Social Work Education, 1978.

Olmstead, K. A. "The Influence of Minority Social Work Students on an Agency's Service Methods." *Social Work* 28(4): 308–312, 1983.

Patti, R. J. "Who Leads the Human Services? The Prospects for Social Work Leadership in an Age of Political Conservatism." *Administration in Social Work* 8(1): 17–29, 1984.

Pierce, Dean. *Policy for the Social Work Practitioner.* White Plains, NY: Longman, 1984.

Roff, L. L., J. P. Adams, and D. L. Klemmack. "Social Work Students' Willingness to Have Government Help the Poor." *Arete* 9(1): 9–20, 1984.

Sancier, B. (Ed.). "Building on the Strengths of Minority Groups." *Practice Digest* 5(3): 3–19, 1982.

Sancier, B. (Ed.). "Working with Gay and Lesbian Clients." *Practice Digest* 7(1): entire issue, 1984.

Schram, S. F., and J. P. Turbett. "The Welfare Explosion: Mass Society versus Social Control." *Social Services Review* 57(4): 614–625, 1983.

Stack, Carol. *All Our Kin: Strategies for Survival in a Black Community.* New York: Harper & Row, 1974.

Steiner, J. R., T. L. Briggs, and G. M. Gross. "Emerging Social Work Traditions, Profession Building, and Curriculum Policy Statements." *Journal of Education for Social Work* 20(1): 23–31, 1984.

Warshawsky, R. "Social Justice and the Welfare State." *Urban and Social Change Review* 18(1): 20–24, 1985.

Weiner, Adele. "Are BSW Students Sexist?" *Affilia* 3(1): 69–78, 1988.

Weiner, Adele. *Racist, Sexist, and Homophobic Attitudes of Undergraduate Social Work Students and the Effects on Client Assessments.* Unpublished Doctoral Dissertation, New Brunswick, NJ: Rutgers University, 1988.

Wilson, P. A. "Towards More Effective Intervention in Natural Helping Networks." *Social Work in Health Care* 9(2): 81–88, 1983.

Withorn, A. "Beyond Realism: Fighting for Human Services in the Eighties." *Catalyst* 4(2): 21–37, 1982.

Zimmerman, S. L. "The Reconstructed Welfare State and the Fate of Family Policy." *Social Casework* 64(8): 459–465, 1983.

PART III

Social Workers in Action

PART OVERVIEW

In the previous sections we have looked for the connections of social work and society. Our search focused on exploring professional purpose, the human and social need to manage the changes that affect people's social functioning, and "societies" and services as contexts for practice.

The area of need served by social workers was defined as dealing with managing the change that takes place in one or more of the interactions between a human system and one of the subsystems that makes up that person's social environment. These changes, whether they are needed or have occurred unexpectedly, create problematic social functioning for people.

Purpose was used to define social work as enhancing people, linking them with social resources, and making the operations of structures more just. Along with purpose, the human and social need to manage the changes that affect people's social functioning serve as the bases for developing a model of social work practice. The model covers the place of values, knowledge, and skills in carrying out the generalist problem-solving method, which takes place in a series of practice relationships that are akin to limited partnerships.

Practice was discussed as occurring in the contexts of "societies" and services. The interaction among purpose, diverse societies, and welfare services and resources creates a contemporary and relevant practice. Practice is shaped by social workers, according to professional purpose, within these two contexts.

We have reached our goal of developing ways to find social work and its connections to society. Another goal of the book has been to engage you in an active examination of your response to what we have presented about social work. In applying the ways we developed for finding social work, Part III offers practice illustrations and asks readers to respond to how they would feel carrying out the actions of these social workers.

The first chapter in this part explores more fully how social workers have created a contemporary practice in a relevant profession by confronting significant changes in people's lives and in policy. The ways that purpose guides practice in relation to people's resources and to structural change are explored.

As noted in Chapter 1, the material obtained in interviews with social work practitioners is used differently in this part. Two entire chapters are based on that material. The final two chapters in this part present the practice experiences of several active social workers. This material has been developed from interviews with these workers. The illustrations in these two chapters cover a range of practice fields, resources, and client populations. These stories of the activities of social workers are organized according to purpose, people, problems, and policy.

CHAPTER EIGHT

Practice Activities: Managing Change in People, Policy, and the Profession

A memo to a higher office
Open letter to the powers that be
To a god, a king, a head of state
A captain of industry
To the movers and the shakers—
Can't everybody see?

It ought to be second nature—
I mean, the places where we live!
Let's talk about this sensibly—
We're not insensitive
I know progress has no patience—
But something's got to give.

***

I'd like some changes.
But you don't have the time
We can't go on thinking
It's a victimless crime.

***

Folks have got to make choices—
And choices got to have voices
Folks are basically decent
Conventional wisdom would say.
Well, we read about
The exceptions
In the papers every day.

***

It's hard to take the world
The way that it came
Too many rapids
Keep us sweeping along
Too many captains
Keep on steering us wrong
It's hard to take the heat—
It's hard to lay blame
To fight the fire—
While we're
Feeding the flames.

from SECOND NATURE
by Neil Peart

CHAPTER OVERVIEW

This chapter uses all the ideas about generalist social work that have been developed in our search for the profession's connections to society. These ideas are used to organize a description of the following practice activities:

Working directly with people and linking them to resources.
Creating resource system policy and procedures.
Developing the profession.

As social workers help people and society manage the changes that affect the social functioning of people, at the same time they also manage the effect of change on their own profession as changes are created by the profession's interaction with societies and services.

These practice activities are summarized according to professional purpose, which calls for activities to strengthen people's social functioning abilities, to develop and use social resources, and to manage and structure change in social welfare. Practice activities include direct interventions with clients and indirect work in the management and development of social services. It also involves developing appropriate knowledge of people and policy for use by individual practitioners in their growth and development and to guide the ongoing development of the profession itself. This latter area of practice activity is implicit in social work's professional purposes.

In this chapter, a way of organizing illustrations of how social workers help to manage change in people's lives, in society, and in their profession is introduced. The sections of the chapter that cover interventions used by social workers to prepare people to confront changes in their lives, to use resource systems, and to help society manage and change social welfare structures are illustrated with contemporary case situations. Using these illustrations, connections among the various generalist interventions are highlighted. Moreover, the effects of people, problems, and policy on developing the profession and its practitioners is discussed along with the practice activities used in doing so.

PRACTICE ACTIVITIES TO HELP PEOPLE, MAKE POLICY, AND DEVELOP THE PROFESSION

You know how social work is connected to society. You know some of the diverse societies served by social work and what they face from society's response to helping with people's social functioning. It remains to discuss and illustrate practice activities more fully. The activities of social work practitioners include more than direct or indirect involvement with client situations. Helping clients is served also by the ongoing growth of individual practitioners and the development of the profession. Critical social work activities include interventions to help clients, actions to change policy, and approaches to develop practitioners and the profession (Pierce, 1984; Schorr, 1985).

We have explored the social work profession's sense of meeting human and social need, especially the need to deal with change. The profession's purpose in helping people and society has been spelled out. Using the language of need, the purposes of social work can be stated as follows:

Helping people to develop the knowledge and skills to handle changes in their lives.
Obtaining the supports people need to meet change.
Guiding change and determining its directions in social structures.

As we examine practice activities, we use interventions related to each of these purposes to illustrate direct and indirect work with clients and social structures.

We have also said that contemporary practice is shaped in the twin contexts, or crucibles, of "societies" and "services," our shorthand for the diverse people with whom social workers deal and the entire range of social welfare services, opportunities, and social resources practitioners use in helping people to manage changes in their lives. Each of the contexts is like a crucible, a hard test or trial. The test or trial for social work comes in maintaining the integrity of its professional purpose in light of emerging problems and specific needs of people and in face of an ever-changing sense of responsibility that is displayed in society's policy about how it will help people deal with their problematic social functioning. Social workers shape contemporary practice by developing themselves and the profession. Illustrations of these activities complete the chapter's survey of what social workers do in practice.

Social workers balance all these activities in their practice by doing the following:

Managing people's changing problems involving their social functioning.
Strengthening social responsibility.
Guiding and changing service structures.
Developing and maintaining their profession.

People need to manage change in their social functioning. Society needs to manage change to make a better response to human need. Social workers help to manage both of these changes as well as needed changes in themselves as practitioners and in their own profession. Social workers use similar problem-solving steps in each area of practice with:

People.
Policy.
Profession.

In our discussion of a model of practice, we explored how knowledge is used to assess problematic social functioning in terms of changes in system interaction. A number of subsystems compose the social environment of a given human system, whether an individual, small group, family, or community. In a given human system some, all, or none of its interactions with its subsystems may be affected by change. Any change, however, leads to diminished or disrupted social functioning among all of the subsystems.

When people's social functioning becomes inadequate because of a change in the interaction between them and one or more of the subsystems in their social environment, then social workers step in to intervene. An assessment of the problem by the social worker leads to the development and implementation of intervention plans.

In our discussion, interventions are grouped according to purpose. As social workers apply the problem-solving approach in their practice, interventions are selected, or created, and used according to people, problem, need, and goal. It is useful, however, to organize our discussion of interventions according to the professional purpose they serve.

Practice activities that are related to policymaking use a similar problem-solving approach. Policy-related interventions are based on identifying an issue or problem, selecting a policy change goal, and devising a plan to get the system in control of needed resources to allocate them to a policy of concern (Pierce, 1984). Moreover, problem solving is used in the self-assessment and professional growth and development activities of individual practitioners.

We consider practice illustrations by focusing on the following:

A variety of interactions between human systems and subsystems in their social environment.

Problems people might have in these interactions that create inadequate social functioning.

Knowledge used in problem solving to assess and develop interventions to deal with these problems.

Interventions that might be used.

In addition, the illustrations lead to a statement of the people and policy issues contained in them and how social workers address them to develop themselves and their profession. These activities include those that promote practitioner growth and development of the profession.

PREPARING PEOPLE TO CONFRONT CHANGES IN THEIR LIVES

As noted in our preceding discussion of direct client work, certain activities are useful in enhancing the ability of people to function in their social environment.

Teaching new behaviors, providing individualized support, developing support groups, confronting, and role playing are a few interventions used to enhance people's social functioning. These interventions are used to achieve the goals of promoting optimum growth and development of people, helping them face and handle stresses associated with changes in their lives, developing new skills, or restoring formerly adequate abilities to cope and solve problems. Although these goals are quite general in nature, they reflect some of the more specific goals that grow out of the assessing and planning stages of the problem-solving process used by generalist practitioners in direct client work. Direct work with people is involved in administration, planning, or community work. The people involved, however, are less likely to be clients.

Direct work takes place with human systems of various sizes, including individuals, families, and small groups. Similar types of interventions are used to enhance these different-sized human systems. For example, consider a case situation in which an adolescent parent needs to grow and develop because of a lack of sufficient parenting skills. We cculd diagram the interaction as shown in Figure 8.1. The social functioning of this person is problematic due to the inadequate interactions between parent and child, as well as development needs within the parent. The social worker's assessment is based on knowledge of developmental psychology and of social parenting role theory. Part of the worker's assessment includes human diversity factors that are relevant to the parenting of the adolescent. The intervention plan may include being supportive through individual counseling or group sessions. In addition, intervention activities to teach the client the required new behaviors are developed. The goal in this case is to promote the growth and development of the parent, providing the client with required skills. At the same time, necessary supportive services are obtained for the client. (Obtaining these is covered in the upcoming discussion of how social workers use resource systems.)

An example of how inadequate social functioning is caused by changes in the interaction between the client and another human system is an elderly person who faces the death of a spouse. This interaction would appear as shown in Figure 8.2. Based on an assessment of the strengths and needs of the elderly

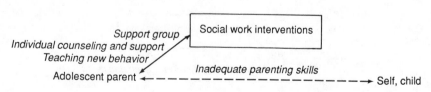

Figure 8.1

person and the worker's knowledge of developmental psychology, ego psychology, and issues of death and dying, the goal may be to help the client face the consequences of losing a relationship with a loved one. Depending on the worker's assessment, actions may be to confront the client or use individual or group support. Moreover, new behaviors would have to be developed through a teaching intervention.

Changes in the interaction between a human system and a social system is exemplified by the breakdown of a family, leading to an adolescent's running away. Our perspective in this case situation is the runaway, and our goal is to restore the family system, which has been vastly changed by the adolescent's behavior. The situation can be seen in Figure 8.3. Focusing on enhancing the adolescent, interventions may include a family group counseling session, role playing to learn new life skills, and developing peer supports.

An example of problematic interactions between a human system and a social welfare structure involving a new client, who lacks the skills to negotiate a welfare agency can appear (see Figure 8.4). The worker can develop interventions to teach new behaviors or to strengthen the client in a support group. The assessment is based on knowledge of organizational theory, bureaucracies, and social welfare resources, as well as discriminatory factors involved in the treatment of certain clients in the delivery of services.

Problematic interactions between an adolescent lesbian and the majority "straight" cultural system results in an inadequate self-image and lack of skills in interpersonal relationships for the adolescent. Knowledge of developmental psychology, human diversity, and the effects of homophobic oppression are used in the worker's assessment. Teaching new behavior, individual support and counseling, support groups, and role playing are possible social work interventions. The situation can be shown in Figure 8.5.

Each of these case illustrations is incomplete. We have discussed only practice activities used by social workers in enhancing people's abilities. Part of assessment focuses on factors in the people themselves, in their growth and development patterns, their strengths, and their personal needs that can be altered or used to help them better face their problematic social functioning. In addition, and coincidental with direct practice activities to enhance people in

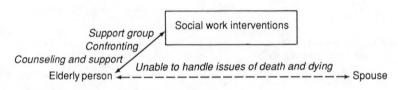

Figure 8.2

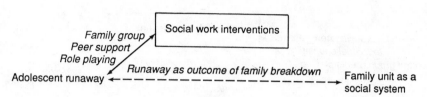

Figure 8.3

the worker-client relationship, another set of practice activities is performed. As indicated in the foregoing illustrated cases, these activities are associated with using resource systems.

USING RESOURCE SYSTEMS

In some of the preceding case situations, we noted that the workers may also have to connect clients to needed resources. Resources include all kinds of social welfare services used by people in meeting their needs. (See Dobelstein's discussion, 1985, about social work's separation from welfare resources.) Many of these resources were introduced or discussed briefly in our coverage of social welfare and of services. Resources, in addition to the skills and abilities of the social worker, include the following:

Services of other professionals, such as medical doctors, lawyers, nurses, therapists.
Opportunities for specialized education or training.
Shelters for the homeless or for abused women.
Programs that provide nutritional services.
Peer counseling and support groups.
Indigenous resources.
Financial assistance programs.

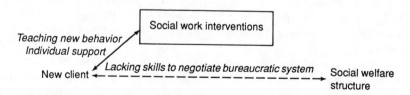

Figure 8.4

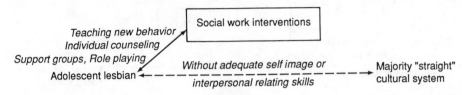

Figure 8.5

Community centers.
Senior services.
Family service agencies.

In their professional practice, social workers carry out a number of activities that connect people to such resources and deliver on that part of professional purpose. As will be discussed later, connecting people to resource systems leads to political and social action. Of course, the social worker does not know what resources are needed by the client until after an assessment of the situation. Before work with clients, as an ongoing part of practice, workers will have developed the following:

Resource files.
Networks and agency contacts.
Information about resources.
Skills in referral and follow-up.

In other words, some of the practice activities that are used in linking people with resources involve a great deal of preparation on the part of the worker before client contact. Knowledge about resources, development of useful contacts in other resource systems, and refining support and referral skills are basic to the effective use of resources in practice.

Consider the case illustrations we used earlier. In each instance, we could diagram additional practice activities involved in linking these clients to needed resources (see Figure 8.6).

In obtaining resources, social work intervention activities replace or supplement the inadequate interactions of the human system within its social environment. Sometimes, through means of the intervention, the worker connects the client to a resource system that lies outside the existing subsystems of the client's social environment. Several of our case illustrations indicate such an occurrence.

If necessary, the adolescent parent may have to be connected to a parenting group outside the worker's agency. The parent may also require additional social resources such as shelter and financial assistance. The practitioner may be involved in activities to coordinate the case, make referrals, follow up on referrals, and identify additional needed resources to maintain adequate social functioning.

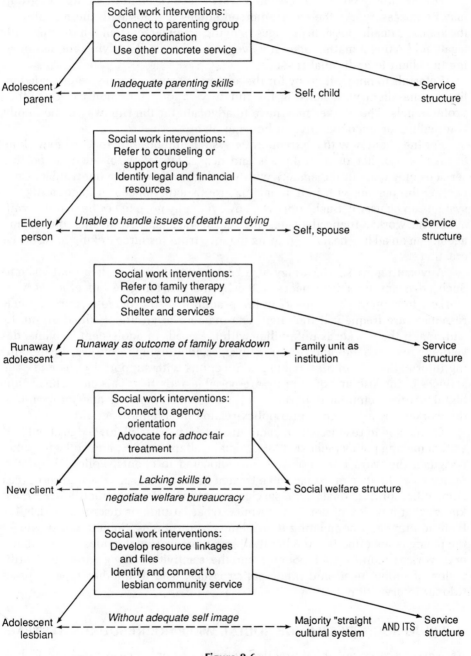

Figure 8.6

For the elderly person, a referral to a skilled counselor or to a support group may be necessary. As the elderly person comes to grips with the meaning of the spouse's death, possible changes in living arrangements and in dealing with legal and financial matters may involve the worker in identifying and connecting the client to additional resources.

Referrals to family therapy for the adolescent runaway may be preceded by linking the client with housing for runaways and/or the counseling of other professionals. The worker may have to advocate for the runaway if the family is unwilling or uncooperative in housing plans.

For the client new to a bureaucratic system and needing to learn new skills to take care of her or his interests and needs, few of the needed supportive services may exist in the agency with which the client is having trouble. Connecting the person with individuals or groups experienced in negotiating the system can be useful. Such supports, however, may not exist or be readily available. The worker then advocates for the needed help from the troublesome agency on an ad hoc basis, beginning to move from resource linking to resource creating.

Advocating for services may also be necessary for the adolescent lesbian. Such advocacy would be necessitated by the unwillingness of other service workers to support the requests of the practitioner to provide resources. Such responses are frequent if the client is a member of an undervalued group. In addition, if the worker is unfamiliar with the needs of adolescent lesbians, developing resource files and resource linkages, identifying resources, and obtaining information about and making connections with support groups and peer services in the lesbian community are possible activities. This case illustration highlights the potential importance of indigenous resources and implies how the worker begins to move into policy-related intervention activities.

Connected to resource-using activities is the worker's knowledge about and skill in making policy (Schorr, 1985). Social welfare, agency, and collegial policies guide the ways that resources are allocated to clients. Policy also determines how clients can expect to be treated in receiving services and resources from other professionals and service structures. Hence, practitioners must know what a policy of concern permits, what latitude or discretion exists for them to pursue in connecting their clients to resources. Sometimes, however, the policy is not effective in what it offers or fair in how it guides service delivery. Workers monitor such policies, and these activities, along with the identification of unmet need and other policy issues, lead to another type of practitioner intervention.

HELPING SOCIETY CHANGE SOCIAL WELFARE RESOURCE SYSTEMS

As workers carry out their practice activities to enhance people and to link them with needed resources, they accumulate knowledge about the needs of the people they serve, the existence or availability of resoures to help them, and the effectiveness and fairness of the structures that deliver resources and services to their clients. The third type of interventions includes practice activities to change systems and create policy to serve a group or number of clients who are in need of the same resource or policy change (see Document 8.1).

DOCUMENT 8.1

Social Policy Center Is Focus of Fundraising

NASW has begun a campaign to raise $10 million to fund a National Center for Social Policy and Practice and associated programs, as a result of action at the January board meeting. The center will collect, analyze, and disseminate information derived from social workers' firsthand experience.

"There have been, in the evolution of social work, two streams that have not been very well related," says Bert Beck who heads the campaign's steering committee. "One of them has been concerned with helping individuals and families . . . and the other is concerned with attacking social causes of social despair." The center, he continues, will tie these two streams together by assisting NASW members and community decision makers in dealing more effectively in the arena where policies control the resources made available to clients. "An informed membership will make data available. This will be collated, analyzed, and used by policy makers and legislators at national, state, and local levels."

The center will make a "systematic effort to rigorously analyze practice data and use it to impact on social policy," Beck says. "In the past, NASW policy has been dimly related to everyday practice. In the future, NASW and others interested in policy will have access to the learning that comes from the day-to-day experience of social workers."

Although the campaign will be formally kicked off this spring, some NASW leaders have already made substantial contributions, including several ranging from $5,000 to $10,000. The campaign will request contributions from NASW leaders, members, and staff, social work professionals and concerned citizens, and will seek grants from foundations and corporations as well.

Using data collected from practitioners, the center will determine how existing social policy is affecting clients. It will analyze social policy proposals for effectiveness. It will influence social policy by arming federal, state, and local decision makers with the information. And the center will develop alternative policy proposals to be introduced at federal, state, and local levels.

The center will also create and manage a clearinghouse of information for NASW members, chapters, collaborating practice organizations, and subscribers. It will give the media selected analyses, position papers, evaluations, and studies, for maximum exposure.

"I've spent decades . . . asking for the profession to become a powerful force, not in the political arena in the sense of supporting candidates . . . but . . . in its knowledge and its ability to provide analysis on pivotal social issues," says Daniel Thursz, a member of the campaign steering committee and executive vice-president of B'nai B'rith. "That expert knowledge of the profession—which no one else has, really—has to be delivered in the Washington systems in an effective and powerful way."

Organizers say the center should be seen as an instrument through which practice and social policy are linked to produce change in both. They say it should be a vehicle for a new image for social workers as deliverers of needed, accurate, reliable, and useful information to the policy processes of the nation.

"NASW needs a way to gather and develop information from the practice knowledge of its members and from any other sources in order to then develop recommendations for policy and advocacy work," says Gail Champlin, the NASW board member who heads the National Center for Social Policy and Practice Task Force. "One problem has been that we have had no good way to gather the data except on an ad hoc basis, and this center will provide the means to do it more systematically and effectively."

One observer saw the center as a way for "social workers to get credit for what they know and do."

The participation of social workers is one of the elements crucial to the center's success.

"We have to enlist not . . . just the leaders, not just the deans and the people who run programs, but the ordinary social workers, in supplying the information, and the (center's) research people (will) see how to get at this systematically and see what conclusions you can draw," Beck says.

Corinne Wolfe, a New Mexico social work activist and member of the steering committee, agrees: "I think we have to have more than just a single practitioner's view of something."

Besides gathering data for social policy analysis, the center will also make the information available to social workers. "I would tell members that if they're going to be successful . . . there ought to be a place where they can get information quickly, where they can exchange information, and where they can find out what new ways of doing things might work, rather than just doing it on their own, and it should be a national source of information," Wolfe says.

"We often sit and we wring our hands in our local NASW chapters of communities, saying, 'Nothing is happening. The world is falling on our heads,'" says Thursz. "Here's an opportunity for us, collectively . . . to know that we are participating in a very clear and important function. Secondly, . . . hopefully the center will influence social policy and that, in turn, will result . . . in a better quality of life for the people we care about, better services, and an opportunity for the profession to use itself appropriately and in a meaningful way in the service of the people.''

NASW Director Mark Battle says the center ''is not an academic think tank. It is not a theoretical research organization aimed at competing for grants with universities.''

He says the center would be unique as the only national institution devoted to using the substance and data of social work practice to inform social policy, as well as to give social work practitioners access to the national data that their colleagues have collected, analyzed, and prepared for use.

The center will eventually offer fellowships and internships to social work practitioners, managers, researchers, educators, and students in a variety of special fields.

The *NEWS* will carry a feature in a forthcoming issue giving details about the center and the campaign's goals.

(SOURCE: Copyright 1987, National Association of Social Workers, Inc. Reprinted with permission from ''Social Policy Center is Focus of Fundraising,'' Vol. 32, No. 4.)

In reconsidering our case illustrations of enhancing people and linking them to resources, the following *groups of clients* become the focus of our policy-related practice activities:

Adolescent parents in a given state.
All elderly people in a given service region.
All potential runaways in the United States.
All new clients served by a given agency.
All adolescent lesbians of a particular city.

Policy-making activities are aimed at getting a particular social structure that has needed funds or other resources to allocate them to the services sought by the worker. To do so may call for modifying or creating policies in that particular social structure.

The intervention plans developed by workers include activities appropriate to influencing the policy-making process of that structure. Such activities appear in Figure 8.7. The interventions and the assessment and planning that precede them, are of a slightly different character from other practitioner activities. This is so because the social work assessment, in part, looks for the cause of the problem in the environmental structures with which the human system interacts while obtaining resources to use in overcoming problematic social functioning.

For example, many adolescents who face parenting responsibilities may not have received the needed socialization in their own families or schools, or the

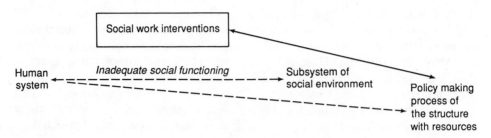

Figure 8.7

pregnancy may have made it too late for the expected development of parenting skills to occur. Hence, another structure of society must become responsible for helping to provide resources for such parents. The structure with the needed resources becomes the focus of the worker's interventions.

Although family units or educational institutions could receive the needed resources and pass them on to our group of clients, a special program or service may have to be established. The new structure would be provided through the institution of social welfare. Helping society to create and change social welfare structures occurs when social workers carry out policy-related practice activities.

In each of our previous examples, all the knowledge sources used by the workers in their assessments and planning would also apply to assessing the needs of the entire group of affected clients. In addition, knowledge of bureaucratic operations, organizational theory, social problems, social welfare resources, social psychology, organizing, planning, and policymaking would be used in making an assessment and planning an intervention. This knowledge would be used to develop the needed program or service, decide which policy-making group to approach about getting it adopted, and plan the policy-related intervention to encourage policymakers to adopt it. In our case illustrations, as re-stated to apply to the entire group of affected clients, policy-related interventions appear in Figure 8.8.

If a social worker wanted to help all the adolescents in a state by developing resources for them, then he or she could adopt an intervention plan to get state legislation passed to provide for a parenting skills program along with other needed social services. Drafting the legislation, possibly through the state chapter of the National Association of Social Workers, would be one intervention approach. Another might be to lobby, testify, or influence legislators on behalf of legislation that would create such services.

Or a social worker might aim at influencing a regulatory welfare bureaucracy responsible for issuing guidelines regulating the services available to the elderly. The sought-out regulation would mandate that education about issues of death and dying be provided at all senior centers receiving funding from the welfare bureaucracy.

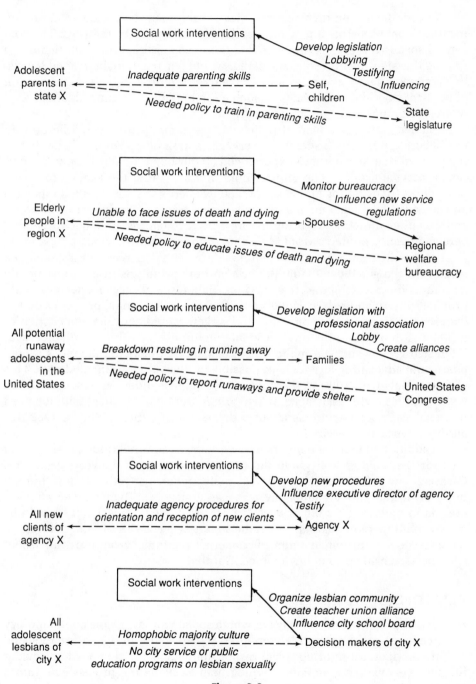

Figure 8.8

A third illustration involves activities to create legislation aimed at providing a national reporting and shelter system for adolescent runaways. The concerned social workers, having assessed the needs of this group of clients and finding this significant resource lacking, would engage in lobbying and legislative activities. These activities might take the form of working for the election of political candidates favorable to such a social policy, creating alliances with interested groups, and influencing legislative staffs.

Practice activities aimed at policymaking in an agency would be used in our illustration in which social workers take action on behalf of all clients facing problems similar to those experienced by our client who was new to a particular service agency. The effort would aim at getting the agency to create procedures for orienting and welcoming new clients in a way that is supportive and considerate of what novice clients face in the agency. Influencing the board and executive director and bringing pressure through resource network members and agency contacts would be some of the worker activities.

For the situation where the client system is all the adolescent lesbians in a given city, the goal is to create policies and opportunities in appropriate city structures to provide supportive services. Public social service agencies could provide support and public schools could provide educational programs on lesbian sexuality and public homophobia. Workers would consider such activities as helping to organize the city's lesbian community, creating an alliance with interested groups such as public school teachers, influencing the city's school board, and advocating as widely as possible for the entire group of clients. This example deals with a group that may have established its own resources or be willing to do so with assistance. It also brings workers in contact with the need to alter basic social attitudes about a diverse group. (See Withorn, 1982, for alternate types of interventions.)

In addition to making policy, some workers, as administrators, manage and monitor the policies that guide the operation of service delivery structures. Creating new policy may make service delivery more effective or just, but administering the policy adequately also has a sizable influence. The changes created in policy by the administration of service delivery agencies would be more evolutionary in character than the adversarial activities found in bringing policymakers in line with a policy of concern. Creating new administrative constituencies is critical to policy change (Gardner, 1984).

DEVELOPING THE PROFESSION

We have already introduced ways in which social workers shape contemporary practice by responding to the diversity of societies and to the nature of social welfare services. Monitoring social responsibility and creating needed services involves policymaking activities, which help to shape the profession's future (Patti, 1984; Hughes, 1983). We noted how important to practice is keeping abreast of knowledge developed by other workers in helping new client populations and strengthening society's sense of responsibility for helping with people's social functioning. Social workers need to educate themselves and members of the public (Brawley, 1983).

To shape practice and to shape themselves as practitioners, social workers engage in practice activities that are not easily subsumed under the categories of helping interventions, direct or indirect practice, or policy-related activities. These activities involve the following issues.

Practitioner growth and development.
Professional association involvement.
Knowledge development.

Such activities keep practice true to the purpose of social work by developing responses to the input of societies and services and by developing the profession itself (Steiner, Briggs, and Gross, 1984). These activities include the following:

Self-assessment.
Consulting with, supervising, and teaching colleagues.
Professional association involvement, including holding office.

Social workers employ self-assessment to examine how effective their practice is and how relevant it is to the needs of their clients. Such examinations reveal what additional knowledge and skills the worker should learn. Self-assessment is akin to the problem-solving process used in direct work with clients or in analyzing and developing a policy of concern. The goal of the data collection and assessment is to evaluate the practice of a given social worker. The needed skills or knowledge can be learned in workshops, as introduced in a preceding discussion. Many workers faced with an emerging social problem, such as adolescent runaways, or one that involves oppression and inadequate knowledge development, such as lesbian sexuality, need to engage in a professional self-assessment of their practice knowledge and attitudes.

Some social workers engage in supervising other social workers. Such activities do not involve clients directly, but these activities are critical to the delivery of professional services and to the growth and development of social work. Other social workers provide consultation to colleagues or agencies, instructing them on better ways to perform their jobs and deliver services. Consultation also gives direction to the development of the profession.

Another activity involved in practitioner growth and development and the enhancement of the profession is developing new knowledge. We indicated earlier that information about new client populations, their needs, and available services was often shared with colleagues and contributes to the development of the profession. Knowledge is also developed in a more systematic fashion by workers who engage in research activities.

Some social workers are research specialists, whereas others apply research skills in the development of policy and programs. All social workers learn research and can apply it to the systematic development of knowledge. Presenting the knowledge so gained at conferences, workshops, and in professional journals is another activity involved in developing social work knowledge (Basom, Iacono-Harris, and Kraybill, 1982).

In our case illustrations, knowledge of the various client populations and their needs is essential. Our examples include knowledge about adolescent pregnancy and parenting, elderly people facing death, adolescent runaways, bureaucratic treatment of new clients, and lesbian sexuality and self-image. In addition, policymakers would have to be helped to understand the special needs of the teenage parent, runaway, and adolescent lesbian. Social workers guide the profession's response to these issues by developing social work knowledge about them.

Social workers are also involved in the activities of the professional associations mentioned in our discussion of social work as a profession. These activities include working on committees and planning workshops, developing policy stances and organizing lobbying activities, campaigning in support of social work political positions and candidates, and serving as officers in the association. Involvement can be at the local, chapter, or national level. Such involvement helps to develop the profession through the power of the association's membership. Workers also mobilize professional associations to take action on the social justice issues of family problems, welfare bureaucratic treatment of clients, and rights of minorities.

This chapter has explored some of the typical activities of social workers. Those who choose to become social work practitioners are motivated by wanting to help people. We have outlined ways social workers go about the business of helping, and we have discussed several types of interventions in addition to those used in direct work with clients.

Social workers employ a range of interventions to help clients directly and indirectly. They enhance people's abilities to function adequately in their social environments, and they develop skills in finding out about resources, managing information about them, and linking people to them.

Social workers also engage in activities to use and make policy. Sometimes their clients are involved in these activities; at other times social workers ally themselves with other interested parties. Social workers focus on creating policies that will change systems to make them more effective in service delivery and fair in their treatment of clients.

In addition, social workers develop their own practice abilities and the entire profession to serve their clients better. Social workers use a range of activities to shape a contemporary practice in a relevant profession. We noted that professional self-assessment is one activity used in practitioner growth and development. Some of the questions that were posed in earlier chapters for your consideration and the intent of those questions are similar to an assessment by a practitioner.

How do you see yourself in relation to these practice activities? Which do you think you would most like? Had you thought about learning about resources and managing this information for the benefit of clients? If not, do you think you would enjoy such activities? What about policy involvement? It has been stressed throughout this text that social change and policymaking are critical to meeting professional purpose and to maintaining professional integrity. Do you believe you would like to learn how to influence others? Would you like to try to do so? Would you like to write a proposal or testify in favor of a piece of legislation? Would you be interested in attempting to convince members of an agency's policymaking process to support the policy you want? What about developing knowledge? Do you like to research and write? Would you like to teach colleagues your new ideas about practice? And what about self-assessment? How introspective are you? Can you evaluate and guide your own behavior?

For Further Study

1. Identify as many resources as possible offered by your community for a given client population. Add to this list indigenous resources from the "societies" of the client population. Also discuss which workers would have to create a network in order for effective worker-client use of these resources.
2. Discuss how generalist practice interventions in direct client work to strengthen people, in work with resource systems, and in actions to develop or modify policies and procedures are connected.
3. Explore how sources of knowledge about human behavior apply in practice situations that aim to strengthen poeple, link them to resources, and create services or change policy.
4. In what ways are developing the profession and promoting the growth of individual practitioners related to the purposes of social work?
5. Do a self-assessment of your knowledge, skills, and experiences that will help you in your social work career.

Bibliography

Basom, R. E., D. A. Iacono-Harris, and D. B. Kraybill. "Statistically Speaking: Social Work Students Are Significant." *Journal of Education for Social Work* 18(2): 20–26, 1982.

Brawley, E. A. "Alternative Routes to Public Recognition for Social Work." *Arete* 8(2): 1–9, 1983.

Brownstein, C. D. "The Social Work Educator: Social Worker and Professor?" *Social Service Review* 59(3): 496–504, 1985.

Dobelstein, A. W. "The Bifurcation of Social Work and Social Welfare: The Political Development of Social Services." *Urban and Social Change Review* 18(1): 9–12, 1985.

Gardner, S. L. "The Future of Human Services: Building New Constituencies." *Public Welfare* 42(1): 38–41, 1984.

Hughes, J. J. "Organized Social Work and the Welfare State." *Social Thought,* 9(2): 47–55, 1983.

Patti, R. J. "Who Leads the Human Services? The Prospects for Social Work Leadership in an Age of Political Conservatism." *Administration in Social Work* 8(1): 17–29, 1984.

Peart, "Second Nature," from the album *Hold Your Fire,* by Rush, Polygram Records, 1987.

Pierce, Dean. *Policy for the Social Work Practitioner.* White Plains, NY: Longman, 1984.

Schorr, A. L. "Professional Practice As Policy." *Social Service Review* 59(2): 178–196, 1985.

Steiner, J. R., T. L. Briggs, and G. M. Gross. "Emerging Social Work Traditions, Profession Building, and Curriculum Policy Statements." *Journal of Education for Social Work,* 20(1): 23–31, 1984.

Withorn, A. "Beyond Realism: Fighting for Human Services in the Eighties." *Catalyst* 4(2): 21–37, 1982.

CHAPTER NINE

Helping People Deal with Change and Managing the Resources They Need

The social worker should serve clients with . . . maximum application of professional skill and competence. . . .

The social worker should act to ensure that all persons have access to the resources, services, and opportunities which they require. . . .

NASW Code of Ethics (1980)

CHAPTER OVERVIEW

The illustrations in this and in the following chapter are drawn from the careers of the social workers whose words have appeared in the interviews called "I Am a Social Worker" in the preceding chapters. Although careers of these workers, as well as their lives, represent diversity, these illustrations cannot perfectly represent the entire range of people, problems, and policies involved in social work practice. These illustrations, however, offer insight into what being a social worker entails and what it means to several people who are practicing social workers.

The examples in this chapter illustrate dealing directly with changes in people and in managing resources to help people live the sort of lives they desire. Actual names of clients have been omitted to maintain confidentiality. The names of agencies and co-workers have similarly been deleted or changed. The careers of the workers illustrated in this chapter do not focus exclusively on changing and/or supporting people. As noted in the preceding discussions about practice and interventions, the generalist practitioner does not engage in direct practice activities to the exclusion of resource development, system change, or professional involvement. The following illustrations emphasize direct client work as much as possible.

Each interview is preceded by a brief introduction. The introduction summarizes how the ideas about social work that you have encountered so far in this book apply to each illustration. The introductory discussion covers how purpose, interventions, policy, practice contexts, knowledge, and values are used. The intervention(s) used is diagrammed.

WORKING WITH PERSONS WITH AIDS (JOE HERNANDEZ)

The provision of hospital social services to persons with AIDS is illustrated by the practice of Joe Hernandez. Joe's work with PWAs started just when the AIDS crisis began. Hence, he had to deal with a new problem and the changes it posed for people while developing and delivering new services to them. In his work, Joe stressed self-assessment and individual growth and development as he came to grips with the impact of the AIDS crisis on his clients, his colleagues, and himself. He had to deal with his own values and feelings and to propose modifications in hospital policy in order to deliver services according to the values and purposes of social work. Like many social workers in other practice fields before him, Joe was in the vanguard of promoting the development of the profession as it helped society deal with the enormity of the changes coming from this national health crisis.

JOE'S WORDS: Shortly after I completed my MSW, I went to work at a New York City hospital, a large facility serving Harlem. The positions I interviewed for were obstetrics-gynecology or with children. At that time, however, the hospital was beginning to deal with persons with AIDS in larger and larger numbers. I was asked by the director of the department to see a supervisor for another position. In that interview, the supervisor asked how I felt about working with the terminally ill. At no time did I guess the type of caseload. I guess it was handled in that way purposely to avoid frightening me away.

Looking back on this experience, I'd say I emphasized self-assessment in my practice because of the feelings that were aroused in me and in others because I was working with persons with AIDS. I felt depressed. I was frightened of what I didn't know and of what I was learning about AIDS. I was worried for myself and my family. I reached outside the hospital to get support from colleagues to deal with my own feelings. Even my own family was uncomfortable with me for working with this population. I brought material home to help them learn and overcome their fear. I did a lot of self-assessment and monitoring of my practice and of my own feelings. I guess I had such fears for the first nine months I was there. I overcame these by studying, carrying out research, and seeking and developing support.

Early on I noted a need for a better cultural and language fit between clients and workers. Many of those with AIDS in this hospital were Hispanic or black. The workers weren't. In a sense, I tried to change the hospital's policy regarding the social workers they intended to hire on the newly created AIDS team. I made an effort to get a bilingual worker hired when they were putting the team together. They intended to hire only one social worker. I negotiated with them to hire me, because of my experience, along with another bilingual worker. They did hire me, but the second worker from the clients' cultural background did not materialize.

One situation comes to mind that typifies my practice with persons with AIDS. One client system, a Hispanic mother of a thirteen-year-old and a four-year-old, had three sisters and a mother and father in her family. Her parents were alcoholics and her sisters professionals. She herself was a drug addict and developed AIDS. I had to intervene with the entire family because on her death someone would be needed to care for her children. I needed to get her sisters more involved, to assume responsibility or to help plan for the future of her children. I needed to reach out to her parents, whose concerns and abilities were different from those of her sisters. I first worked with the sisters to discover their own feelings about their sister and about AIDS. I spoke to them individually and as a group on two consecutive weekends because of their jobs. I discovered that they were willing to become involved, and I developed contracts with them to split responsibility for their sister's children. In addition, the children needed to be linked to social services, provided medical follow-ups, and transferred to new schools. I made many contacts with other systems.

With the client, the work was not so easy. She would not accept her diagnosis. To tell a person that they have AIDS is difficult. Although the MD reveals the medical diagnosis of AIDS to the patient, the social worker must deal with the patient's feelings and acceptance. This particular PWA stated that her doctor had made a mistake and denied that she had AIDS. I confronted her with

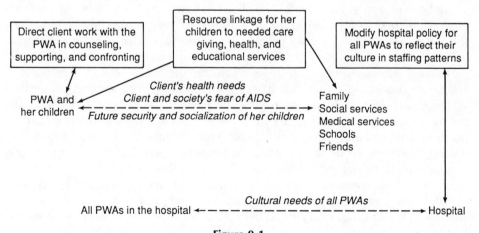

Figure 9.1

the evidence as a dually diagnosed patient, one with a drug addiction and with AIDS. In dealing with this client system, I acted as a counselor, supporter, teacher, and broker.

Joe's practice includes the aspects shown in Figure 9.1.

SOCIAL WORK IN EDUCATION (SUSANNA HUESTON)

Whereas Joe Hernandez's work illustrates a drastic change in the lives of people, Susanna Hueston's practice focuses on the changes that accompany the physical and psychological growth of children and adolescents. The nature of the issues faced by school children have changed during her practice career, and Susanna explores how her skills in social work practice and in developing knowledge help her to keep up with changing client needs. The school uses a team approach to deliver services. In the direct client work illustration she presents here, the inability of the client to handle changes in her life created a life-threatening situation. As Susanna worked with the client and her family, she also had to deal with her own feelings and values regarding the client's situation. In so doing, she used the strength of a collegial relationship to promote her own growth and development.

SUSANNA'S WORDS: I am currently working for a junior high school in Westchester County, New York. The children in grades 7 to 9 range in age from twelve to fifteen, with some sixteen-year-olds. I have been in this system since the fall of 1973, taking a year off when my son was born. The population is mixed in terms of socioeconomics, from very affluent to very poor. The largest percentage of the students are from white families. The recent movement of Hispanics has brought them about even with Blacks, with a small percentage of Orientals. This division represents the part of the community where the school is located. The community itself is a prosperous suburb, with an affluent northern part and an inner city of Blacks. The students at the school live within walking distance. None are bused, as are Blacks to another junior high in this community. Basically the school reflects its neighborhood.

I do a lot of crisis intervention with students in terms of disruptive behavior and fighting, poor peer relationships, and personal problems. I do quite a bit of work with the families in trying to help students adjust to the school, make the transition from elementary to junior high school. I do a lot of referrals to outside counselors and agencies because of the type of services offered by the school.

It is not possible to provide complete services to the families. The school's hours, 10:00 A.M. to 3:00 P.M., are not convenient for working family members. I am able to follow the children for three years while they are in this junior high school. When they have been serviced in elementary school and transfer to junior high, the elementary school's social worker and I meet. I pick up the case at that point. This is true when they graduate from junior high. I meet with the high school social worker to try to make that transition as smooth as possible.

In terms of policymaking, we meet as a group in the social work department to clarify our approaches and procedures in dealing with the kinds of problems a child may be experiencing. There are limits to what matters I can affect. For example, the approaches required to prepare a child to go before the special education committee are fairly rigidly determined. There are federal and state laws and bureaucratic guidelines prescribing what a social worker can do. My role is to provide a social history to the team, along with the psychologist and learning specialist.

During my years in the school system, the kinds of presenting problems of the children and the social problems they face have changed. In terms of "fighting," much of what children engage in is an, "I said—you said," exchange. So, using groups, I help children to sort out their patterns of interaction and to learn to communicate differently.

An emerging problem of even greater proportions is drug abuse among children and parents. In dealing with the drug issue, I have a little spiel in which I tell children I am not there to be critical of them. I try to let them know that I understand that they want to experiment as a result of peer pressure. In those instances where the family must be involved either in the child's drug or alcohol abuse, I inform them that I have to let my superiors, my principal and assistant principals know. Depending on the child, I tell the child that I reserve the right to inform their parents because that may be the best course of action to help them.

An interesting case I worked with was one involving a little white girl who was anorexic. I initially became involved in this case when she was in the fifth grade. At that time I was working in the elementary school she attended. To begin with she did not exhibit the signs of an anorexic but was nervous and tearful. She had attended a parochial school where she was seen by a psychiatrist. She had no learning disabilities, but when she transferred to the elementary school she was seen by the social worker who was there before me. At that time she talked about family problems. Her father was a compulsive gambler and had some problems with alcohol. The mother was a housewife, attractive but obese. Her older brother was married, another brother had left the home and maintained no contact, a sister was severely hearing impaired and had problems wearing a hearing aid and adjusting to it. The girl I worked with was quite bright, very compulsive in doing her work. I saw her for a full school year in her fifth grade. She would come to me when she felt overly tense or depressed.

In September of her sixth grade, I passed her in the hallway and did not know who she was. Later I commented to the school psychiatrist that it looked as if one of our students was anorexic. Her head was large, her facial features sunken, her body very frail. When I realized who she was, I contacted her mother.

When I met with her mother I was informed that her daughter had stopped eating over the summer. Her mother said she acted as if she were suspicious of her cooking, questioning what the mother had put in it. She bought a scale to weigh her food. She ate only fruit at lunch. I had attended a conference on anorexia at a local agency and contacted them.

Working with the family presented other problems. The mother could not face the father's gambling and drinking, which involved other women. The family was a strict Catholic one. The mother confessed a lot to the priest, who along with me tried to help her. I referred the little girl to an eating disorder program in a N.Y.C. hospital, where she was admitted. I was not entirely comfortable with how they handled children in this program. I literally took the family to visit her in the hospital. The father would not attend the family sessions there unless I did so. His participation, however, led to further deterioration on the girl's part. When the family's insurance ran out, she was discharged from the hospital's program.

The school psychologist and I carried the child and her parents from this point on. It was a very draining case. I found that my anger at the mother and father got in the way of my being helpful. I recognized my feelings and, because I was working so closely with the school psychologist, found I could bounce my frustrations off him.

The child graduated that year and started junior high, but was not able to establish a close working relationship with the social worker in that school, and the child's mother maintained close contact with me. The junior high social worker called me in to do follow-up. A year later I transferred to that school. By then the girl had lost so much weight that I sought another eating program for her. I got her accepted into an outpatient program in a county medical center. The psychiatrist got her admitted as a patient in the hospital. In that program her weight increased, her attitude changed. The feeding program worked better, and this was reinforced by her sharing her room with another anorexic. This gave her a greater sense of reality.

Unfortunately she started to regurgitate. She continued in outpatient services through the ninth grade. The psychiatrist stayed in contact with me also. I was able to talk to him about my anger and frustration and my feelings about overweight people and about overeaters.

I had become overly involved in this case and developed a lot of anger at the parents and child. I came to believe that the girl should forget about the craziness in the home, live within it, and get out. Her school work was honor roll status, and she continued to be compulsive about her grades. The mother

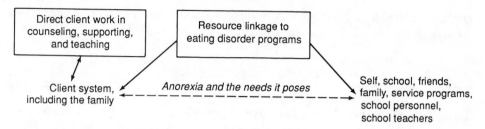

Figure 9.2

tried to involve me into the girl's tenth year. The girl could not relate to the high school social worker.

In a sense I realized I had overidentified with the child. My own self-image and feelings about weight were exacerbated in this case. The case was emotionally draining. I felt that I could do no more and prayed they would not contact me. I asked the high school social worker not to involve me. That was difficult but necessary. My supervisor and the school psychologist helped me to terminate.

I now feel comfortable that I did the most I could for the girl. It was a great learning and growing experience for me. My attitudes changed. The case revealed more to me about my strengths and weaknesses. It sharpened my ability to assess whether or not I should be involved in a case. The case strengthened an already vital relationship I had with a colleague. We developed a healthy interdependence of support and collegial help.

Her practice is summarized in Figure 9.2.

CHILD WELFARE AGENCIES AND GENERALIST PRACTICE (TRACEY JOHNSON)

The work of Tracey Johnson illustrates practice in a number of different child welfare settings. In most of these, Tracey dealt with the impact of poverty and how it changes the growth and development of people. She describes herself as a social worker and an advocate. Tracey used resources both within and outside the agencies where she worked. In several instances she attempted to shape agency policy to make it more responsive to the purposes of social work. Tracey consistently assessed client problems as stemming from their interactions within their social environments. To her the environment, including social welfare structures, becomes a chief part of assessing and intervening. Her career goal has been to find a setting where she can practice completely as a generalist, incorporating social work skills and values in her practice.

TRACEY'S WORDS: I have had several jobs since completing my BSW. I assessed each carefully about how close it came to my ideas of social work. First, I worked for recreation and parks in Columbus, Ohio, as a playground leader. I worked with children aged six through eighteen. This job required only two years of college in any field. The job basically required working with children because the older kids attended infrequently. The biggest turnout was kids six to twelve.

There were a lot of children from families on public assistance. Although it was not part of my job description, I was more tuned in to some of the outside problems the kids had. The problems of the kids were of no interest to the other workers in the program. The other workers did only what was on paper. For example, there were a few kids who came in hungry over a period of several days. I came in one morning and found two kids, one six and the other seven or eight, eating out of a big garbage dumpster. I got in touch with my supervisor. I found out that the mother was turning tricks, and the kids ate at fast food places, if at all. I got involved but almost lost my job because those in charge at the agency said it was not part of my job to be concerned about the kids not having food. I threatened to call the state department of Social Services to see what could be done. They were frightened of any notoriety, any effort to change their own policy. I was supposed only to introduce the kids to the skills of sports and facilitate their participation in daily activities.

I moved to New York City and worked in a group home for retarded adults. Although I had the BSW, the pay on this job was low and my professional autonomy nonexistent. I put in a lot of hours and stayed overnight because of my hours and being on call. After a while I came to believe, contrary to the title of the job I had been hired to do and my efforts to act like a social worker, that this was not a social work position. I did no planning for clients. Although carrying out plans was important, it was not social work. I learned a lot about myself in working with this population. I functioned a lot like a teacher, using examples on how they should function. I learned patience. I was promoted to an administrative position, but I still wanted direct contact with clients as a social worker. Although I had direct client contact, it was not like a social worker to me.

My next job was with emotionally disturbed children, aged nine to twelve, who in many ways had rejected authority. As a substitute parent, my role was a caregiver. They had emotional problems leading to hyperactivity, introversion, or undisciplined acting out. There were also a few children who were borderline retarded.

I also worked in a large public agency, providing protective services to children. It was next to impossible to deliver services in this setting. The caseloads were gigantic, the amount of required paperwork equally huge. It was difficult enough just getting to all of the clients, without even considering the delivery of concrete or long-term services. Again, I did not see this as the sort of social work I wanted to do. I could make decisions, but the contacts and assessments were aimed only at the agency's definition of protection. Decisions to remove children, either into foster care or temporary placements, were made, but follow-up with the parents either to help them or monitor their change was hit-or-miss. New cases came up; old ones were shelved or minimally attended to. Agency expectations, given the caseload, were unrealistic. I did a home visit, made an assessment if the child should be removed, did the paperwork, and transferred the case to another care unit. Delivering effective services to 50 cases was not possible. So, workers need the space and time, and respect of the agencies who hire them, to use their professional skills. I thought I was getting closer to real social work—to make a plan and implement it. I also had been attracted by the salary, but I discovered in a sense the agency exploited the trained social worker and used nontrained social workers who imposed their values on clients and followed agency prescriptions unquestioningly.

Recently I've taken another child welfare position. It seems to be the social work position I've been looking for. I handle concrete services in an after-school program doing tutoring as well as observations and counseling. It operates as a truancy prevention program. I work with the families and the children. Unlike the protective services agency, I am really involved with the families. I actually develop and implement plans, doing hands-on interventions myself. For example, a mother's name was called in to the state registry for delivering cocaine in her home and for neglecting her children who were not attending school. I put the daughter in our after-school program, confronted the mother, counseled her, and helped her get into a drug program. I've been on the case about six months. Although our goals and many of the clients' tasks have changed during that time, I can see that real progress has been made by the mother and daughter. Finally, I'm able to complete the entire social work process of helping people work up a contract and set goals, work with them on realizing them, and evaluate how the plan is working.

A good example of what I consider to be social work practice is a family I've worked with for about nine months. The family lived in a series of hotels and shelters. The kids had not been in the same school for an entire academic year. At times the kids were truant from school. When I first worked with the kids, they were shy and did not want to talk. I involved them in our after-school program with the mother's permission. It had taken me a while to discover why they refused to do homework. As I worked with them, I discovered that the kids could not read, could barely write, and lacked all math skills. The mother also was illiterate.

The family has been living in a "temporary" residence for about a year.

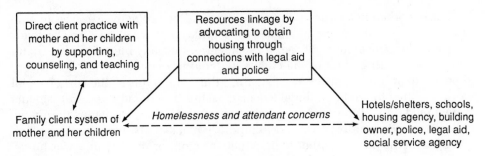

Figure 9.3

Recently I advocated for the family about their housing. The family had signed up with an agency which would take their housing grant and use it to find them housing. They got the housing. Later at the same time a problem arose in their housing grant I discovered that the agency, which was supposed to be paying for the new apartment, was not doing so. That was the reason they were being evicted by their new landlord. The housing agency was mishandling their money and misinterpreting why the family was uncooperative. I took the family to legal aid and found out their rights. Procedures for eviction had not been followed by the landlord or the agency staff, both of which were harassing the family. I also uncovered that the landlord lacked proper licensing. My own actions on behalf of my clients uncovered the two interrelated "scams." I involved the police as a support system because as I applied pressure the landlord and agency were illegally taking her money and harassing her. I got her settled elsewhere and those two "crooks" in trouble.

In a sense I was doing the same thing for clients—advocating for them against agencies—as I did in my first job. The difference is that my current agency supports me.

Her practice efforts are shown in Figure 9.3.

SOCIAL WORK PRACTICE WITH THE ELDERLY (ADELE WEINER)

Adele Weiner has an extensive background in direct client practice and group work, agency administration, and in social work education. Currently, she teaches but also works as a consultant to an agency dealing with the elderly. Adele discusses her sense of policy and social welfare and offers an illustration of a case where the problem (elder abuse) is new and the systems (social agency and police) are still working on how to address the problem. She poses questions about how to deal with the specified clients—the elderly parents, and their daughter, who is also a "client" in need. A number of issues, resolved and unresolved, surface during her work on this situation. Her work involves a variety of direct contact wth the parents and a need for contact and engagement with the daughter.

ADELE'S WORDS: I conceive of social welfare in its broadest possible meaning. As such, all the services that a society provides for its members (including social control, education, medical programs) are all part of social welfare. I think that it is important for people to understand that all members of a society receive the benefits of social welfare programs. As the modern industrial society has become more complex, so has the social welfare structure. I believe that social workers serve a vital function in having knowledge about this structure and helping individuals secure benefits they are entitled to. I have often thought of this function as "finding the loopholes and shoving the clients through them."

Cases of elder abuse are both challenging and intriguing for the social worker. These cases are not always clear-cut and easy to solve. Mr. and Mrs. J are 72 and 68 years old respectively. They have three grown children. Their two sons have not had contact with them in several years; one is in a cult in California and one is married in Pennsylvania. The abuse problem seems to be with their thirty-three-year-old daughter.

The daughter is a I.V. heroin user who has been getting methadone in a clinic. She has been diagnosed as having AIDS. Additionally, she is a lesbian who has recently lost her lover of seven years. According to the parents, the lover introduced their daughter to drugs and deserved to die. They are totally nonempathetic to the daughter's loss. The father seems somewhat upset about his daughter's impending death, but the mother is fairly egocentric, caring only about herself.

Until recently, the daughter lived with her lover. But when the lover died, the apartment was lost. She now lives periodically with her parents. The problem arises because of her welfare benefit payments. The daughter gets two checks, one with both her and her father's name on it for rent expenses. She gets another check for personal expenses. The problem occurs when she comes to get her money. The father refuses to give up control of the checks. Rather, he cashes them and doles out the money $20 at a time. He feels that he has to do this or else she will spend all the money on drugs. The worker has tried to get him to understand that this is helping to create the conflict.

When the daughter shows up at the house on drugs, she is verbally and physically abusive to her parents. She has hit her father, spit at her mother and choked her mother. The parents did get a court order of protection, but she ripped it up in front of the police. The parents have sworn out two complaints against her, but the police won't touch the daughter because of the AIDS. The parents do not want the daughter to go to jail, but they don't know what to do. When the daughter is not on drugs, she is not abusive. The parents would like to force the daughter into a residential drug treatment program but are not realistic about her life span. They are ambivalent about who she is but want her to be able to come home to them to die.

The family in this case needs many different services, none of which are all offered by the same agency. Additionally, many of the solutions involve tradeoffs. The district attorney's office is unsure whether they can have her arrested, brought to court and have a drug treatment program agree to take her, without her having to go to jail. There is a possibility that no drug treatment program will take her because of the AIDS diagnosis, and so she would end up in jail in an AIDS treatment ward. The daughter has not been seen by the worker because her parents are concerned about retribution. Thus, while it appears that the daughter needs much support and help, the worker has not been able to contact her or speak with her directly. The parents feel unable to ask her to speak to the worker as they are afraid of her reactions if she finds out they have asked for help. Agency staff are also concerned about her behavior if she did come in to speak to the worker. The parents do not seem to understand who their daughter is. The father carries her high school graduation picture in his wallet while the mother talks only about herself. Both parents seem unable to accept the daughter's sexual lifestyle and have offered no support to her in her loss of a long term relationship. The father is caught between trying to take care of his little girl (including her finances) and protecting himself. Giving up her checks may also mean that they will lose control over her life and/or contact with her (as has happened with their sons).

Confidentiality is an issue on several points. First, the father thinks that the daughter is selling half her methadone and using other drugs, and he wants to inform the methadone clinic. The worker had to convince him not to do this,

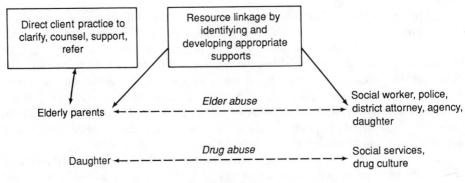

Figure 9.4

as the clinic is the only support resource that we know that she currently has. Second, although the father reports that the daughter has AIDS, there is no way to confirm this. And last, there is some concern that the daughter is continuing to spread AIDS through shared needles or possible prostitution to get money for her drugs.

The worker is caught in the middle of this. Interventions up until this point have involved trying to get clarification on the problem, partialization, gaining information about possible services and implications. Explorations of outreach to the daughter seem appropriate, but this service is out of the mandate of the particular agency that the parents approached and there is concern about the safety of the parents and the worker.

Her practice to date is shown in Figure 9.4.

CONCLUSION

As noted in the chapter overview, a generalist's direct work with clients to strengthen them or to link them with resources also entails working with other systems to create resources or to change their policies. Joe did so in the hospital where he worked, Susanna described how she and other workers developed and used policy, and Tracey attempted to change policies and practices in agencies where she worked. This chapter, however, focused on those aspects of their practice that directly supports and changes people to improve their social functioning abilities. In so doing, worker attitudes and values about clients and the other systems they work with play a role. In addition, the knowledge they have or must develop is also critical to helping clients. Together, their knowledge, values, and generalist practice skills meet the social work purposes of enhancing people and connecting them to needed resources.

For Further Study

1. In thinking about the practice of Joe Hernandez, how would you have handled the feelings he had about working with PWAs? Consider other situations in which the worker's family or friends react negatively to some aspect of the practitioner's work. Describe how Joe handled human diversity issues in working directly with his clients as well as in his relationships with hospital staff members.
2. Susanna Hueston provides insight about collegial relations. Apply the material you learned in Chapter 3 regarding the relationships of social workers with their colleagues.
3. Compare and contrast the experiences of Susanna Hueston and Tracey

Johnson in their work with children. How do you feel regarding Tracey's advocacy for clients against agencies?
4. In what ways is the practice of Adele Weiner similar to and different from that of the other workers?

Bibliography

National Association of Social Workers. *Code of Ethics.* Washington, DC, 1980.

CHAPTER TEN

Resource Development, Policy Change, and Professional Involvement

The social worker should act to improve the employing agency's policies and procedures, and the efficiency and effectiveness of its services. . . .

The social worker should protect and enhance the dignity and integrity of the profession. . . .

The social worker should advocate changes in policy and legislation to improve social conditions and promote justice. . . .

NASW Code of Ethics (1980)

CHAPTER OVERVIEW

The interviews in this chapter emphasize resource development, policy change, and professional involvement. As was stressed in Chapter 9, the careers of those interviewed for this chapter do not focus exclusively on a single part of generalist practice. It is hoped that the examples offer insight into social work practice that does not focus entirely on direct work with clients.

For example, the career of Graciela Castex could be summarized as moving from work with Cuban refugees to conceptualizing services for Hispanic populations. Although Bernice Goodman has an extensive private practice with lesbian women and gay men, she also has been an activist within and a developer of policy for the National Association of Social Workers. Bette Harlan, currently a supervisor, also has a direct practice background. A very active leader of the profession, as president of an NASW chapter, is Irma Serrano, who also serves as an administrator of programs for children.

WORKING WITH HISPANIC POPULATIONS (GRACIELA CASTEX)

The career of Graciela Castex illustrates how to work with the needs of an individual as well as the needs of a community. In the following account, the needs are those of the first group of refugees who came to Miami from Cuba. They

233

entered a city and its social welfare service structure that were unprepared to deal with this group of Cuban people or their needs. Graciela's discussion of her work with individuals and the development and implementation of policy demonstrates the dynamism of social work and its practitioners. Graciela learned about her professional self in relation to agencies and services. She also learned about policymaking first hand by being involved both in a needs assessment and in the implementation of a new policy. Her policy involvement represents the need to develop new resources for an unserved population. The skills she learned in resource and services development were applied in the next programs where she worked. She expanded these resource and policy development activities to include service creation, education of the public about social work, teaching, understanding of the strengths of special populations, and knowledge development. Throughout all aspects of her work her commitment to people—the basic value of the profession—is clearly evident.

GRACIELA'S WORDS: As a social worker, originally my focus was the family and how society sees it both as responsible for causing problems and that which would lead the family out of problems. For example, in terms of children and youth, if there is a drug problem it is because of something being wrong with the family and the family is expected to work out a solution. It was from seeing the family in this context that led to my trying to understand what happened in the small system of the family and how that family system hooked up with other systems in society. The family was a great interest in my earlier career—both in education and in practice.

I began with an undergraduate degree, a BSW, working in a psychiatric center in Miami, Florida. Because I could speak Spanish, they gave me cases that perhaps could have been better handled by someone who had a bit more practice experience. So I found myself having to deal with a lot of complex psychological issues as well as life issues that these migrant families were experiencing. My clients were Cuban refugees who were part of the first Cuban group that came. A particular member of the family, the identified client, would be having horrendous problems in adjustment. For me, what I began to see was how those problems touched on every part of the family, and that this particular person's problem had something to do with the amount of money that came into the family, the resources in the community that were available to meet their needs, and who could take over when this person was taken out of the family. That introduced me to the whole idea of linking people with community resources.

A case that comes to mind that was certainly challenging was one I had when I worked at the center. A mother came in with a four-year-old child who was becoming totally frightened by dogs. She could not figure out why this child would black out whenever he saw a dog. What made her worry was that even when he would read a story in a book where there was a dog or see Lassie on television he would just freak out.

Part of my job in working with this Cuban family was to do a complete assessment of the child, including the family's history. One of the things that came out was that the mother and father were divorced and the child had visitations with the father on weekends. These weekend visits created strain for the parents, who were having a hard time with each other.

I also had sessions with the mother and child. After many weeks of working with the child and using play therapy techniques, one of the things that became very clear was that the child was having sexual intercourse with a dog and that this experience was taking place on the weekends when the young child visited the father. Eventually what came out was that the father was forcing the child to have intercourse with the dog.

There was a lot of work in terms of consulting with the father and helping the father express the kinds of ways in which he showed love for his child, for whom he had always maintained great affection. Using that approach and those words, I worked with the father for several sessions helping him to tell me how he loved the child, how he showed emotion to the child, what kinds of things he would do with the child. Finally, he was able to talk about how he would have his dog have sexual intercourse with his child as a way of loving his child.

A lot of things happened with this case. One was that I went to court, testified in family court that these were the experiences that the child was having when he was with his father. The father had to stop seeing the child for a while, and then the court ordered the father into therapy and denied him access to the child until he was reevaluated by the courts.

I worked on this case a long time. It involved many systems—the school, mother and father, court system, lawyers, other medical facilities, physician to treat the child's infections. It involved services to an individual in the context of the many other systems involved in his life.

About that time I also became involved in seeing how policy changes were made, funding sought and allocated, prioritizing done on issues, and programs developed. Although it happened very quickly, for me it was like a mini-lesson in terms of how to implement policy and how to get services to the persons who were in need of them. It was a very exciting time in that sense and in the growth of the community.

In making policy, I was involved in several task forces in the community that assessed what was happening in and what the needs of the community were. This was with the United Way Special Task Force that was composed of various educators, service providers, and some business people who were appointed to try to begin to look at the issues. This was done on a community-wide basis. We gathered information from the census on immigration in terms of the numbers of people who were coming in. The federal government was involved in trying to supply ideas about the resources available and what money could be allocated. This was the first time this had been done in Miami.

There were no housing, no schools, no transportation, no way to communicate with the refugees in their own language. Medical services were needed for their people. The emergency rooms in hospitals were filled with people who would just kind of line up. There was need for child care and day-care centers. Employment opportunities needed to be made available for people. It put a burden on the existing resources. Suddenly 50,000 people came in—a tremendous number that landed in Miami. Resources had to be stretched to the limit.

Staff had to be hired in agencies on a part-time basis. Policy was changed not only in terms of agencies expanding services, but new issues emerged and had to be dealt with. People who were not residents needed service, people who were not "legal." In which language services would be provided came up. Traditional ways of providing social services were questioned. Hence, it was a practice change as well as a policy-resources-services change. It was a change of policies in all ways.

After my MSW, I worked in a hospital and after that for a children's psychiatric service. Again, I was involved in policymaking, in program creation. I wrote a grant to provide special services for this population. That was exciting because it was something new. We had to develop a whole way of providing service to children that would not alienate the family. These families were very different from many of the clients the clinic had been seeing. At this agency, the white middle-class mother would bring the child to the clinic, drop the child off, go shopping for an hour, and come back to pick up the child and go home. Now it meant providing services to a family, to a cluster of people who many times were not blood relatives. In other words, we had to think about how a family was defined, who was a family, and be very flexible how that was seen by the agency. In a sense, I was helping the federal government understand what a family was and to look at it in a different sense. I was trying to influence the federal government about how they handed money down to people; who they considered to be a family member all of a sudden had to be expanded.

Later I worked for a hospital in Georgia. I was hired by a physical rehab hospital to set up a social services department. I was its director, and it was an exciting opportunity. Again, I was involved in figuring out how to provide services, given the resources made available by the hospital. It was an opportunity to design and implement. Also, while in Georgia, I began to do a lot of speaking in the community on public relations work for the hospital. I went to hospitals and other places where we could get clients to come to the rehab hospital. I went all over Georgia. Partially what I did was talk about social work. What I would "sell" was not the hospital, the physical part, but rather what the department of social services provided to the patient and the family. The department became the selling point. What led others to refer patients to the hospital was the way we conceptualized the delivery of social services.

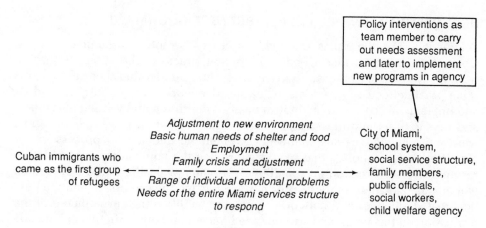

Figure 10.1

It was easy and exciting to do this. People valued what I had to offer in the way of the department's services, valued that we would look at a patient as an individual, look at the patient in the context of where she or he came from, how that touched all of the other systems—family, employment, future goals, everything else this person did in life. They liked that, and I think that is social work.

I consider teaching as social work practice and have practiced as a teacher. After I left Georgia I wrote three welfare training grants. They were funded, and I worked under them. Again, the excitement was to work with people and turn them on to social work. I thought that what we do is exciting. It makes people's lives better. When people are learning about that and can feel a part of that, it is exciting. It reinforces my own sense of feeling good about myself. I was able to share my own knowledge. My students are enhanced, and they are excited and feel good.

Recently I have begun to think more deeply about what it means to be a Hispanic person in this culture and about the issues connected to that label. This includes the specific problems that population has in terms of language, in terms of education, in terms of legal status in this country, and in terms of participation in the economy. So I'm currently very much involved in pursuing a deeper understanding of that. Eventually I want to try to conceptualize a model of how to practice and provide services to this particular population.

Figure 10.1 is a diagrammatic summary of her practice.

DEVELOPING AN NASW POLICY (BERNICE GOODMAN)

Taking action on the issues and needs of clients is rooted in the private social work practice of Bernice Goodman. In that practice, she supports lesbian women, women of color, and gay men to define and value themselves. This same practice focus was evident when Bernice worked to get NASW to adopt and implement a policy to facilitate a positive definition and valuing of lesbians and gays within the profession of social work. Her patience, efforts, and spirit were quite evident as she followed a systematic and logical process to get NASW to adopt a policy that would guarantee the application of association resources to the creation and facilitation of such a positive image of lesbian women and gay men. In these efforts, she educated the profession and the public, created alliances and networks, helped to facilitate the development of the profession on this issue, and strengthened herself and others in this policymaking process.

BERNICE'S WORDS: I am in private practice. I believe that the issues I face in my private practice I must also address in larger arenas. I have done that in terms of work with NASW, in helping create the Institute of Human Identity, in being involved in the creation of the National Lesbian and Gay Health Foundation, and other local lesbian and gay organizations. It seems to me that an action on my part that is likely to make a significant change across the board is extremely important to social work.

It occurred to me in the 1970s that NASW, at that time an organization of 90,000 people, needed to do something that would have an across-the-board impact on lesbian and gay people. Once it was forced to adopt a public policy statement on lesbian and gay people, then it should begin to develop programs to support, facilitate, and help members of this population. I was deeply involved in getting the policy accepted and in efforts at getting chapters and the national organization to take action on implementing it. I wanted to use this action in NASW as leverage to bring about change at other levels in society. Once adopted and once NASW started further educational and supportive activities, then there could be across-the-board impact on other issues related to these populations, such as child custody.

I spent a great deal of "blood, sweat, and tears" working with NASW for years on this issue. At the Delegate Assembly in 1977, the policy was adopted. At the time, one other person and I pushed this whole thing through the Delegate Assembly of NASW. We had a lot of help from other people, of course. This included those who were not willing to come out of the closet along with some wonderful straight women and men who were secure in who they were and who were willing to support the passage of this policy statement. These straight people were able to commit themselves to supporting this issue because of their belief in a human value system that thought something was very wrong in mistreating people simply because they were lesbian or gay.

We had a lot of difficulty. We went to every caucus there was at the Assembly in an effort to drum up support for the policy. We went to each caucus to present our case and seek votes. Of course, there were some people I would put on my "hit list" because of their opposition. We knew we would have difficulty in getting two sections of the statement accepted. One involved the use of the language that "homosexuality is equal to heterosexuality." This became a real issue for some people, and they worked hard to exclude its use or defeat the entire policy statement. I never really thought much of this wording anyway and agreed to alter it. The second issue, and a more difficult one, involved children. It talked about adoption, which was changed to read adopting their own children. One person headed a caucus of eastern social workers. In meetings with them, they agreed to support the statement if changes were made in these two sections.

On the floor of the Assembly, however, that person moved to table our motion. I was ready to blow up. What happened was that an ad hoc committee was formed to redraft the policy resolution. The chair of that committee was really wonderful, and it was her help that pushed the policy statement through. It passed. Still included in the statement was a section that stated that a task force on lesbian and gay issues had to be established. I had put that wording in the policy statement because I wanted to be sure that NASW would do something about lesbian and gay people. Without a task force, NASW really would not have to do anything about the issue.

It took about another two years to force them to set up the committee, but we did it. Policy is extremely important because once you get people in an organization to commit themselves to a policy then you can work to get them to put into operation programs that are based on that policy. That is why in the 1977 policy statement I had insisted that the creation of a task force be part of it. The two years were necessary to convince NASW that the real policy was the creation of the task force, not just the remainder of the statement. In this effort there was an extremely helpful member of the national NASW staff. She insisted that the organization had to take a position and act on setting up the task force. Again, she was a person who acted professionally from a set of values that assigned worth to all people.

My involvement with NASW on this issue should be thought of as a process. First came the work prior to the 1977 Delegate Assembly, then the effort to get the policy statement adopted, and finally the two-year effort to get the task force off the ground. After that we worked on priority statements for national and chapters to follow. We also worked on a manual to be published by NASW that addressed lesbian and gay issues. It seemed like the publication of the manual was blocked at every turn by NASW, but we finally got it into print. Next the effort was to get the task force turned into a permanent part of NASW. We

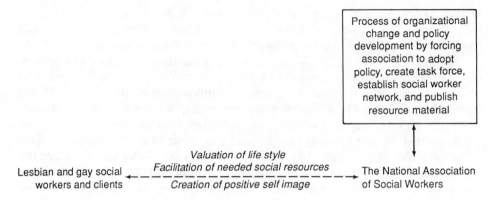

Figure 10.2

wanted to have the task force turned into an NASW commission, but we com-
promised on it becoming a standing committee. A colleague and I appeared
before the Board of NASW to argue that the lesbian and gay task force should
be made a permanent part of NASW. There was resistance, of course, but again
we succeeded.

Another effort we carried out successfully was the creation of a network of
lesbians and gays across the whole country. We did this by having the task force
hold an open meeting to involve as many persons as possible. This meant that
those who attended, other than actual members of the task force, had to pay
their own way. Many, many people attended, and the network was created. A
staff person of NASW opposed such open sessions, but it went ahead anyway.
At the open meeting we had about twenty-five to thirty people show up at their
own expense. They came from all over to indicate that if they were paying dues
to the organization they expected recognition of their existence and needs and
that the organization should be responsible to take action on these needs. At
this point, a new staff person was assigned to the task force and worked very
hard on its development and continuation.

The whole task was an enormous one. In a sense my entire involvement in
this issue was like a second practice. I carried out my private practice as well
as helped create a network of lesbian and gay social workers across this country
within a professional association that was responsive to their needs and interests. Our success was grounded in a lot of committed people.

The process in diagram form appears in Figure 10.2.

AGENCIES AND ADMINISTRATION (BETTE HARLAN)

Bette Harlan's sense of social justice is evident in both her direct client practice and in her indirect supervisory and administrative practice. Her sense of justice plays out in her conception of policy that views regulations and services as matters about which worker and clients should be informed. The focus on accurate assessment is evident in her individual work and in policy development. Moreover, her patience is also applied to these two aspects of practice. She uses the problem-solving approach and the concept of systems in both. For her, the critical context of practice is the institution of social welfare and its services. She frequently refers to its impact on clients and the need of workers to make an impact on it. She does so from the values perspective and professional purposes of social work.

BETTE'S WORDS: Good solid grounding as a social worker allows one to move into practice with the entire breadth of populations. I have been a social worker in family service, public welfare, school social work, special programs for the elderly, and mental health settings. If one has basic skills, one can move into different settings and use one's social work ability.

I am client-oriented. Because I am currently working in a state hospital as a supervisor of social workers, my client orientation means that I see my role as taking the brunt of administrative pressure to leave my workers free to focus on client service. I think of clients as a system. From the time I worked in rural Colorado I learned that you have to think in terms of client totality. I also believe that clients' basic needs must be considered before their psychic needs.

I see the social welfare system as existing to provide some of the basic needs of clients. As a social worker concerned with social welfare, I must be able to maximize that system on behalf of clients. I believe that every social worker should know all the "regs" that apply to their clients. As a public welfare director, I did everything I could in order that workers would know about the system and assist their clients to take advantage of every benefit possible.

In terms of engaging in problem solving with clients, my work was to provide clients with knowledge of policy and to provide support and encouragement as they tried to impact the system to get what they need. With workers on my unit, I see a real partnership of each doing what he or she can in the system to get the most done for patients. My part is to protect my workers from administrative hassles. I will help my workers with direct patient care when they are overloaded.

Two cases provided me with the most learning. One came right after I completed my social work degree, the other when I served as a community mental health worker. Both involved individuals who suffered from disabilities. The first was a young woman who was referred to the agency where I worked because she had difficulty keeping a job. She was attractive, personable, articulate, and presented a truly sharp image. The reality, however, was that she was developmentally disabled, with an IQ of about seventy. Because of her appearance, it was difficult for her, her family, or those who wanted to hire her to see that she was limited. So she would get herself into job situations where she was doomed to failure. Getting an accurate assessment was the first task. The second was working with her to help her identify the "liabilities" she faced without taking away her strong, positive self-image. I did not want to make her feel inadequate. I tried to help her see how the "problem" developed. I worked with her so that she came to realize that not acknowledging her limitations placed her in situations that ended up undermining her confidence. The next step was helping her accept the liability that she had and move into using the strengths she had.

The other case involved a woman who had brain damage that affected her speech and her ability to read. In this situation, however, the family was really making trouble. Instead of identifying the problem as a disorder, they insisted that she was crazy and kept getting her into the mental health system. At this point her self-esteem was excessively low. She could not identify anything positive that she could do. The major strengths she'd had were gone after years of being told that she had nothing. I used behavior modification, confrontation, reality therapy, and a lot of supportive work. The behavior modification came with taking the newly formulated assessment and emphasizing what the real problem was. Then whenever she would come in for her weekly appointment, I would ask her what she had done that had been positive. Inevitably she would discuss what had gone wrong. I decided to ignore her when she began talking that way. So, when she started discussing any negative things, I would pick up a pad and pen and begin working on writing or start some other task but not make a word of response. After the end of the interview, I would tell her that the next time I would be ready to hear about positive events in her life. This went on for only two weeks, at the end of which she came in with a positive to report. I reinforced that report. Within two months I had linked her with a volunteer group in the community. I could not hook her up with a job because her reading skills were still low and she could not handle pressure. In the volunteer setting, she was able to develop skills in a low-pressure situation. In a year this woman who had previously spent most of her time in mental hospitals was named one of the city's volunteers of the year. She was honored at a banquet by the mayor and others. Ultimately she married against her family's wishes. With time, she was able to handle crises significantly better. Even now, at Christmas she sends me a homemade present to show me her capabilities and her appreciation for where she is now.

In my work as a supervisor who tries to create policy that my workers can use in their practice with clients I apply the same sense of realistic assessment

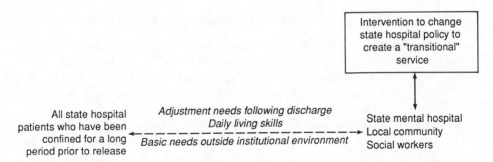

Figure 10.3

and problem focus that I use with individual clients. I also apply the same degree of patience. For example, for reasons of budget the state hospital where I now work decided to place security in charge of patient care on the unit. Granted that the security people have little idea how to treat the patients, nonetheless for cost reasons the decision was made. Hence, there is a real problem in the delivery of service when decisions are made on the basis of budget or convenience rather than on the basis of what patients need. Another problem is dealing with other workers who are incompetent and don't do their jobs and also hurt patients and cause frustration for other workers. Moreover, legislators make decisions about mental health and mental health issues without consulting mental health professionals, causing problems for workers and clients alike. They sometimes seem to prefer to base decisions on the sensational case or on their emotions. I am also concerned about having to do and redo paper work for those who can't make up their minds about what they want the data to reflect. I work in a state that is fiftieth in its expenditures for mental health care, resulting in serious staff shortages. This budgetary shortfall also means that not enough is done in the area of patient aftercare. Without sufficient community supportive services, patients are likely to end up back in the hospital or join the homeless.

Within the hospital I am quite involved in the policy dimension. It took me about three years to convince hospital administrators that patients should not just be dumped out on the streets after having spent a long time in an institution. I worked to get a policy that would reflect the need for a transitional period for those who had been in confinement of some sort before their release. When it comes to this sort of policy involvement my advice is—don't give up.

Figure 10.3 shows her practice as a supervisor and policy advocate.

LEADERSHIP IN A PROFESSIONAL ASSOCIATION (IRMA SERRANO)

Although the career of Irma Serrano began in direct client work, she now practices as an administrator in children's psychiatric services. She currently heads a children's unit in a hospital's community mental health center. At the same time, she has become extremely active in NASW, serving as the president of New York City's chapter. In that post she has established three interrelated goals. Their ultimate purpose is to develop the profession and to educate the public and its representatives about the essential worth of social work. She frames her efforts to do so in terms of the profession's purposes. She has not lost sight of the values of social work or of the role of the advocate within the profession. Change—within the lives of her youthful clients, in the makeup of New York City's population and its problems, or in the social services context of the profession—is a constant part of her outlook on the enhancement and development of the profession.

IRMA'S WORDS: After completing my MSW at Columbia, where I had gone to learn to become a school social worker, I took a job in a hospital, that was part of a college of medicine. In graduate school, I did a school placement but changed my mind about being a school social worker. I did a second placement in psychiatry, and said I'd never work in psychiatry. But my first, and only job it turned out, was in psychiatry.

I have been involved in psychiatric services to children for over 16 years. Now I am in charge of the children's unit in a community mental health center. We have different units within that children's component, according to age. The community mental health center is part of Albert Einstein College of Medicine, which is with Yeshiva University. The college of medicine has a department of psychiatry. I am employed by that department. The community mental health center was established in 1967, the second in the Bronx. The center started as a rehabilitation center for patients coming from a state psychiatric hospital who could be helped to function independently. The center also has outpatient clinic services for the community, a geriatric program, workshop and services for the chronically mentally ill from state hospitals, and the children's services.

The children's programs serve those aged two to eighteen. We have nursery—preschool programs for kids aged two to five who have any developmental problems such as in separation, language development, or management problems. We have a classroom. The program includes individual therapy for the children and their families, as well as parent groups. We have outpatient clinics in each location to serve children aged six to eighteen. We get referrals from community agencies and hospitals. Two years ago we were funded for an on-site school program. We send social workers to the schools. We are serving four area schools presently. We serve nonspecial education students.

I started at Jacobi Hospital of Einstein Medical Center in 1971 as a line worker in the children's and adolescents' unit. This was during New York City's fiscal crisis. I worked two years in that clinic. I then worked for inpatient services for children in the same hospital for a year and a half. I then moved to a coordinator position in a community mental health center in 1974 on a grant. In that job, as coordinator of a program that was written to serve adolescents and children of this community, I served those who were involved in family court.

After a year in that program going to family court, I discovered that the area did not have that many kids involved in family court who needed services. We had a site visit from the federal government, and I told the federal representative that it was a shame we were getting that money because it could be used better in the South Bronx. Usually you don't say such things. At that point I think I started developing what I later came to consider better ways to develop services and allocate resources in this area.

From there I became coordinator of the whole children's unit, to acting director, and now assistant director. So, for more than seven years I have been very active in the policy making area, creating positions, writing grants, getting money, and determining which areas of need the center should work on.

The problems have changed. In the past we got kids who were misbehaving in school. Now we are seeing kids who are really sick, psychiatric kids. There are a lot of suicidal kids, and contrary to popular belief that it is only a suburban problem, it is here in the Bronx and is epidemic. This center's programs do not deal with drug problems as such. We are not funded to do so. The center has started a program to deal with alcoholism in children. It treats individual children as well as families who are dealing with having an alcoholic member. We have dealt with a few children with crack problems.

I am trying to make the regular funding sources realize that many of the treatment methods we've used with children have to be changed. With adolescents, psychotherapy is difficult, more so with the newer problems. When adolescents have an emotional crisis, for example, and are seen in the emergency room, we offer them hospitalization in a psychiatric setting, but they frequently do not get the type of service they need. Their crisis usually lasts up to a week. An open-door drop-in program or a respite center with a few beds where they could stay overnight or for a few days is needed. Their crises create the kind of situations where kids run away, times when dangerous things can happen to them. We need to consider their needs and appropriate programs quite carefully.

Another example of such a program is a state funded one we developed. It will fund a social worker to provide preventive services to preschool children who are coming from hotels and shelters. The workers will deliver services within the Department of Social Services. This program exemplifies helping the funding sources recognize changes in need.

Another issue that needs recognition by funders is how child welfare workers are trained. They are trained how to fill out papers, not about child development, about needs, and how to recognize them. Workers need to learn how to assess children, determine new issues and problems, and help bureaucracies meet new needs and develop new approaches and not ritualize service delivery.

In addition to being active in NASW and other professional organizations, I also started teaching in schools of social work about 10 years ago. I teach about Hispanic lifestyles and serve on the state's minority committee on mental health.

Recently I began duties as president of NASW. It is a lot of work, a lot of responsibility. I work with the board of directors to set policy and provide NASW with direction. I consider it an honor to be representing a profession with 7,000 to 8,000 members in New York City. I have to mold and get people's opinions together.

One of my aims is to work on several major priorities during the next three years. One of the problems with the social work profession is that we think we can save the world, but we don't accomplish very much. We have to set priorities, decide on a few things to do, and increase our impact on the world.

One of my aims is to get governmental offices, especially the city administration, to see social work as a profession that has a lot to say about social issues. Presently the profession is more reactive than proactive. One of the things I'd like to move on is changing this. One of the recent problems in New York has been with school social work. It was decided that others than social workers could get social histories. I consider that a big threat to social workers because what the Board of Education is saying is that anyone can do social work. We have a lawyer, have filed a brief, and will go to court. We are not saving positions, we are fighting for a profession. Social work has been extremely important in the world of education for a long time; New York City has been a big employer of them.

We are also very involved in the whole reorganization of the Human Resources Administration. One of the things I would like to convey to social workers in HRA is that we are experts and know how to use resources. It is time that we sit down and talk to them and say, "We know how to do it." I think that must be our message. It is not that we are going to run for office or make unreasonable demands. It is not that we are saying that those in charge are not doing their job but that NASW has committees that can offer ideas. The committees are well known in the field and can offer suggestions to HRA for its reorganization. We are willing to share. We need to educate administrators about what we can do as social workers. To do so, as president of New York City's NASW chapter, will be a full-time job.

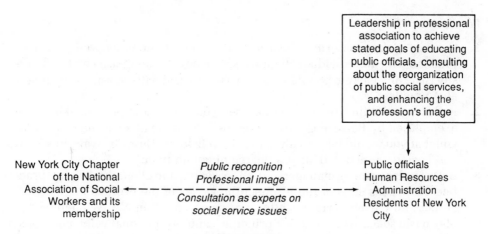

Figure 10.4

A final priority in the chapter is enhancing our professional image. I emphasize that we need to communicate what we do and how it is valuable. We all need to understand our profession and how to present it in a positive fashion to those who do not understand or appreciate it.

Her leadership is diagrammed in Figure 10.4.

CONCLUSION

These four social workers have rendered services to individuals, developed their professional selves, and became involved in the creation of resources and policies and in the strengthening of professional associations. Graciela has moved from services to individual persons from Hispanic populations to conceptualizing practice with and service delivery to this population. Bernice continues in private practice but has carried the needs of her clients into a larger arena within the profession. Bette supervises workers in a way that frees them up for the delivery of services to clients while she attempts to create more effective and humane service delivery in the agency. Irma heads a chapter of NASW and does so in practical ways that are designed to strengthen the profession. Their actions make a powerful case for the necessity to clients of the totality of social work practice.

For Further Study

1. Graciela Castex describes several policy interventions as well as direct practice with an individual client. Describe how her emphasis on the diversity issue of Hispanic populations helps her to deal with all aspects of generalist practice.
2. Reflect on whether or not you can see yourself in the policymaking role exemplified by Bernice Goodman. Is there an issue of such importance to you that you would take on an entire organization? Describe ways in which you have demonstrated such a degree of commitment.
3. Bette Harlan reflects management, supervision, and client work in her practice. How does each of these reflect the values of the profession?
4. Discuss how Irma Serrano's efforts as president of an NASW chapter display basic social work practice principles and professional value positions.

Bibliography

National Association of Social Workers. *Code of Ethics.* Washington, DC, 1980.

CONCLUSION

CHAPTER ELEVEN

Determining Your Direction: Commitments to Social Work

Federal retrenchment has been implemented from a budgetary perspective, with little consideration for how the voluntary sector and individuals and families will cope. . . . [I]f the ostensibly vast untapped reservoir of effort, talent, and good will does exist, additional resources are required to mobilize and coordinate the expanded role of the voluntary sector. . . . [C]ommunity leaders could become aware of the scope of social ills as they attempt to raise funds, train and supervise volunteers. . . . Social workers and other human service providers are being told that their efforts are of decreasing value to society and that their functions could be carried out effectively by efficient managers, well-intended citizens, and caring family members. . . . Social workers should resist embracing these trends as viable solutions to pressing social ills.

Schilling, Schinke, and Weatherly (1988)

CHAPTER OVERVIEW

We have completed the first part of our journey to discover social work. We selected the ideas of purpose, change as a needs area, and societies and services as practice contexts to guide our search. In our initial statement about this journey, we pointed out what direction these words would take us and that other ideas might be excluded from our consideration.

Using these ideas, we developed ways to search out social work's connection to society, explored these connections thoroughly, and applied them in our examination of social workers in action. You know something about professional purpose, the human and social need to manage the changes that affect people's social functioning, social work's knowledge and value base, how diverse societies and social welfare services interact with purpose to shape contemporary practice, and some of the activities social workers use to deliver on purpose and to develop themselves and their profession. If we diagrammed these connections we would see the flowchart in Figure 11.1.

The second major goal of our journey was to help you to determine your place in social work. To facilitate that process, you were offered opportunities in each chapter to reflect on what it had cov-

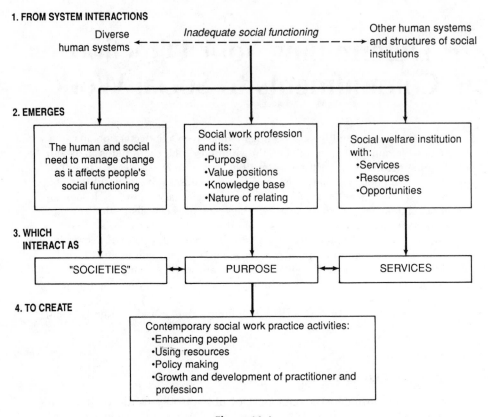

1. FROM SYSTEM INTERACTIONS

Diverse
human systems

Inadequate social functioning

Other human systems
and structures of social
institutions

2. EMERGES

The human and social
need to manage change
as it affects people's
social functioning

Social work profession
and its:
•Purpose
•Value positions
•Knowledge base
•Nature of relating

Social welfare institution
with:
•Services
•Resources
•Opportunities

**3. WHICH
INTERACT AS**

"SOCIETIES"   PURPOSE   SERVICES

4. TO CREATE

Contemporary social work practice activities:
•Enhancing people
•Using resources
•Policy making
•Growth and development of practitioner and
  profession

Figure 11.1

ered. You were asked to examine your thoughts, attitudes, and feelings about the chapter's discussion.

In a sense, this final chapter pulls together all those reflections and asks you one final question: What is your commitment to social work? A commitment is like a pledge to pursue one or more chosen directions. You now understand the directions required by generalist social work practice.

Can you commit yourself to them?

SOCIAL WORK COMMITMENTS

A commitment is deciding on and sticking to a particular direction. It entails promising to do something, pledging or binding oneself to a particular course of action. Social work provides several such directions and demands that practitioners be committed to them.

To social workers, practice sometimes means less people contact and more paper work than they would like. At such times, practitioners require a lot of courage and common sense to continue their commitment to the profession. The profession demands a great deal of those who decide to become professional practitioners. Clients also have high hopes regarding what social work can do for them. And members of society expect a great deal out of social workers. Practitioners must exhibit the highest level of commitment to social work (see Document 11.1).

DOCUMENT 11.1

Best Way to Enhance Social Work's Image Is Job Well Done

Dorothy V. Harris

For years, social workers have been concerned about our "image." Despite the public recognition accorded social work's professional status by licensure and the public acknowledgement of the demanding and difficult jobs social workers must perform, we continue to worry about how our profession is portrayed in television, movies, and print.

Every place I go in my extensive travels as NASW president, colleagues ask me, "What are you doing about our image?" They want to know what NASW is doing, and what I, as president, am doing, to "improve the image of social workers in the eyes of the general public."

This kind of question baffles me. I have never had the kind of concern about our profession's image implied in such a question. I feel that if we are doing what we know how to do and doing it well, respect will come from our work.

Recently, while traveling across the country, I sat next to a corporate executive who asked me what I did. His response to hearing that I am a social worker was to recount that he had had some particularly difficult problems with one of his children and, after a number of frustrating experiences in his attempts to get help, had finally received exactly the help he and his family needed—from a social worker named Phyllis Clymer at Sheppard and Enoch Pratt Hospital in Baltimore.

The incident impressed on me just how surely our work will speak for itself.

I can think of no stronger proclamation of our image than the quality of social work practice performed by Phyllis Clymer and by my fellow social workers in every part of the country in a wide range of settings. I firmly believe that this is what determines our "image."

The comment "What are you doing about our image?" implies that image improvement—if this is, indeed, a valid concern—is *my* job, or the *job of the association,* to be done *for* members. This concerns me because NASW is an association in which we all have ownership. We are not consumers in NASW, we are *constituents.* This organization is ours, and if improving our image is a priority, then we all have a responsibility for achieving that goal.

Several years ago, NASW's Office of Public Information produced a flyer which implores members of our profession to "say you're a social worker." It points out that too many of us identify ourselves by saying, "I work with troubled children," or "I counsel alcoholics," or "I manage an employee assistance program." If we would all preface such statements with "I am a social worker," we would do for ourselves far more than any expensive public relations program could ever do for us.

I am troubled also when I find that social workers prefer to identify their practice as "psychotherapy" or "therapy." These social workers are suggesting that "social work" in and of itself is not important enough, does not bespeak sufficient education, and does not have sufficiently high status for their professional purposes. It is my conviction that we need not apologize for being social workers who provide essential services to diverse populations.

While some social workers seek to associate themselves with seemingly higher status professions, others are not members of NASW because they perceive the association's membership to be made up of people who indeed view themselves as having higher status because of the settings in which they are employed or because of the clients they serve.

This feeling was best expressed to me by a social worker employed in the public sector. She wrote in a note to me that she was not active in her local NASW chapter because the concerns seemed always to be about "licensure, vendorship, and how many more prestige bucks can be made. I often feel distanced and looked down upon despite the fact that *I know* I am as qualified, as professional, and as competent as those who are in private practice. Why don't our colleagues recognize this?"

We must not allow an inordinate preoccupation with status to distance us from colleagues who serve the most vulnerable people in communities across the country or to blur our responsibilities to people in need of our services.

What I want for our association is a strong profession which is responsive to the needs of people, a profession which is able to provide the *quality of services* true to our historical traditions, and a profession which will ensure that all people, regardless of class, race, age, gender, sexual orientation, or place of residence, will have access to those services.

If we put our efforts toward these goals and work with the diligence and dedication social workers have traditionally displayed, I believe our "image" will take care of itself.

(SOURCE: Copyright 1987, National Association of Social Workers, Inc. Reprinted with permission from "Best Way to Enhance Social Work's Image Is Job Well Done," Vol. 32, No. 1.)

There are several possible levels of commitment to the profession. A person can be committed to some directions of social work and not to others. Commitment to social work should not be considered as being of only one sort. It is better conceived of as a continuum, as a range of commitments to social work.

We can use several social work directions to gauge a person's commitment to the profession. These directions are the ones most associated with social work, including the following:

Human and social need to manage change.
Professional purpose.
Problem causation in people's social functioning.
Sense of social justice.
Value positions.
Nature of helping relationships.
Range of practice activities.

As we covered each of these directions in our search for social work, you were asked to question your own attitude and orientation. A summary of these highlights each one, and permits you to reexamine where you stand.

In introducing the idea of change as an area of need, we observed that evidence in the form of ideas about dealing with change indicates that change is seen as a fundamental part of contemporary human existence. Every person undergoes change as a natural part of his or her life. All social structures undergo change as a natural part of their operations. Social work exists to help people manage change in themselves and in their social environments. Social work requires a commitment to learning about and teaching others that change is okay and that the need to manage it is okay.

We discussed how professional purpose also emphasizes the need to change social structures, never a particularly popular activity in this country. Effective and fair delivery of service is a specific change called for by professional purpose. The changes conceive of effectiveness in human terms, especially meeting need and treating people fairly. Not all people agree with change or with emphasizing effectiveness in human, not financial, terms.

In addition, the purposes of making people stronger and of linking them with resources have different meanings to others who come in contact with social work services. To those, enhancement of people is interpreted in terms of ending welfare dependency, using resource availability as a goad to individual motivation, not as critical social support to ensure adequate social functioning.

Connected to these directions provided by purpose are opinions on problem causation. Problems in people's social functioning may be seen as stemming from a lack of motivation on the part of individuals in trouble and/or from the operations of social structures. Social workers believe problems are caused by the interaction between people and the systems that make up their social environments. Most members of American society like to believe that their success is based on the high level of their motivation; the failure of others or their lack of it. The social work commitment is to locating problem causation in the balance of the interactions between people and institutions, fully acknowledging the role played by society.

Allied to problem causation are conceptions of social responsibility and social justice. Rationales for how responsible society should be in helping with people's social functioning are partly based in the belief that if people cause their own problems then they, not society, are responsible for helping themselves. Social work finds society to constitute part of a complex set of contributions to the inadequate social functioning of people and is thereby responsible to help those with problems.

Moreover, social workers believe that those who receive social welfare services have a right to fair and just treatment and to have input about their treatment and their future. Such treatment becomes a major part of social work values, which comprise another critical direction to which social workers are committed. Major social work values are placed on human diversity, self-determination, and social and political change. These positions grow out of purpose and need. An emphasis common throughout the other directions we pursued in our journey to discover social work was on people and on the value of their differences. A commitment to diversity as a source of strength rather than problems is also not a universal one in our society.

We discussed that social workers in helping people establish relationships. Most people are conditioned to view helping as being an interpersonal activity. To relate to individuals in other fashions is to be "cold." To think of relating to people who are not clients but who are involved in social work helping relationships as partners may leave them dissatisfied as well. Commitment goes beyond the interpersonal to partnerships that secure resources and create change.

Commitment to the practice activities we outlined go beyond direct work with clients to interventions that require using resources and making policy. In addition, activities that lead to the growth and development of practitioners and of the profession itself are required. Paralleling people's commitment to personal helping is a commitment to direct interventions.

Persons other than social workers are in contact with social work clients, social service agencies, and social welfare programs. These people also face some of the factors that are most characteristic of those who demand a particular commitment of social workers. On a regular basis they face many of the same issues that characterize social work helping.

Such persons may or may not hold the same commitments on these issues as social workers. They have a different set of commitments than those that are essential to a social worker. Exploring these differences helps to summarize and review the commitments required of the individual social worker.

For comparison, consider the extent of social work commitment among the following:

Volunteers.
Supportive lay people.
Resource system decision makers.

It is not possible to make generalizations that will fit all volunteers, all lay people, or all resource system decision makers. Our analysis aims to identify the potential among such people to develop commitments that correspond to those of social workers and to help you visualize how you might have to stretch yourself in order to make a commitment to the practice directions of the profession of social work (see interviews on pages 257–260).

I AM A SOCIAL WORKER
"Recommendations to Students"

GRACIELA CASTEX: If I were talking to someone who was considering social work as a career, I would ask them to think about a couple of things. One of the important things to be considered, broadly speaking, is what they want to do with their life. I think that social work is a commitment to people, a commitment to social justice, a commitment to contributing to society. We do that through an agency or through an educational institution, but still it is a commitment to society as a whole. One has to think about whether they want to make such a commitment to society. The person would have to compare making such a contribution from this perspective with other things they may seek in life, such as more money or more notoriety or visibility. Social work may not necessarily be the vehicle to do that. But I think that once a commitment to contributing to society and to social justice has been made, then one begins to think about oneself as part of this larger group of people who are trying to help people survive better in this particular environment.

Social work is the discipline or career that asks such a commitment of people. How one selects a field or a setting I think is a second element that takes a lot of thought. But that can also be decided as you go along. I don't think that one needs to decide right away where one wants to work, such as in a hospital or with youth. I think that the commitment for the betterment of society, to social justice should be there first. Once that is in place, once that becomes the primary purpose, the rest will fall into place easier. By talking to social workers who are practicing in diverse settings, you can get some indication as to how they do it. Also, talking to recipients of social work services is an excellent way of finding out about fields. Also talking to colleagues and to professors is helpful. If the commitment is there, you can apply that to any setting or group you work with. The setting may change, but you will find your place if the social work perspective or commitment to social justice is there.

BERNICE GOODMAN: My recommendation would be to hang in there and stay committed to making a social statement with your social work practice. You can add to yourself all the other pieces—the knowledge base, the skills, and the experience. Yet they have to be added to a basic sense of commitment to the creation of a better living environment for all of us. Don't lose that sense; don't let anyone take it away from you.

BETTE HARLAN: Learn regulations and learn policy for the purpose of making them work for your clients. Find the loopholes and know the vulnerable points in a policy. If you think that a policy will not be of value to clients and you decide to try to change it, don't give up fighting to get it changed. In order to change anything and in order to make any kind of impact, document what is going on in your practice and with your clients. Documentation is valuable when you are trying to make a case for your clients. Keep precise and careful documentation. Don't just trust to an impression, but get facts for your documentation. I also would recommend using system ideas at whatever level you work. Don't waste anger; save such energy for when you want to make an impact. You may want to save your anger, but don't save your sense of humor. Laughter will help you survive the system; otherwise you will be prone to burnout. Finally, in thinking back to my first placement, it was my field instructor who taught me to realize that I should not underestimate myself or my clients. Remember you will have another chance to make it right, and remember that you and your clients will be able to make it work.

JOE HERNANDEZ: You will need good verbal and written communication skills. You have to be able to talk to people with empathy. When you talk to someone about a concern of theirs, you have to know whether or not you can relate to such a person. In thinking about a career in social work, you need to check out in advance how you communicate and relate to others. Another area would be written communications. There is a lot of writing in social work, and workers have to be able easily and adequately to state what has happened with their clients. You need to think about writing and whether or not you can handle a lot of it. Basic to social work are communication skills. Check out how strong yours are.

SUSANNA HUESTON: The most important thing in deciding about a career in social work is to decide how you feel about yourself. You must like yourself and in turn you must like people. Liking other people and working with them must provide joy for you. I believe that in whatever we do there must be joy;

without joy nothing is worth doing. You must also have a willingness to give, and this must be something that is fulfilling for you. Social work is not all roses, of course, but enjoying people and being able to derive joy from helping others will help deal with the pain.

In choosing social work, one must not be lulled into a false sense that it is easy to get through. Social work can be frustrating and it is not easy. You have to know that gratification in social work cannot come if we pass on our own insecurity or depression to the clients we are working with. Lacking joy in ourselves minimizes our ability to work with those who do not have it in their lives.

It is not a profession where you will earn big money. The joy has to be in the gratification you get from helping others. Some social workers make good money; while many go into private practice to do therapy or counseling. As a social worker, you have to be sure enough in your own professional worth and competence that you avoid competing with other counseling professionals, such as psychiatrists and psychologists. Don't get caught up in proving who you are; focus rather on doing social work. Don't pat yourself on the back; do your job and others will. Cooperate with your colleagues, be complementary with their skills.

TRACEY JOHNSON: I would recommend to anyone thinking about a career in social work not to think that your first job or interest has to be the final one. Do not be afraid to find what suits you. In your undergraduate field placements, do a little bit of everything unless you absolutely know what you want. I think it is important to try as much as possible and get a feel for yourself and for social work.

IRMA SERRANO: If someone were considering a career in social work, I'd have a couple of thoughts for them. First of all, I'd say you have to look at yourself as someone who must accept individual differences; it's not only liking people or liking to help people. So many say they go into this profession because they like to help people. What we have to do is accept differences, which is a complex and difficult thing to do.

The second thing, drawn from my own experience, is that what you believe about yourself when you're younger may change because you change. When I was younger, I always said that I could never work with people because of my personality and my sheltered background. I wanted to be a technologist in a lab. When I was in college I did not think I could work with people. Social work is a good profession to find out different things about yourself.

I feel very good about being a social worker, having grown as one, and once you get your degree or training, go ahead and call yourself one. Be proud of your work and your title. Don't buy into the negative image; educate others what the title of social worker means. Perhaps all of us need to learn how to enhance our profession's image, beginning with our own understanding of its value.

ADELE WEINER: It is extremely important that students explore their own needs and feelings about being in the field of social work. I have always said that I can teach any student skills and knowledge but I can't teach caring. Social work as a profession is stigmatized, the monetary rewards are few, and the stress and burnout are high. Thus, the rewards one gets from being a social worker come internally from knowing that one has done one's best to make this world a better place for oneself and for others.

The purpose of this discussion is to indicate the usefulness of a range of commitments to the issues, problems, services, and people served by social workers. It is not the intention of the discussion to disparage those whose commitments are not the same as those of a social worker. By highlighting the differences among such commitments, it is possible better to pinpoint those of the social worker. Moreover, as a person who performs many different roles, it is quite possible for a social worker to be a volunteer or a member of a decision-making body. In one of those capacities, the social workers could also display a different commitment from that expected of him or her as a social work practitioner. Only in the sense of a commitment to the values of the profession and its stated aim to create just social conditions for all members of society could the social worker be more critical of those who do not share those outlooks.

VOLUNTEERS AND INDIVIDUAL HELPING

Social workers come in contact with clients and colleagues in the social agencies or programs where they work. We have already noted how different from social work are clients and colleagues in some of their outlooks and perspectives. Persons within agencies who are also somewhat like social workers in some of their activities are volunteers. We noted earlier how volunteerism contributed to the development of professional social work practice but how gradually social workers "professionalized" their discipline by becoming salaried and trained to perform their jobs.

Volunteers still deliver services to people and match some of the commitments of social workers. On other factors, however, they are committed to directions other than those pursued by social workers. Most volunteers are committed to helping out with human problems, quite to the exclusion of working on broader social problems. Much of their volunteering involves working with individuals or providing resources and support to them personally. They are likely to view problems as rooted in factors of individual motivation and inadequacies and are eager to help.

Their involvement argues for a sense of responsibility, maybe not in the form of supplying resources and services in social welfare, but certainly one delivered through personal involvement. Charity-type work once motivated most volunteers. Now their motivations are more complex. Frequently, the motivation comes from the belief that people have a duty to help others but not necessarily that the collectivity should do so.

It is possible that volunteers' "on-the-fence" commitment to social responsibility could be shaped into a commitment more compatible with the social work perspective. In a similar fashion many volunteers, motivated by a concern for those less fortunate than themselves, need assistance in translating their viewpoint about people into one that is free of "isms" and lacking in paternalism. Volunteers engage in helping through personal relationships and individual or small-group activities. Their commitment is to individual helping.

Although in some ways the volunteers share with practitioners commitments to social work, there are also serious differences. The primary emphasis on individual helping tends to exclude social factors in determining problem causation, could lead to a personal sense of responsibility to help with the problems people have in their social functioning, and may develop a lessened commitment to social change and policy interventions. Nonetheless, volunteers share with social workers a critical aspect of professional practice—a commitment to helping people deal with the issues they face in their social functioning.

THE SUPPORT OF LAY PEOPLE

Many lay people who have contact with social work like it a great deal, yet they never make the same commitments as practitioners. The support of lay people of this persuasion, however, is significant to the profession. They serve as members of boards of directors of social service agencies where social workers practice, or they are members of the news media. The latter, for example, usually have limited contact with social workers, aside from their personal acquaintances. For members of the news media, many of the issues they deal with relate to social work practice. Persons based in social service agencies, on the other hand, may have had greater contact with social workers.

Generalizations about the commitments of lay people to social work are difficult to make, even for those who have regular contact with the profession. Among them are those who tend to be committed to social and institutional aspects of the human and social need to manage change as they appear in social work's purpose and in its practice activities.

Board members of social service agencies are more experienced with social problems and understand more about how problems in people's social functioning may originate in the operation of social structures. They and members of the news media are in touch with the problems people have in negotiating economic, political, and social change. Their exposure to this side of the person-environment equation is greater than that of volunteers. Similarly, board members are faced with similar resource issues as are social workers. Also, like so-cial workers they are involved in policymaking. It is in this latter capacity that they often deal with social workers and the concerns of social workers.

Although the potential exists for these two groups to develop similar com-mitments, such a development does not always occur. In terms of social respon-sibility and social justice, board members might tend to personalize involve-ment and be neutral toward or oppose developing the institution of social welfare. In part, these stances derive from how they conceive of their responsi-bilities as decision makers who must be concerned with *cost* effectiveness in the delivery of services. Having the responsibility to decide about scarce re-sources, they are not so committed to the social work values of human partici-pation and self-determination. They are not so committed to creating service delivery structures that define effectiveness in terms of meeting human need from the perspective of those in need.

It is possible to conclude that because of having regular contact with social work or with the issues facing practitioners lay people often make some of the same commitments as social workers. On significant commitments they differ markedly. These differences are critical, but they should not detract from seeing the potential among such lay people to support social work commitments.

RESOURCE SYSTEM DECISION MAKERS AS ALLIES

Decision makers in systems other than service agencies, those persons who make policy concerning resources social workers seek for their clients, are another group who have regular contact with the profession and its prac-titioners. Policymakers in such systems as local Community Chests, state and federal legislatures, and state and federal welfare regulatory bureaucracies make commitments on some of the same issues facing social workers, although they do not share quite the same commitments as do social workers.

In many instances, decision makers are mixed in their commitment to the human and social need to manage change. As these decision makers allocate resources to create programs to help people and face the rapidity with which problems emerge and services have to be changed to meet them, there emerges a greater sense that managing change has a social as well as a personal compo-nent. In a similar fashion, as they establish programs, they must commit them-selves to how responsible society should be.

The decision makers in these other resource systems are likely to possess a commitment to political or social change to help people. From their perspective as decision makers who act on behalf of the public, they are not entirely favor-able to strengthening and extending social welfare structures nor do they usu-ally possess as strong a sense of society's responsibility as do social workers.

Because of their involvement in resource decision making, they also come in contact with large numbers of diverse people and their needs. Given the limited resources they have to allocate, they tend to evaluate service delivery structures on the basis of cost effectiveness. Their commitments in policymaking are to economizing. In this sense, they do not always share social work's commitment to human diversity and the fair treatment of resource users.

Their commitments can be summarized as creating delivery structures that are cost effective and serving people in such a way as to avoid bringing about any dependency on social welfare services. To a limited degree, their commitments to change give them the potential to be allies of social work.

PUTTING THEM ALL TOGETHER: THE PROFESSIONAL SOCIAL WORKER

In several places in this text, our discussion has compared social work to the magic of a juggler whose task is to balance the following sets of conflicting factors:

Professional purpose versus expectations of people.
Social problems versus individual motivations.
Professional values versus popular ideas regarding social responsibility.

A final balancing act involves studying the various commitments people have to social work, making a decision about your commitment to social work, and creating the supports and alliances needed to buttress your commitment to it.

You must decide whether you wish to make such a commitment. In seeing how the commitments of others fit together, you can grasp the totality of the commitment social work expects of its practitioners. At the present time, your commitment may be only to pieces of social work, similar to the commitments of volunteers, lay people, or policymakers.

Professional social workers must expand people's view of human needs to include the human and social need to manage change. At the same time, volunteers and interested lay people must be helped to understand the significance of managing change to create service delivery systems that are just and fair in their treatment of people. Those who come to hold such commitments can help to lobby, write letters, and join alliances with social workers in their policymaking efforts.

Social workers can help some people to expand their sense of how responsible society should be for helping people. Included among them are those who have a potential to share social work commitments or who are neutral or mixed in their commitment to what causes problems in people's social functioning, or who share a commitment to the practice activities of using resources and making policy. In addition, they can become allies in working for an end to oppressive conditions and to supporting greater client participation.

They can also be moved in the direction of recognizing the importance of policymaking in the overall scheme of helping people with their social functioning, and they can be made to recognize social work's place in that scheme.

Persons who are committed to these directions and to obtaining the commitment of others to them are truly social workers.

What about you? Where do you stand? Are you like a volunteer? Can your commitment be summed up as to individual helping? Are you, rather, more like a supportive lay person, having some commitments to social work's sense of helping people and society? Or are you like the decision maker in a resource system who in some ways is a potential ally of social work in its commitment to change and policy making?

Or do you already have extensive commitments to the directions taken by social work? If your commitment lies with social work, then you are committed to strengthening the commitments of others to social work. If you have this commitment—welcome aboard.

For Further Study

1. Review all the social workers' interviews. Discuss how any words or terms used in the text were used differently by them in their statements.
2. Summarize the commitments displayed in the practice illustrations drawn from the social workers' interviews.
3. Reflect on the recommendations offered for your consideration in this chapter. Discuss which are new to you and what you will do to consider them.

Bibliography

Harris, Dorothy V. "From the President: Best Way to Enhance Social Work's Image is Job Well Done." *NASW News* 32 (1): 2, 1987.

Schilling, Robert F., Steven Paul Schinke, and Richard A. Weatherly. "Service Trends in a Conservative Era: Social Workers Rediscover the Past." *Social Work* 33(1): 5–8, 1988.

Index